BY
ANOTHER
ROAD

The Medfield Sermons
2016-2019

Rev. David W. Chandler

StrongVoices

Medfield, MA

Strong Voices Publishing
P.O. Box 731
Medfield, MA 02052
www.strongvoicespublishing.com

Credits: Front cover photo "Spring Equinox 2019" by David W. Chandler.
Back cover and inside photo by Sally Orth Chandler.

ISBN: 978-0-9905361-8-5
eISBN: 978-0-9905361-9-2
Library of Congress Control Number: 2019943560

To my wife, Sally
And to the people of First Parish UU, Medfield, MA

Right now.... the portal is open to who we really are, and to how things really should be. In the moments most crowded with people, with memories and expectations, with tasks and travel, with events and epiphanies small or great, we are headed home. Like the Magi, we are called to journey by another road to that place, and thus can safely proceed past all danger and delay and despair.
— "The Ritual of Renewal," Nov. 26, 2017

Introduction

Rev. David W. Chandler was our minister at First Parish of Medfield, Massachusetts (Unitarian Universalist) from 2016 until his retirement in 2019. During those three years, he preached the sermons that are now collected in this volume.

Unitarian Universalists are spiritual seekers who look for wisdom from a variety of religious traditions and, while they agree on their denomination's Seven Principles (printed here on the next page), they can hold vastly differing positions on religious questions. Unitarian Universalist preachers therefore cannot do a weekly exegesis of some sacred text; they must draw on their own resources of reading, experience and reflection. This collection of sermons shows the depth of resources Rev. David has to draw on, a well of wisdom from which we can now continue to drink.

David Chandler's unmistakable voice comes across clearly and vividly in his "Medfield sermons": we hear his wry perspective on congregational life and on life in all its facets; we hear words of encouragement, reminding us of the human, all-too-human characteristics that we share, our weaknesses and failures, but also our strengths and successes. He reconciles us to the human condition and directs us to find comfort in spiritual community. He instructs and delights us; he makes us smile and makes us think; he makes us appreciate the gift and the burdens of life.

He wears his learning lightly, but his extraordinary selection of readings that accompanied his sermons and his many references to a vast archive of American music give us a glimpse at the deep scholarship tucked away behind that dry wit, compassionate humanity, and well-timed delivery we heard from our pulpit during these three precious years.

We thank Rev. David for the many gifts he has given us, and for the great blessing he has been to our congregation. We will cherish and share this collection of his sermons as a gift that keeps on giving.

Fritz Fleischmann

Acknowledgements

Thank you to Fritz Fleischmann and to Thea Iberall for making this written collection possible. And to Shirley Riga, Helen Beedy, Darline Lewis, Margaret Rolph, and David Russell for help in preparing the manuscript.

David W. Chandler

The Seven Principles

WE, THE MEMBER CONGREGATIONS OF THE UNITARIAN
UNIVERSALIST ASSOCIATION, COVENANT TO AFFIRM AND
PROMOTE:

1. The inherent worth and dignity of every person;
2. Justice, equity, and compassion in human relations;
3. Acceptance of one another and encouragement to spiritual growth in our congregations;
4. A free and responsible search for truth and meaning;
5. The right of conscience and the use of the democratic process within our congregations and in society at large;
6. The goal of world community with peace, liberty, and justice for all;
7. Respect for the interdependent web of all existence of which we are a part.

Principles [Excerpt from, Statement of Principles and Purposes,
Adopted as a Bylaw by the 1984 and 1985 General Assemblies.]

The Six Sources

From the Statement of Principles and Purposes. Adopted as bylaws of the Unitarian Universalist Associate, 1984, 1985, 1995.

THE LIVING TRADITION WE SHARE DRAWS FROM MANY SOURCES:

- Direct experience of that transcending mystery and wonder, affirmed in all cultures, which moves us to a renewal of the spirit and an openness to the forces which create and uphold life;
- Words and deeds of prophetic women and men which challenge us to confront powers and structures of evil with justice, compassion, and the transforming power of love;
- Wisdom from the world's religions which inspires us in our ethical and spiritual life;
- Jewish and Christian teachings which call us to respond to God's love by loving our neighbors as ourselves;
- Humanist teachings which counsel us to heed the guidance of reason and the results of science, and warn us against idolatries of the mind and spirit;
- Spiritual teachings of Earth-centered traditions which celebrate the sacred circle of life and instruct is to live in harmony with the rhythms of nature.

TABLE OF CONTENTS

The Congregational Garden

The Pretty-Excellent Church

04 Dec 2016

In the late 1990s I taught the sixth and seventh grade Sunday school classes in our UU church. The "middle school" years are notoriously hard to deal with and we had the normal challenges, with one wrinkle. We were teaching the Bible to those UU kids. It's true—the "pedagogical task" was to connect the Old Testament narrative to the life of Jesus. The highlight each year was Cecil B. DeMille's Biblical epic, "The Ten Commandments." We'd bring bagels, the kids would bring sleeping bags and everybody sprawled on the floor for two Sundays in a row—it's a long movie.

One of my favorite memories is watching their mouths literally drop open as the Angel of Death—in the form of some very nasty-looking green smoke—passed by the Israelite doorways even as it claimed every Egyptian first-born, animal and human. The kids were stunned. Who would have thought that would happen? Never underestimate the power of story—and over-the-top Technicolor spectacle.

DeMille—"C. B." to his friends—specialized in gloriously hammy Hollywood spectacle. One innovation was the use of crowds—"thousands of extras!" as the posters cried. He had a trick to get those crowds to sound surly and restive, vaguely threatening but also uncertain—ripe for a new dramatic turn in the action. It was a word, the word "rhubarb." Each one would repeat it over and over. Voila—an ornery unsettledness.

Want to try it? Come on, we can do it—*rhubarb, rhubarb, rhubarb, rhubarb…*

This bit of silliness has a point. Groucho, Chico and Harpo might remind us silliness *is* the point, but there is more. We deal here with matters of life and death, but we do not carry them in glum despair. The power of experience is our power. It is our power when we live fully and draw on the resilience of our own spirits and the care and support of those around us. When we make some noise, move around, sing as well as speak we embody that power. "Incarnate" is the religious word—*incarnate* the spirit.

I remind you this can be the Holy Spirit, but does not have to be. It can be the Spirit of Life, Gaia, the Goddess or any other expression of the divine. It can be your own individual spirit—no outside intervention required. You and I—every one of us—has as a human being a priceless gift, the compelling power of spirit.

A religious community is a place where we bring forth that great gift.

To accept this premise as foundational is to ask the logical follow-up question: How are we doing? How well are we nourishing the gifts of the

3

spirit—and how well are we putting them to use among ourselves and in the world at large? Is our strength of spirit growing or diminishing? Is our work in the world truly inspired or is it punching a time clock? Are we embracing other people or merely tolerating them? Are we *present*?

Deep in New England heritage is the "halfway covenant." At first the Puritan elders required a documented "conversion experience" for entry into church, but this rigor soon gave way to a more practical standard. It became enough to attend worship services, to accept a certain social discipline, to adhere to the outward forms of religion. Our inheritance from this halfway covenant is the "pretty-good" church. It is a friendly place—except when it's not. It is filled with people who are nice—except when they are not. It acts generously and even with some courage in the public sphere—except when it does not. It looks to a future that will be pretty much the same—except it will not.

The inescapable lesson of our time is this: *Pretty good is not enough*. We know it in our bones. The future—that sooner or later place—will belong to the excellent. We will talk another time about why this includes churches, but let's for today just assume it is so. Let's stipulate, as lawyers say, that you want an excellent minister in your pulpit. Will you be an excellent congregation? How will you know? How will you explain?

Here is a framework to ponder, adapted from Sarai Schnucker Rice of the mainline Protestant Congregational Consulting Group. These are some benchmarks:

- Discerning *and* decisive. It is crucial to ponder and discuss, to keep the body politic in good order and harmony. But it is also crucial to *decide*. Good process leads to recognition of those critical moments when something indeed must be done. Trust must underlie a commitment to following through on the decisions.

- Self-aware. This is the "know who you are and what you are about" clause. The important related aspect is to grasp the *process* of self-awareness. There is no all-purpose, for-all-time call, but rather a series of options and opportunities. Steadfast goals require flexible methods and openness to following the heart.

- Organized. Well yes, a church is an organization. Too often we forget or overlook this reality, relying on sweat or single-mindedness instead of clear policies and procedures. We undermine effectiveness by being nice people who dilute accountability. We fail to plan, thus encouraging muddled improvisation.

- Resilient. Ambiguities and uncertainties accompany all life, and the life of a faith community is no exception. Taking risks, trying new things, learning from success and failure is required. Being open to positive and negative feedback is essential. As I have already stated, the spiritual search is at the heart of all.

- Expressive. This I have also touched on. However you are moved, we need to know it in all the ways humans communicate passion, insight and inspiration. An excellent church resists the impulse to delegate its spiritual expression to its minister. It is work we do together. Sharing requires authenticity by all parties.

- Public. "Why don't we do it in the road?" Someone *will* be watching us. If we are excited about what is happening here, we will give generously of time and money to help it soar. If we are excited to be who we are, everyone we know will see it.

- Strategic. This quality forms a trio with *discerning* and *decisive*. Yes, we have to watch where we put our feet, but we also have to have our heads up. Where are we going? That means a vision of the whole—rewarding, not merely renewing. Every component of church needs to be asking, what's the *best* that we might be?

- Clear. One tangible fruit of the bedrock of trust and compassion is the freedom to speak plainly. Your ideas may be weak and your behavior at least occasionally is a bit much, but *you* can never be unwelcome or unloved. How hard this is! How essential it is! We must drive out fear, to be free to be honest about who we are.

- Congregationally oriented. This is the point of it all. We shouldn't be here if we don't want to be together. We shouldn't open the door unless we want new people to join us and be welcome. The life we control is not eternal. It is right now. It is right here. It is indeed complicated and hard—but it is in our power.

This "pretty-excellent" church is certainly in your power. Many of these qualities are ones you have already demonstrated. So much of who you are is already caring and welcoming and energetic. People *will* come if you genuinely do what is promised every Sunday—if you carry the flame through the week ahead in your own life and gather again next Sunday to rekindle it with others. So many long for—so many look for—what is already here. More skillful church life can be learned. We have reason to try.

Amen. Blessed Be. Shalom. Salaam.

The Thing with Feathers

11 Dec 2016

Saturday morning television when I was 10 or 12 years old was unencumbered by adult supervision. My younger brother and I would park in front of "Tarzan," with Johnny Weissmuller. We watched "Sky King." In between was a documentary slot for boyhood dreams like rocket sleds, the X-15 and land speed records at Bonneville. I learned the jingle for Paul Parrot shoes, which I can still sing—but I will spare you.

I think it was "Jungle Jim"—another Weissmuller studio safari into "Darkest Africa"—that taught me about quicksand. When you step into quicksand, here's what *not* to do: Don't count on the manly hero just happening by—unless you're the heroine. Don't lunge up and down and wave your arms—that will be glug, glug and goodbye.

How to actually escape? Lie flat on your back to distribute your weight and "swim" your way to firm ground. Unless you are the dastardly villain, it works. I always felt well prepared for any quicksand I might encounter around suburban Philadelphia.

Actual quicksand is not common in the world. It is, however, very often encountered in life. The muck of adversity comes up over our shoes. What previously seemed reliable—our health, our job, our relationships, our car that starts on cold mornings—are all aspects of human *terra firma* known to turn wobbly. This is not the thunderclap of disaster. It is more a negative trend we properly describe as a "sinking feeling." Things seem to be "going to hell in a hand-basket," as my mother used to say.

Congregations experience quicksand, according to church experts. This is not a fire or an act of violence or theft. It is a sense the community is—like the infamous political polling—"heading in the wrong direction." These are some warning flags:

- The ways people belong to the community seem to become less clear and less certain; the sense of connection may feel less fulfilling and satisfactory;
- Communication seems less effective; things said are not always heard; things needing to be said are not always spoken, or not where they need to be;
- Making decisions for the group gets harder; feeling unheard or second-guessed becomes too common to support the trusting relationships of shared governance;

- The role of the professional clergy may be challenged from diffuse directions, which makes appropriate responses harder to formulate and less satisfactory.

These signals of anxiety may sound familiar. I dare say you have experienced them, which is painful and a disappointment. I want to reassure you they are a normal turn of the wheel. In the lifetime of any congregation, there are natural cycles. The body of the church itself is born, matures and declines. Congregations seldom die, but a church fight can leave them dark stars, bereft of the energy to provide more than a glimmer of mere survival. The blunt term is, "burying each other." Those shocking words have a purpose—to remind us this is a fate you do not want for your church.

How to avoid it begins with understanding this is indeed what happens if we don't make happen something different. The foundational book on congregational life cycles is called *Taking Your Church to the Next Level* by Gary Mcintosh. The subtitle is right to the point: "What got you here, won't get you there." Cycles are inevitable; what we do about them is a choice. Somewhere in the maturity of a congregation, it can choose to renew itself rather than decline. Any church can do this—best to arrest decline before it sets in.

Plateaus are also normal church cycles—periods of consolidation, or rest even, of discernment that should precede a new direction. The danger is when they turn into drift. To avoid drift, embrace transition. Choose a time to get ready leading to a time of new vitality. "This too shall pass" is Biblical wisdom for when things are not going well. It is equally good to remember we have the power to help this happen. We are going from here to somewhere different— that's a transition. It's a good thing to make.

The congregation is always in its current cycle rather than some earlier one. Without assuming the earlier ones have gone away—they never do—each of us must be opening up to the ways in which the cycles of our lives and the opportunities of our congregational life are moving into alignment. What you *want* may still be coming into focus; what you *dream of* may still be preparing to appear. It should be this way for all of us, all of the time. In an ideal world, what we want and what we dream of would always be going on simultaneously, both leading and guiding us. They would be linked by *what we are making happen*, or gathering the energy to make happen, in an endless cycle of renewal. We would see ourselves as protean creators, even on the days we rest.

"The darkness around us is deep," as William Stafford put it in a poem read earlier this year, but he reminds us we are not "following the wrong god home." We will not "miss our star," as long as we are willing to know the kind of people we are and stay properly attentive to "the parade of our mutual life." What a memorable phrase!

This that is right here in front of us—this *parade*—is what we have charge of. We are not immune to history, or outside it. But this little corner of history belongs to us. We have the capacity to know well what we have inherited. We can be skilled and dedicated to shape the best present that is within our power. We can be inspired and faithful to the needs of those who will come after us. Small things these may be in the larger scheme, but they are our possession, our responsibility and our opportunity.

They are the hope perched within us.

We don't forget about the quicksand. When we do step into it, the situation carries some urgency. We can't stand there; we can't wait for somebody else to solve the problem. We can't whistle past the graveyard and expect some other day to work out an answer. Experts recommend this focus: What will be missing if we stay the same?

That is an opening to perceive opportunity, not loss. What calls out profoundly to our spiritual selves, individually and in community? What is indeed "perched in our souls"? If we get caught up in "fixing" things, we'll never know. There's no use changing a flat tire if the oil is low. You won't get far. No mission to the future can get under way without a comprehensive long-term strategy—not on a flipchart, but in our hearts.

Unlike quick and delusional fixes, plans take time. They call for patience as well as vision. We have to be willing to live in some tension and uncertainty, to sit close enough to the fire to feel the heat—and succeed. We can do that by actively helping each other—community is as community does. That sacred promise—that covenant—starts with accepting responsibility for ourselves. Don't be afraid to change your whole point of view—being horizontal is something the mind won't naturally embrace, but you can go there. Spread out—the wider the effort the better the results. Paddle, for Pete's sake—nothing is going to happen otherwise, and you will only be wet and muddy that much longer. Repeat as often as needed: There is firm ground out there somewhere and we will find it. Quicksand is scary but it is not forever—unless we let it be.

Remember this first and last: The thing with feathers called *hope*—"it never stops at all." It perches in your soul and mine—and certainly in the soul we share. Hear in your heart the closing line: "Yet, never, in extremity/It asked a crumb of me." Emily Dickinson's hope is perched in the soul of the eternal. That's why it is always there for us. In a season of hope, let us be unafraid to name our hopes—and follow them home.

Amen. Blessed Be. Shalom. Salaam.

Sending Up Sprouts

05 Mar 2017

I personally am 100% in favor of things that grow, including churches. It seems this is in harmony with an essential element of the universe itself, and certainly of the life within it. Everything living is also growing, and although no one knows the exact origin of life, we do know its trajectory—from the chemicals to the cells to the creatures, from the sea to the land to the stars.

Of course, there are seasons and cycles. Winter must come and all that lives must also die—how would we otherwise appreciate the amazing gift? Not to die is not to have lived. What we are called to do is align ourselves as we may with the energy of life.

I like planting things myself. We had a tree in Pennsylvania that literally came home in a Dixie cup from our son's preschool. I stuck it in the ground on the side of the house, right next to the outside faucet, to avoid running over it with the lawnmower. Later it went to a permanent location, and right before we moved in 2006, we took a goodbye picture of Ben standing next to it. Both son and tree had reached a considerably larger stature after 15 years. A decade later, the son is about to be a father and, in the photo our neighbor sent not long ago, that tree towers over the house.

All the vigor of growth will be on display all around us, we hope—coming soon to a season of spring near you. We do remember some cautions. First, of course—there are no guarantees. Farmers and gardeners know that, and so does every parent. It's where the gray hair actually comes from. But the way of growing things is just like any river, starting small and getting bigger, whether you are watching or not. The Parable of the Mustard Seed, told by Jesus, reminds us the seed grows by day and by night. That small phrase is the key to the metaphor of God's unceasing love.

It does help to watch—to do what you can with what you can provide. This is the human responsibility so clearly embraced in Unitarian Universalist faith and practice. There is work involved in growing—that too is essential to our tradition. We often hold ourselves to have no power at the central mystery. I don't see it like that, but we are all free to choose in this matter. Let us agree we are appointed to be present to mysteries, especially this one. "Spirit of Life" is how we address it. Further, we agree perfectly that we are always called to the tending and the nurturing, to the encouragement and the caring. Our human lives are a sentence to considerable vexation about the wind and the weather, the drought and the flood. Ultimately, we can be sure all life stubbornly insists on unfolding to its own design, not necessarily to our wishes, no matter how explicit.

This is one obvious lesson. It will be what it will be. Here is another: It will be stronger, and in the end, more successful if you remember to allow for some growing room. Clench your teeth if necessary. Trees will never grow strong roots if too much protected from the wind. We all have to learn much the same lesson about children. The hardest part is learning this for our own lives—adversity makes growing room.

And what lesson about churches? How could a church not be a place essentially engaged in continually growing? If not a place where our souls are stirred, why would we come to church? If not a place to get larger in heart, in mind, in caring, and in the making new of what the world needs, what would a church be? It's a hard bench if you are just sitting for an hour, never rising, as we say, "in body or spirit." That rising is an engagement in growth. If the companionship here proves steady and sustaining, why would we not seek more of it? Being with new people, and being with people you already know but are coming to know in new ways—that is engagement in growth. If wisdom falls lightly on us—or experience lands with a thud—why would we not want others around us to share the enlightenment and the burden also? We come to life singly and leave it that way too, but everything in between is entwined with other people. To bolster their number and make the ties richer is an engagement in growth.

Growing is what a religious community is for. It is the central purpose. Seasons and cycles come to congregations too. Some of them are seasons of adversity. You have been through one. In some ways, it is still with you. It is not the first and I hope none of us is so naïve as to think it will be the last. "Violently sweeping out your house" is what Rumi tells us the animations of adversity do. It is how you know they are real. The real adversity that hurts, real fate, and the real people who say and do things that cause us pain—these events and actions are what clear the way for new growth. These are, as Rumi also reminds us, the authentic "messengers from beyond."

Strength is often overrated. It is *resilience* that sustains us most. Go around telling everybody how strong you are and you are begging to get busted. Understand in your bones how resilient you are and you will be tested—but you will already know that. You also already know how to meet the challenge. One of the classic books about congregational growth is called *What Got You Here, Won't Get You There*. It is by Marshall Goldsmith. It is a cogent explanation of how and why seasons and cycles are perfectly normal in church life. The most essential wisdom is to recognize that and learn together how to make the most of them—how to harness this natural movement to flow in the direction you want. It is not actually that hard: Don't take it too personal, don't give up on each other, seek opportunities not obstacles, go with what is working, ask for the future instead of avoiding it. Well, okay—it is a *little* hard.

Not trying is what is fatal—being frozen. Sometimes we are inspired and sometimes…not. Sometimes we pull it off and sometimes…not. Sometimes we are truly kind and caring and sometimes…not. *This does not matter.* I mean the falling short—it doesn't matter because only we are here. Just as there are no sinners in a Unitarian Universalist congregation, so there are no saints. All of us are here being only human.

This question is posed in a way I love: What will you be in this year's garden? What is the seed within you? Almost certainly there is more than one—will you pick or will you let sprout whatever is vigorous? Will you make yourself ready, that the sprouting will happen? Will you help make the soil and the water and the sunshine ready, so others may send up the sprouts they are abiding? And here you know is where we must be called to what does matter—not for any kind of perfection but our straightforward willingness to be responsible for what we can help the future be.

Ministers are expected to have big thoughts once in a while, so here is my big thought on the subject: The seas will boil dry someday, but not likely in my lifetime or yours. Until it happens, we are actually in charge of most of the universe, because we are responsible for the corner in all the vastness where we actually live. We are simply tourists in the rest of it, which is all either very, very tiny or very, very far away. We are, I hope, appreciative observers, but we live only right here with each other. There are always uncontrollable storms but the vast majority of the future we will experience we will control. We will make that future with the people we choose to have around us.

"Good people," says Hildegard of Bingen, "Most royal greening verdancy…" It is the quite proper way to address good people, because royalty is who we are and greening is what we do. Add good soil and good energy and get verdancy. Here and everywhere, we are the seeds and we are given the garden. We are all together made for sprouting.

Amen. Blessed Be. Shalom. Salaam.

Mission Unpredictable

19 Mar 2017

In Junior High School I had the same Social Studies teacher two years in a row. I cannot for the life of me recall his name, but I can see him plain as day. I remember his daughter attended Wheaton College. He was very proud of her.

I can still hear him plain as day, too—fifty years later. He must have intoned these words two hundred times: "All progress is change; not all change is progress."

That old TV show began with these words, "Your mission, should you choose to accept it…" My teacher's mission was quite clear: When it comes to change, the "not accept" option does not actually exist. Change happens. The "progress" is up to us.

Where might First Parish find progress in the midst of change? We choose this theme for the Annual Fund Drive: "Now more than ever, we need one another." What do we ask of every member and friend? "Connect." Whatever we dream, we must dream together. Whatever we want to accomplish, we must do it together. Whatever we commit, we must all commit together—every link in the chain is crucial to the whole.

All together, you are now moving. Movement is essential to every organism and organization. Life is dynamic. There is no standing pat— tomorrow will be different. "Mission" then, is your choosing. You own the responsibility and the opportunity. It does not belong to a minister—whoever or whenever that minister might be. It is yours.

Start with "Caring"—as in, "caring for each other." This is a central value of church—indeed it may seem to be the essential value of any church. So obvious and so fulsomely asserted, caring mission can masquerade as standard operating procedure. I assure you, it is not. Some churches indeed do not hold this value as most important, and many churches who say they do are more talking the talk than walking the walk.

That usually happens because the critical discerning questions are never asked, or never answered. *Why* are we a caring community? *What* is our shared belief about the need and the possibility? *Who* is receiving caring, and who is giving it? How much of caring is a way we *are*; how much is what we *do*? How is caring living and visible?

Here is a second component of mission—"Equipping." This term may not be immediately familiar, but it covers everything we say and do with an ultimate purpose of helping us improve our lives. It is our learning how to be Unitarian Universalists, and how to carry that into the world. It is our learning to be better people and doing it beyond Sunday morning. It is both profound insight and connection—to each other, to the future and the past, to the cosmos and the community. It is equally quotidian and practical—what are those Seven Principles (see page iii)? What is a Welcoming Congregation? How about a Green Sanctuary? How important is shaping who we will be after walking out the front door from Coffee Hour? What are the most important tools we need—what is our religious equipment for ordinary living, and also for the everyday extraordinary?

From any perspective, mission is, like those Seven Principles, a circular concept. It cannot be represented as a list. Each element is intimately tied in with the others, and each both affects and reflects the others. Each element is necessary to the whole.

To complete our circle—at least for today—I suggest "Justice-making." If Caring tends to prompt the phrase, "for each other," it is Justice-making that is reflexively followed by, "in the world." The essential question is, "What difference does it make—not for us, but for other people?" How important is making the world a better place? What is our dream of "better," and what part of the world are we transforming? To change any large part of the world, you must plan carefully and persist. To be good stewards of some small part, you must focus correctly and act rightly. In either case, good intentions are not enough, and any lack of clarity invites a fatal drain of energy.

However we frame our mission, we must live in genuine welcome. An excess of Justice-making demands other people live the way we see fit. An excess of Equipping constricts the conscience. An excess of Caring fixates on who has already come, an inoculation of "how we do it here." Genuine welcome is an invitation to mutual growth.

Caring, Equipping, Justice-making—these are vital components of mission. Each incorporates the reality of change and the possibility of progress. How should the balance be struck among them? Most important, whatever the balance struck today, remember it will be something different tomorrow—or the next day at the latest. Real mission is like life itself—a journey unpredictable at heart and variable in expression. Who will be the same in a month or two, let alone a year or two? None of us. Nor will our world. Our mission is not impossible, but to grow into our dream it must be flexible and evolving, changing form and emphasis even as circumstances change over time.

Dream together? We can. Lean forward? We should. Move? We must. Amen. Blessed Be. Shalom. Salaam.

What We Talk About

02 Apr 2017

I bought a car in 1970 for $150. It was an old Volkswagen Beetle. It was painted orange with black spots—in other words, as a ladybug. When I say "old," it had a 1959 engine and a 1956 body, which had been towed out of a farm pond.

Early Volkswagens had certain peculiarities. You may remember they had two small rear windows, not one larger window as in later years. My Bug had one windshield wiper, maybe 6 inches long. It had no radio and no discernible heat. Instead of a gas pedal, I pushed my foot down on a small roller wheel made of hard rubber.

More pertinent, the car had no fuel gauge. It was very thrifty on gas, but obviously would not run forever. Refills sometimes came only 25 cents a pop—so this question was always crucial: Do we have enough gas to get there?

Will we have enough gas? It's the annual pledge-time question. A small group like First Parish is an early model—an antique even. We are willing to stand out in the crowd. We can go anywhere we choose, although not necessarily fast and not with as many creature comforts. We are thrifty and reliable, determined and adventurous. When things break, we fix them. We do worry about the gas. Will there be enough?

One time at 3 AM the ladybug did coast to a stop on the interstate a couple miles short. A buddy and I were returning from a blues club in Chicago. The Wisconsin State Patrol stopped almost immediately, toted us up to the all-night gas station and brought us back with the jerry can. He couldn't have been nicer. Recall that time—1970—and think skinny me with mustache and ponytail. I am still reminded help sometimes comes from places unlooked for, and people you might not immediately be comfortable with.

Still, this congregation has to keep going on its own hook, setting your own vision, employing your own assets and dialing up your own momentum. Fortunately, you have that history. You have believed in yourselves; you can plan for it to continue.

What we actually talk about though, when we talk about the future of First Parish—that is the critical question. I've pinched the image from the late Raymond Carver's groundbreaking story collection, *What We Talk About When We Talk About Love*. As with falling in love, the prospects are wonderful but there are pitfalls. The possibilities include the amazing, but also some confusion, frustration and even "failure to launch."

On the other hand, as with love, who would want to miss the experience?

When you talk about the future of your church, don't think of it as words spoken by your mouth. Think of what you might say—and what others might say to you—as coming from the heart. Think of it as conversation, as sharing in your community. Every human being faces central questions of life and death, of origin and fate. Each of us seeks purpose and meaning. So does every gathered human community. Every congregation occupies a continuum of time. Each individual moves through the present moment as a portal between the past and the future. So does the church. It too is always moving. It too will "never set foot in the same river twice."

Like a family, a congregation lives beyond the years of individuals. We inherit. We also bequeath. In between, we create. We don't worship what we were given, we reshape it into what we need and remold it into what we want to arise in the world. This is important: We are not given custody of Lenin's Tomb. We are not here just to dust the corners of some perfect shrine. Everything human is always under construction. As Unitarian Universalists we say this has to be, because that is how we understand the universe itself. In motion—that is how we see the spark of divinity. In the flame of our chalice we affirm the essence of life inside and all around us. It is all becoming new.

These are the questions that go with "becoming new": Who are we? Where are we going? How will we get there? In this context, think of them as *mission, ministry,* and *stewardship.* These are not mutually exclusive categories. Each one is also part of all the others. Different people use the terms in slightly different ways, which can be confusing. It helps to define them consistently and repeatedly for our context.

"Who are we," for instance, is at its core a statement of essential identity. The agreed purpose of a living body of people must be a declaration of its animating values. What do we believe that truly moves us? The minute we start moving, fueled by the energy of our values, we enter into ministry. It is everything First Parish does. Every act—personal and communal—must be infused with the spirit and practice of ministry. As a church, there is no other reason to exist. An old jazz song offers worldly wisdom: "Be nice to the people on your way up, you gonna see 'em on the way back down."

"Where are we going," then, is about what we do and how we act. It draws on mission for direction. It draws on stewardship for resources. "How will we get there?" That is the question of stewardship. It is what we choose, of time, energy and money.

The first point of emphasis is the choice—we always have one. We have to cope with circumstance, but we are never its prisoners. "We don't have enough… (Fill in the blank)" is actually a statement of *feeling.* Feelings are important and should always be heard, but they are not statements of fact. I never had enough gas in my old car, but I always managed to get where I wanted to go. You will, too. Time, energy and money always strike a balance—more of one, less of another. You must talk about the balance.

This balancing is for now and also for the future. In this case, "future" is defined as a three- to five-year period. If that seems like too short a timeframe, I assure you expert opinion is unanimous: Churches almost never plan even three to five years ahead, not really. Congregations overwhelmingly assume—often without ever explicitly saying so—the future will be a continuation of the present. We plan for next year by taking the current budget and adding or subtracting around the margins—a few percent more or less. This may be an understandable rebellion against the change that seems to overwhelm our lives in almost every other way, but it is doomed to ultimate failure. I'll offer one definition of failure: It is to lose what you cherish. What do you cherish too much to lose? You need to talk, to listen to your heart and spirit and then speak out.

You have a crucial success in what you have accomplished, in where you have already arrived. The future will always arrive, but how will you shape it? You have a preferred frame of endeavor—a professional minister, a very part time but still professional staff, and a congregation generous with its own energy in the life and leadership of the church. Exactly how much? In what ways? For how long? You need to talk. Among other reasons, there will never be any permanent answer. There has to be a process of conversation, ongoing, regular and resilient enough to anticipate new circumstances and respond to new challenges and opportunities. We have to *steer the barky*—it isn't going to go there by itself. You have to keep making all this happen.

And you have to talk about fuel. High mission and high ministry can't co-exist with low stewardship. Sooner or later—more likely sooner—the three must reach a comparable level. There is absolutely no wrong level of these qualities. What is wrong, what is not in any way sustainable, is to assume they can be disconnected. It is not possible to invest in or attain any one of them without the others getting the same attention. Now is the time to talk about how you will make that happen. Please join in.

Amen. Blessed Be. Shalom. Salaam.

Red Light, Green Light

21 May 2017

"Low and slow." "Low and slow." This is a phrase you do not want to hear when landing a jet plane on an aircraft carrier. The margin for error is vanishingly small. Too low and too slow means your plane may hit the "round down"—the stern instead of the deck. They call it a "ramp strike," and it makes an awful mess.

Carrier pilots are the most carefully selected and intensively trained flyers there are. Why do ramp strikes still happen? 50,000 pounds of F-18, moving 150 miles an hour on a black night and trying to find a very small and very dark landing space that is heaving and pitching on the open ocean—well, what could possibly go wrong?

What goes wrong is in the brain. Under stress, our "working memory"—what we have available to process and cope—erodes to a more and more narrow field. In a fascinating book called *Deep Survival*, author Laurence Gonzales explains how that can lead even the best-trained and most experienced pilots, river guides and mountaineers straight into disaster. Anxiety rapidly reduces perceived options. The pilot fixates on the deck—the place of physical safety, the emotional home—and literally never hears or sees all the blaring alarms going off to warn the approach is "low and slow."

These are experts, mind you. What about us? Ordinary people doing ordinary things—like living in religious community—can also suffer tunnel vision and "target fixation." It is especially important to note we are living with other people. Anxiety—like all emotions—is contagious. It can shoot through a group of people faster than the flu, and with equally painful results. How do we avoid becoming an anxious system?

Some of the answer lies in personal self-control. Remember the first time you drove a car? Do you feel that apprehension today? No—you have learned to manage the task and the anxiety. You can't—and shouldn't—make the fear go away. It is a powerful motivator to stay "on task" and thus keep safe. Controlling your own fears must also mean not stoking the fears of others. Again, this is not denial. It is about not encouraging panic. If we stampede for the exit, nobody will get out. Walk—don't run.

And of course, as healthy people we try in every area of our lives to construct systems and relationships that help us manage our emotions. The second law of thermodynamics reminds us everything heads toward chaos, but we try to slow it down.

Big decisions faced by a group—the kind requiring difficult choices—can be huge sources of organizational anxiety. Complex options—no answer perfect or painless—invite a crucial spiritual system for preventing overload. It is called "discernment."

As your congregation makes big decisions, it might be useful to review how discernment works, why it might be a better process for successfully identifying what exactly are those decisions, and coming up with the best available answers. It might be better, at least, than other decision-making processes we are familiar with or might just default to without even realizing we are doing that. Of course, we must then choose.

Discernment rests on a foundational commitment to living in a special kind of community that holds together when people disagree, or even act disagreeably. Every religious tradition aspires to this, but UUs must be especially clear on the point. We offer no eternal salvation, no "20-questions" catechism, no remission of sins, no uniformity of adaptable spiritual practice, no ashes-on-the-forehead or dreadlocked social location. Years ago, when I was president of a congregation facing a huge transition, I repeated this phrase at every opportunity, "everybody stays in the boat."

How do we—as a practical matter—avoid throwing people overboard or leaving them behind? We decide not to. Such decisions have an awesome power. Is it simple? Yes. Is it easy? Not necessarily. Is it doable? Absolutely—and it changes everything.

The first green light to discernment is this: Every member of the community has feelings, and every member is entitled to them and is welcome—in the agreed upon time and place—to express them. Being a safe place for everybody to have feelings and appropriately express them is how church is much more like a family—at least a minimally functional family—than a workplace or a neighborhood or a country club. Family is family—no matter what they say, unless it is egregiously violent—they cannot be anything else. A church is a place where we can take off the social mask and lay down the burden of being likeable to everybody in every circumstance of interaction. We are free only to the extent we are willing to show and see real selves, not paper dolls.

The second green light to discernment is this: Every member of the community has opinions, and every member is entitled to them and is welcome—in the agreed upon time and place—to express them. Accepting feelings is essentially an expression of our compassion for each other. Accepting opinions is an expression of our respect for each other. A feeling is something you *are*, and must be heard. It should not be a ploy for agreement because that infringes on the other person's right to his or her own feelings. An opinion is something you want to happen, and must be listened to. It invites by definition the expression of other opinions, which may agree or disagree. An opinion should never assume agreement because that is disrespectful of all other opinions. In a congregation it should not be a call to evidence or argument. We are not lawyers or scientists at work—we want everybody to stay in the boat. That means everybody's opinions have some handhold on validity, no matter how difficult it may be to grasp.

In a congregational setting of discernment, for instance, we present our opinions frankly and acknowledge that is what they are, not eternal truths to be announced to enlighten the multitude. A common technique is for all to speak once before any speak twice, and to ask for new opinions only, not lengthy rehashes of what is already said.

A much more crucial rule is this one: "I" statements only, please. "I feel." "I think." "I propose." Recruiting the choir invisible—"some people" who think or say as you do—is, to be blunt, not helpful. If they are present, "some people" can speak for themselves. If they are not present—well, we don't vote *in absentia*. More important, why do you need invisible allies? Don't you trust us to take *you* seriously? Don't you believe *you* are important to us? Don't you believe we really want to hear *you*—at least the first time? Remember we started with the First Principle—*your* worth and dignity (see page iii).

Then we vote, right? Not yet. In discernment the next step is *discern*. Prayer, meditation, reflection on what you have heard and what is in your heart—that is how discernment unfolds into decision. A space opens when words are sent away for a while, making room for inward working of the spirit. It is the space we fill with love even for people with whom we may have just vigorously disagreed. The goal is not what we want or what they want, but what is *right*. It is not evidence or argument that tips the scales, but community. We want to find what is right for everybody. That we can vote on.

How will you recognize it? It is simple enough. "Right for the community" is the place where you feel you can leave the room having been heard and honored—even if you did not get everything you wanted, or anything except that affirmation. It is the gift of genuine community. To give and receive it, you have to be quiet and open yourself.

Father Hosea Ballou, dead now 150 years, was famous for this Universalist testament: "If we agree in love, there is no disagreement that can do us any injury."

Amen. Blessed Be. Shalom. Salaam.

See You Sunday

17 Sep 2017

When I was a boy, Sunday was the only day my father did not go to work. He would shuffle around the kitchen in a shabby plaid bathrobe, likely as not in his bare feet. He would plug in the electric griddle and pull out the pancake mix, the milk and the eggs. He would flick water onto the griddle to see if it was hot enough, and then pour the batter out into steaming pancakes. When bubbles formed and broke on their surface, he would flip them over. When they were done, he would pile them on a big platter and put out the syrup.

Sunday was not a day my family went to church. This was rather unusual for the late 1950s and early 1960s, the high tide of church affiliation and attendance in all American history. It is far from unusual today. "See you Sunday," is more likely now to mean a rendezvous at the mall, a chat at the supermarket, a wave while walking the dog or jogging around the block. It is less likely to mean gathering in a house of worship.

For many Americans, "See you Sunday" no longer offers any promise of religious community. The New England states have especially low levels of participation.

Many people think that's just fine. My parents did. They both worked and my mother was also putting herself through college. They had three boys and a sizeable suburban house and yard to care for. Sunday morning was catch-up time, recreation time, downtime. They ran the wash and read the paper, cut the grass and got in a round of golf. Today, there seems to be more stuff to do than ever before in human history.

And where does it all get us? We are more accomplished, more entertained, better fed and better dressed. We are more busy—perhaps—and more hassled—probably. We seem to work harder and to play harder. Are we happier?

Being in regular religious community has been known to make people happy. The FDA has not verified this claim, and there is no warranty, express or implied. No promises are made in regard to eternal life or worldly prosperity. Your results may vary. Salvation may be by faith or works or by factors entirely random. See label for important information. Consult your religious professional before undertaking revelation, rapture, enlightenment or nirvana. Most side effects are temporary.

But here is what really matters. Here is how it works: "See you Sunday" means we will miss you if we don't. Really. We will miss you any day of worship, or at any other gathering of this community. We will miss you if you have come ten times or a thousand times, if you were here last week or last summer. We will miss you even if we can't immediately remember your name. (Here is where I remind you to wear your nametag, so we can greet each other by name even in moments of mental short circuit.)

This may seem paradoxical almost to absurdity. You can't remember my name—but you miss me? Well, of course! You are much more than your name. You are how you move, how you dress, how you talk—or don't. Each of us generates a solar flare of spiritual presence and physical being. Each of us carries the Spirit of Life around with us, and each of us lives in the penumbra of all the life we have ever encountered—and much that we have not. "The heart knoweth," is what Emerson said. And our hearts do.

Is this a little too mystical? Perhaps, but here we can return to the practical. On the most basic level, it's not like you are obligated to show up—this isn't work or school—but that actually makes the bond stronger. We all choose to come here. We can therefore be glad to see you in the particular fulfillment of a mutual but unspoken choice. We—like you—have lots of other stuff we could be doing, but we choose to be here. Wherever you come from, whoever you are, whomever you love—remember those words? Humans are choice-making creatures, and we all made this choice today. Right off the bat, we share something important—even crucial. We choose this relationship.

If we don't see you on Sunday, we will wonder where you are and how you are doing. Are you sick or sad or out of town? Are you worn out or up to your neck in alligators? Dan Hicks had a wonderful country rock song called, "How Can I Miss You If You Won't Go Away?"—there's truth there as well. We all need time away. You should never hesitate to take it. Remember, however, you don't leave the penumbra. This is the bedrock of congregational life. Near or far, this community always includes you.

Of course, there is no denying people can sometimes go missing for weeks and even months before that recognition stands up fully formed in our consciousness. I am convinced we are aware, though, even if unconsciously. The first cognitive function babies achieve is facial recognition, and humans are resolutely skillful at it beyond all other capacities. It is your voice and your walk and your mannerisms—it all registers. One measure of vitality in a congregation is how quickly that question—have you seen so-and-so?—becomes a conscious inquiry, and what action follows. The beloved, domineering Minister Emeritus of my Saco church was apparently in the habit of calling through the list of the missing on Sunday afternoons—immediately after the service.

Nobody would need or want this kind of bed check in today's world, but if we don't see you on Sunday, our lives are genuinely diminished. Believe it— a certain richness of experience evaporates. I tend to talk about the "energy of encounter." That is a social perspective that consciously identifies *relationship* as that which changes the world. Indeed, it changes the cosmos. Like atoms, we bounce off and head in new directions. Like billiard balls we rebound to a new position on the big green table. This can more properly be called Process Theology, a framework of understanding very congenial to Unitarian Universalism. The Process Theologians see it all as a dynamic, a becoming, an unfolding. There is no fourth wall between humans and the divine. We are equipped to do more than be grateful to a Creator or a creative force in the universe. We *become* Creators. It is what we are meant to be.

If we see you Sunday, the essential is accomplished. We can share with you the ricochet, the transfer of energy into motion in a different direction. Some days that is all we get—or give. Remember we are in a caring relationship, so it is never a stranger encounter, either good or bad. There is a larger possibility chosen, a conscious opening to something entirely different—that we will "walk together." It's much more than a ricochet, in other words. The Puritans and those who followed understood this as "the congregational way," and used this specific language. Just for fun, let me propose it is more crucial to who we are and what we are about than any theological or political belief. We can proclaim, "We do not stand; we move," and still be properly clothed.

William Channing Gannet in the 1800s and James Luther Adams in the 1900s made this point. They were very big thinkers. You and I don't have to be. We can choose and act today on what is right here before us in our own ordinary lives. If we see you Sunday, we can fulfill our covenant to accept each other in all our humanity. We can practice the central spiritual discipline of living in trust, with each other and the universe. We can journey in company through the wilderness and the garden that are the landscapes of every life. We can even make pancakes.

We will know and be known—timeless language for a timeless gift. The gift of family is what we give one another. See you Sunday. See you at the Meeting House.

Amen. Blessed Be. Shalom. Salaam.

A Sermon on the Amount

18 Mar 2018

"Déjà vu all over again" is one classic formulation attributed to the Hall of Fame catcher—and Hall of Fame language innovator—Yogi Berra. "I've been here before—and before, and before." Well, I have and so have you. Fund Drive Sunday comes around each year. You probably wonder—as do I—what new can possibly be said?

The answer may well be, "nothing"—but we say it anyway. Please don't be cynical about this. Think how many times in your life it is actually crucially important you say something you have already said. Try these phrases for examples: "I love you." "Everything will be okay." "You did your best." "No monsters under the bed." "Your hair looks just fine." There are many more—we could hardly get along without them.

Fund Drive is like that. For those who may be unfamiliar with the concept, let me explain as simply as possible—this is how we pay the bills. The baggy old minister joke about "the sermon on the amount" goes with a pithy truism especially for Unitarian Universalists. "The free church," we say, "is not free." We are justly proud of our free church; we cannot enjoy our freedom without taking responsibility for maintaining it.

Or, it is sometimes necessary to ask, if you aren't willing to pay for church, who will? The person sitting next to you, maybe? Some philanthropist? Old money, new money—drug money? Well, we have to get it somewhere! There is no outside income, except for some renters, a few fundraising events and a very modest endowment.

About 80% of what we expect to spend on personnel and all other operating costs between this July 1 and June 30, 2019, we must pledge now. We really wouldn't want it to be any other way. Churches too rich with endowments historically choke on them sooner or later. Churches too addicted to being landlords *become* landlords. Churches too caught up in unrelenting fundraising bargain away the soul of spiritual community.

But you need to say yes. "Yes," means you consider yourself a member of this community. You attend worship. You come to programs and join activities. You light a candle occasionally for the Joys and Sorrows of your own life and for others. We don't pretend to know exactly why we are here. We don't quite live up to our ideal of being completely welcoming—but we never stop trying either. Our souls sometimes feel lifted and sometimes feel lost—but we make this human journey together. Each of us lights the Chalice and keeps it lit for those traveling with us and for the world. That matters.

23

Tuesday is the first day of spring. It is déjà vu all over again. Every spring is the same, but every spring is also unique. This one, for instance—yipes! It is too early to know much at all about what is unfolding, but we know something is. What elevates our hearts is what we have left behind, what is now underway—and what might be coming.

I did get out for a garden tour before the latest unpleasantness. I avoided the remaining puddles and tiptoed over the places still soft and saturated. I checked out the shoots already emerging—an inch or two maybe, and some buds already formed. There are not as many of either as I hope will be there—there never are. I can't speak for all gardeners, but I often get very depressed during the first few inspections. There are dead tree limbs everywhere. Places are flooded I thought I had filled last summer. Some branches have clearly demised. There is debris everywhere. Much of it, unfortunately, is trash blown in over the winter. The landscape is hangdog and scraggly.

This too shall pass. I remind myself every spring. There are years of love and care invested in my garden. Only a few of them have been by me. Over a hundred came from those before me. Yes, it is possible to look and see how fragile it all is, how easily swept away by any passing storm, by the cold and the snow and the chilling winds. It is easy enough to see how transient it all is, how casually drowned by a few years of neglect, how quickly turned back into weeds and briars. Nothing I do will outlast me by more than a few seasons—unless someone else comes along and takes it up.

I garden in some hope that will happen. I garden in the present tense, in the pure pleasure of doing it—because I enjoy the process on many levels. I garden in the possibilities, teasing them out of the ground, out of the plants, out of my instincts and skills. I garden because a vision comes into view year by year, even as it changes. It is never perfect and it is never finished. Why would I ever ask it to be? What else would I be doing? Where else wait and work so certain something unexpectedly good will come?

So here we are in our garden. It is never perfect and it is never finished. Why would we ever ask it to be? Why would we ever want more than the unexpected good? Where would we ever be more clear it will come, watch it arrive, feel it transform us?

Yogi Berra, also: "When you come to a fork in the road, take it." Let's do that.

Amen. Blessed Be. Shalom. Salaam.

The Deliberate Vision

15 Apr 2018

It is a good thing to have a window that looks out on the world. Mine is at the back of the house, at the end of a narrow second floor hallway. It looks out into the yard. I almost never fail to stop for a moment on the way up and down the back stairs.

In this bashful spring the view from that window isn't changing very rapidly. The daffodils have fully emerged but no blooms yet. The red maple buds—candles of the season—are invisible until you get three feet from the trees. The line of sight to the shopping center still presents a garish intrusion, there being no new foliage. The grass is still more tan than green. A snowdrift lingers, shaded on the north side of the house next door. And I never thought I would be lonely for the first dandelion.

Mine is a tree house view. A large silver maple is right off the corner of our kitchen. It is close enough that I had one major trunk taken out a few years ago, but I love looking out from almost within the soaring branches. I feel part bird. The birds are often crows and seagulls in our neighborhood—no nobility or cheeriness but a certain street swagger I have to honor. I often feel like a very modest version of the Creator God from this perch, but this year I am reminded the energy of life doesn't come from me.

Still, spring is visible. Not with the eyes, of course. Eyesight is a physiological process of the landscape through lenses and optic nerves, but what we see, on the other hand, is a product of our brains. There we pretty much see what we want—what we are used to or expecting or have decided we will see. Recall the classic gorilla experiment, in which the subjects are officiously instructed to pay close attention to two people talking. They do, and when quizzed recall the conversation in great detail. They *never* report the person in a gorilla suit who runs right through the middle of the room. They don't see the gorilla even in a later version, when it actually stops and jumps up and down. There can't be a gorilla—so very deliberately the brain refuses the sight.

First Parish now has a great opportunity in congregational life to see what you want, to shape a deliberate vision of what will be, even if not yet. Vital communities find a window on the world and frame what they will see through it. Don't miss the gorilla, but do become a place of intentional spiritual vision. I've adapted from church consultant Wayne Whitson Floyd five community practices to choose richness of soul.

The first he calls the *Practice of Discernment*. To "discern" is to see things clearly despite distractions, despite fog and darkness, people in gorilla suits, lost car keys and a nagging sense that you have missed something critically important because the Red Sox are off today. I suggest these things are important in their own ways, but they should not be surpassingly important in our lives. We are called to uncover our true selves, to expand our sense and our sensibility, to grow into the people we are capable of being. This is not a task for the faint of heart. It is not the manic collection of stuff. Reflection helps— that still small voice has to be heard. But the central challenge is always to bring "who we are" and "what we do" into closer alignment. Discernment is vision that inspires movement. Seeing requires doing, but which way to go?

The *Practice of Story* is how we gain that sense of direction. The highest quality of a community is to be a vision-seeking people. It is to be on a communal quest, to read and interpret what were long ago called, "the signs of the age." We are engaged in a dynamic of creation, in an adventure in the physical and spiritual world. Every sign and portent is interpreted by story and every adventure gives birth to an epic. Humans are narrative creatures. The stories we tell about ourselves have a significant impact on our life experience. Tales of helpless woe generate greater woe. Tales of challenges accepted do not always generate triumph, but they do generate the resilience we must have.

Vision-seeking communities treasure stories of vision being gained, of trials overcome or at least survived. Their story is of a better future and aid that will abide.

These invite us to understand in turn the *Practice of Proclamation*. What truth lies at the heart of things? How clearly will we testify to what we find? This may seem to presuppose some answer about God, but if so, it is not an answer about the existence of God. It is the nature of God that is more crucial. If we find an angry and vengeful God, our lives will proclaim those qualities. If we find a patient and compassionate God, our lives will proclaim entirely different qualities. Our story of God defines us.

Our story can be of no God at all, but it must be of the transcendent. We must practice a passionate sense we are not alone. We are not all that is. Conscience knows the present moment is not the only moment. It knows the people around us matter. It honors those who lived before and provides faithfully for those who come after.

Conscience nourishes relationship. Relationship nourishes the *Practice of Hospitality*. The universe unfolds moment-by-moment, and so do we. This very next moment brings the opportunity to say or do something different. Are we a community living this truth? Are the "words of our lips and the meditations of our hearts" acceptable in the sight of a people who truly welcome the stranger? How many ways has each of us found not just to tolerate others, but also to include them? Is our narrative one of listening, sharing and understanding? It is hard to express delighted good cheer when others stubbornly fail to see exactly what we see, but we must not chain ourselves to our own habitual view. Our hospitality must be radical: Are other people's needs more important than my preferences? This is the central question of all religions.

We answer loudly with our words and more loudly with our actions. The *Practice of Service* is what enables us to hold up our heads in our community and in the world. To be authentic in welcome we must do more than invite others to join us. We must find paths of service that enable them to invite themselves. To be authentic in gathered community we must do more than allow others to participate. We must find paths of service that encourage them to transform us. We must be as willing to change as we ask others to be. As we are transformed, so must we benefit the larger world. We must be willing to go forth and serve the greater good. Our deliberate vision has a purpose. We are not busy growing souls for their own sake. A *bodhisattva* remember, is one who turns away from earned enlightenment to aid all others to accomplish it as well.

So then, it is a path: *Discernment* that we may see clearly; *Story* that we may take heart; *Proclamation* that we may speak with authority. These are critical practices of spiritual community, of intentional quest for the deliberate vision to strengthen and enrich our lives. The practice of *Hospitality* follows, to offer this vision to others and gain its full reward. Finally, the practice of *Service* helps our own hearts love, and take from this place that hope which all hearts crave. The world cannot live without it.

Whatever we may be without in this season of growing, whatever we may lack or have lost over the winter months, we have reasons to be grateful. That which we have and those who are present are worthy of our appreciation. This is not disrespect of those who are gone. Indeed, it honors them in the best way we can, by living fully the life they gave over into our hands. We are fortunate indeed to have the opportunity to call ourselves a vision-seeking people, and gifted beyond words to have it be altogether possible our visions may indeed come to pass.

Amen. Blessed Be. Shalom. Salaam.

Attitude for Altitude

10 Mar 2019

One of the most sacred responsibilities of congregational ministry is the strategic belaboring of the obvious. Once in a while—not too much and not too little—ministers must artfully state the apparent. Nowhere between birth and death is more challenging than the occasion of the Annual Fund Drive. Most ministers in fact would greatly prefer addressing either birth or death to standing in the pulpit "talking about money."

The whining on our ministers' Facebook page is almost hilarious: "Do I have to do it?" "What do I say?" "Do I harangue them or inspire them—or both?" "Does anybody have any good ideas?" "Does anybody know something to say that actually works?" That's probably my favorite—where, dear colleague, did you somehow get the notion any part of ministry ever actually *works?*

Well of course the magic often appears, which is why we do our best and hope for the best and remember always that after that it is out of our hands. This is actually good wisdom for life in general, for all of us making this road trip from here to there and then wherever, by day and by night, fair weather and foul. My first good idea follows immediately: At least 90% of the good in congregational life is—you guessed it—in *your* hands, in the hands of the people of the church. You bake the cake. The minister should try hard to get the icing on properly. Candles are optional but always fun.

My second good idea is this: "Love Will Guide Us"—but we do got bills. The Fund Drive Committee properly chose the first phrase to inspire and elevate you, to encourage your good spirits and your enthusiasm, to remind you of what is here and what will be here if you continue to bring the ingredients of good will and mix them artfully and with proper care for each other. I could not agree with them more. The love we hold is also love we use—it steeps in our hearts; it takes wing in our words; it flourishes in the work of our hands. First Parish is richly endowed with this love. It is how you save each other; it is how you save the world—this small but crucial part of the world, the place you actually live in and the people you actually live among. Be assured, this matters. It is the only way the larger world and all her people can ever be saved.

In the meantime, there are bills. *Stating the obvious here*—at least I hope it's obvious. Remember I cited the responsibilities of "congregational ministry"? The congregational polity—how we do church in our tradition—rests on that word *congregational*. It rests explicitly on the *Cambridge Platform* of 1648. That is indeed the Cambridge down the road apiece, and it is indeed our discomforting forebears of The Godly Commonwealth. They weren't Unitarians to be sure, and Universalism hadn't been invented. But they denied that anybody outside their church should have the right to tell them what to do. This surely is the core of our lineage to this day. No bishops, thank you. They were prepared to fight, although it didn't come to that.

A church in which the congregation has full sovereignty must by definition be a church the congregation is prepared to pay for. If you want to make the rules, you have to have the gold. Otherwise, somebody else is really in charge.

The headquarters of the Unitarian Universalist Association is close—sometimes uncomfortably so. No matter what they may occasionally imply, they have no authority in your church. There is no religious office higher in the UU world than *minister*. Whatever the mumbo jumbo cited to attain that place, only a congregation can ordain a minister, and every UU congregation chooses its own. When they see fit, every congregation has the right to unchoose its minister. And no minister is ever actually in charge of a church. You, as all UU congregations do, elect your Executive Board. I not only do not get a vote; I only speak at all by the good graces of the Chair. *True fact!*

Per ardua ad astra—that's the motto invented for the Royal Flying Corps in 1912. It remains the motto of the Royal Air Force. The common translation is, "Through adversity to the stars." *Ardua* also evokes the sense of effort or even struggle, of sustained work and the taking of calculated risk, of stretching and seeking even when inconvenient or costly or discouraging. It suggests meaningful persistence. There is no other way to accomplish the *astra*—no other way to reach the stars. They beckon us from the highest altitude there is.

We have to want to get there. There are unlooked-for happenstances, but most of the time the attitude is what has to happen before the altitude is even possible. We have to affirm what is worthwhile to us. We have to understand our actual capacity. We have to take the steps, make the journey, find the answers and light the way. Nobody ever got anywhere important by waiting for every detail to be in order before setting out.

And we only go there together. There is no other destination and no other path.

Stating the obvious here. Amen. Blessed Be. Shalom. Salaam.

Falling Upward

07 Apr 2019

My father inherited a large sailboat from his father. This was not entirely intentional. Grand-pop Chandler had a gift for anything mechanical in his 75 years of life. He tended a large vegetable garden and many backyard animals, but had no discernible interest in boats. My father, on the other hand, wanted a boat all his adult life. He never owned even a rowboat.

After my Dad settled his father's estate, he had five thousand dollars in hand. This must have been the permission—and the found money. He bought a 44-foot double-ended cutter, with a 65-foot mast and a mainsail the size of a Fenway tarp. The *Windover* was welded out of angle iron and steel plates, made by a man who built Chesapeake Bay workboats. It was a Queen Mary behemoth. Indeed, on one of our first outings we did cleanly take out 20 feet of pier when my father misjudged his landing.

Uncle Ed eventually rebuilt the entire interior with beautiful woodwork. My father added all the navigational bells and whistles. My mother agreed to be first mate, and they took that boat a thousand miles up and down the waterway to Florida every year for a decade, and often lived aboard—with a cat named George at one point. That boat—and each successor—was Dad's defining joy every day for the rest of his life.

Grand-pop never knew of course, but that is sometimes the nature of legacies. Each of us is a domino in a long chain. What we do and say has consequence far beyond what might be obvious or even apparent. Needless to say, there are often effects far beyond the intentional. Your life may be filled with sound and fury—as is mine. But life does not "signify nothing"—at least not when considered on the human scale. Most likely none of us will change history, but each and every one of us will change the world.

What we are matters. What we do and say matters. Knowing we are building some kind of legacy in every human encounter of everyday, we are reminded to be both humble and audacious. We are challenged to take care in the small things as well as the great ones. "Little pitchers have big ears" is what used to be said about kids overhearing adults in conversation, and memory has a way of marking us up for publication. Almost everything will be lost, but the "almost" takes in a lot. And remember most of all to be fully human. The best memories, happy or sad, are the ones with real people in them.

"Falling upward" is a phrase I have borrowed from the Franciscan spiritual teacher Richard Rohr. His book by this title explores the crucial idea that the soul work of the second half of our lives needs to be very different from the first half. My suggestion is that we are always falling into the future—we hope that motion is some kind of upward. Of course, how we define *up* and *down* is quite critical. We hold essential power over our own perspective. We can see it this way: Journeying through adult life, we transition from a future that includes us—indeed it mostly centers on us—to a future that gradually does not include us, at least in our limited mortal sense.

Yet if we are wise, we come to know how many ways that future has just as much meaning, that it has dimensions practical and spiritual that transcend our own possibility. We are larger *now* because we think about *then*. We are larger *here* because we accept one day we will *not be here*. We have more *today* because we give more to *tomorrow*. This is intentional legacy building. It is what we choose—to contribute to something larger than our own lives that will be good now but also outlast our own lives. It is what we decide is worthy now and likely to be worthy in the future. Nourishing something worthy is an essential definition of a life well lived. It is, in the universal image, the planting of a tree that will shade the children of children not yet born.

How lucky we are to get this opportunity every year in the Annual Fund Drive. I'm not being entirely facetious—just a little bit facetious. Seriously, your church community has been worthy for a lot of years, and it will continue to be worthy for as many years to come as we can possibly foresee. I'm sure of it. How so? Well, it is *your* church; it is in your hands; it is sustained by your effort and energy and joy. You have a million reasons to believe in yourselves. You are not perfect or all-powerful, but thank goodness there is no need to be. Remember the advice, *fully human*. Communities have that quality as well as individuals. Remember the other quality you need—to be *audacious*. Audacity is how we can believe in the future. Audacity is how we are able to love. Audacity is how we must *prevail*, not just endure, as Faulkner declared.

"Falling upward" is exactly what we are best equipped to do. It is the right direction—the direction of sky and stars. It is the right movement—not limited by flapping our arms but carried by larger forces although we see them not. It is our belief in each other that makes it happen. I encourage you to fly forth freely into your legacy.

Amen. Blessed Be. Shalom. Salaam.

Human After Always

Kingdom of the Sick

27 Nov 2016

Sally keeps NPR on the radio in her car, so I know that is where we were one winter night in 2010, listening to a man speaking who did not have a body. It was ten minutes or so before I realized he did not actually have a voice either. He was breathing through a machine and speaking through a synthesizer.

We were not having a visit from the other side, although we might as well have been. The man's name was Tony Judt. He had ALS—Lou Gehrig's disease. He was utterly paralyzed—no muscle control at all. A few involuntary functions were still going, like his heartbeat, but that was it. Judt described his absolute physical helplessness bluntly but not without a wry humor. He told of being put to bed at night, his attendant turning off the light and leaving the room, and of then lying awake for hours unable to move a muscle—and of what happens when you have an itch.

There was nothing wrong with Judt's brain. He described passing the long hours of night running pictures through his head, and—much of the time—composing his thoughts as a leading historian, cultural critic, teacher and public intellectual. By morning, he had ready for dictation the continuation of his decades of work.

Judt was a brilliant interview subject—lively, interesting, wide-ranging, pointed and present. He died in the summer of 2010, but not before publishing a final major work, and completing the manuscript of an equally well-reviewed memoir of his illness.

In the kingdom of the blind, the one-eyed man is king—we have heard the proverb, and perhaps we think it is the same with sickness: Anyone who is well must be king. But perhaps that reflexive judgment is too easy, too gratuitous and even shallow. Perhaps it is part and parcel of our American cult of wellness, of clinging to youth and almost compulsive activity up to and beyond the point of foolish pain and dangerous overreach. Perhaps it is instead a symptom of denial and timidity, a guarded unwillingness to follow the thread of life wherever it may lead us.

To encounter someone who is sick—especially someone gravely ill—is often to find a startlingly different reality than we may expect or assume. Those in the immediate grip of mortality often shock us by not just craving peace. They may indeed seize it with both hands—displaying a vigor of life's energy that can be all out of proportion to the infirmity of body or even mind. How many times have you heard of, or felt, a gift of compassion and composure, not as the well person gave it to a "patient"—as was presumably planned—but as it was *received* from that patient? There is an ageless reason why we lean close to hear—the blessing is so often actually for us.

You may have heard of the *Jefferson Bible*. Our third president, polymath that he was, compiled a chronological life of Jesus of Nazareth. In cutting and pasting, he dropped the miracles the gospels attributed to Jesus. We may still agree with this Enlightenment view as far as Jefferson took it—that miracles were neither necessary nor proper to prove divinity—but we can also understand those miracles primarily as evidence of healing. The sick can give us a profound appreciation of "healing."

Healing is not curing. The wonders of modern Western medicine are many—including cures for medical conditions that would have seemed miraculous only a few years ago. Look closely at miracles of *healing* and see something else at work: Not the disappearance of illness or injury but its integration, the restoration of wholeness even in diminution, the reconciliation of the self and the social bond. The sick often uncover this gift in the uttermost depths of their illness and despair, and then they offer it up to us. Even those at the end of life—knowing they are at the end of life—find so frequently not an overwhelming sense of loss but a surpassing sense of completion—of passing, however understood, from one phase of existence, to some other phase. We can know in their company life is indeed a biomechanical process, but also something beyond that.

To this lesson of healing, add that of enduring. In the kingdom of the sick, patience is not a passive virtue; it is an active necessity. How many of us go through the day longing to be more "grounded," or "centered," more "appreciative" or "mindful," more "in the present moment"—and less processing regret or stifling apprehension?

Certainly illness can be processed as a project with its own deadlines, goals and action plans—realistic or absolutely deluded. But how much more often does the learning come that patience is essential. We soon learn the human body's mechanisms take time for healing. And the mechanisms of chemotherapy, surgery and rehabilitation are deployed as well over extended periods. A cold will take ten days no matter what you do. Something more serious may take months or even years. Might as well leave this rushing and frenetic world and live out the virtues of hunkering down. Time is elastic not linear. This is a gift we can gain and receive in the midst of illness.

Finally, this lesson practical, social and spiritual: The gift of repairing. To understand the central goal of healing, to appreciate the fundamental mechanism of patience and perseverance—these are dimensions sustained and progressing toward the culmination of putting right what is not, or has not been. What is not right is often the focus. The injury or illness naturally draws the attention—it is why you are off work; it is why we are calling or sending a card or coming to hold your hand.

It will take its course. A goal just as crucial is the repair of what has not been right, sometimes long before this particular episode of mortal life. We know this. Our shared narratives are common—of forgiveness between children and parents, between partners and spouses, between friends or even mere acquaintances. These are truisms because—surprise—they actually happen. Stripped of what we create—the accumulated artifice of constructed roles and mediated reality—we touch what is real between us. Forgiveness postponed bursts to the surface. Absolution denied emerges unstoppably. Strained tolerance—or even total alienation—melts from our hearts. We find our hands touching, our words softening, our relationships knitted up not in raveling of cares but sinuous in resilience and in entwined, inescapable connection.

We suddenly find we are together in only this place in absolutely this moment—the most profound truth available to human beings. Our deepest longing—to escape the pervasive sense of being sundered from others—is suddenly gratified. Perhaps only a few minutes or days, but possibly a long and treasured memory, this great gift secures our hearts and our spirits without hardening them. It is an altogether *bona fide* miracle—to become stronger and more resilient through the mechanism of greater weakness and vulnerability. Who among us can fail to see revelation here, if we have the courage to name it? Who will refuse to recognize a reality so transcendent, if we will accept it?

From the kingdom of the sick then, like the gifts delivered by the Kings of Orient, come these three treasures—healing, enduring, repairing. They are delivered to us if we care to receive them. They come despite our gnarled lives, ignoring our transgressions and evasions, regardless of our worldly accomplishment or lack of it. They come to us because we too are divine. Somewhere within us is that inherent dignity and worth, that all-encompassing grace. They come because we are always sick, but never undeserving.

May the moment always arrive when they come to you and yours.

Amen. Blessed Be. Shalom. Salaam.

Affectionately Yours

05 Feb 2017

I watched a mushroom cloud rise over Washington, D.C. the other night. "Have Yourself a Merry Little Christmas" was sung softly in the background. The scene was on TV, thankfully, not Twitter. The date Dec. 11, 1945 flashed on the screen first, and what unfolded was the season finale of "The Man in the High Castle." The fictional premise of the Philip K. Dick novel was the Nazis winning World War II with their own A-bomb.

An atomic bomb certainly spoils Christmas. That premise is as chilling as the scriptwriters could have desired, and they picked the perfect soundtrack for a horrifying alternate reality. "Have Yourself a Merry Little Christmas" comes from the 1944 film "Meet Me in St. Louis," which tells the fanciful but affecting story of a middle-class family swept up in the 1904 St. Louis World's Fair. Judy Garland did the warbling.

But here's a fact: Garland refused at first to sing "Merry Little Christmas." She declared there was no way the lines, "Have yourself a merry little Christmas, it may be your last…" were coming out of her mouth directed at Margaret O'Brien, playing her spunky five-year-old sister. "The audience will never forgive me," Garland complained.

So the line was changed: "Have yourself a merry little Christmas, let your heart be light." Garland sang a classic—from the grinding last winter of (real) World War II.

There's more: In 1957 Frank Sinatra wanted to record a "jolly" Christmas album, so the songwriter, Hugh Martin, made another change. "Until then we'll have to muddle through somehow," became the cheerier, "Hang a shining star upon the highest bough." Muddling was adequate in 1944, but quite out of fashion in the hyper-confident 1950s.

Popular culture is famously a mirror to what is happening in our lives. It is often cracked or distorted, but on this occasion pivots perfectly on affectionate relationships. Notice the line Garland vetoed is much closer to truth—*any* Christmas indeed might be our last. What Sinatra resisted is also much closer to truth—we do indeed *muddle through* life. But those two consummate entertainers helped create powerful vignettes of ideal family. An older sister sings to cheer up a younger one on Christmas Eve. Stoic passivity yields to small but decisive action—we mostly do star-top the tree every year.

Pause here to note how quickly Christmas 2016 evaporated from our hearts. And this, too: Despite their immense popularity, Garland and Sinatra were deeply unhappy.

That juxtaposition of fame and futility reveals a crucial dilemma—how do we get along with each other? What really connects us? How in the name of God—or whomever you want to call on, from Freud to Elvis—do we make it work? Will we—can we—ever admit how hard it is to be in relationship?

I'll raise this question at the risk of being considered cynical, or pessimistic, or even caught with the family linen showing. I rest my case on experience—mine and yours. Pretending we can't see what life shows us, we can't hear the words we speak, we can't feel the pain we give and take—that may be the easier path by some measures. But it also leaves us fatally disoriented, filled with longings we can neither satisfy nor escape. You can run but you can't hide—but we run and run and run. It is a curse of our age.

I've told this story for years: When I grew up, everybody in the family was happy as long as we had enough cars to go around. The worst I can remember was having a serious girlfriend but no vehicle. They had me over a barrel every time. I would tiptoe through Friday dinner. What kind of mood my parents were in at the end of their workweek could sometimes cause a bit of collateral damage. "Can I borrow the car?" was a question very hard to get on the floor if they got in a spat—and those obeyed no pattern I could ever unravel. I still can't unravel spousal thunderstorms, even my own.

My parents were married more than 61 years until my father's death, so you know they managed to work things out. I do too—38 years now, and still with my first wife, as the joke goes. We have learned more affectionate expectations, and to moderate the occasional friction instead of wasting energy pretending it won't happen. There is a lot to be said—I give this advice freely— for "containing the abrasion." People who have figured out how to do that are going to be way ahead in the staying together department. Garland and Ol' Blue Eyes—for all their talent, magnetism, and wealth—never did.

Adjusting expectations—you and I might learn to do that. The "Peanuts" character Linus Van Pelt memorably proclaimed, "I love humanity. It's people I can't stand." After 50 years you can still get a t-shirt showing him saying that. Charles Schulz perfectly captured a moment of pop culture rue. We are called every day of course, to do exactly the opposite of Linus—to get along with people. They are all around us, while "humanity" is abstract. It doesn't know or care how we feel. Love has no impact on it.

"Love" is a cumbersome word. It might be better said that affection is what our relationships with other people must rest upon, no matter how close or far away. This is a confounding paradox. People who don't matter to us actually have no power to hurt us emotionally. Only the ones we care about do damage. Of course, they are the same ones who uplift us, gladden us, and console us. What did Paul Simon say? "I have no need of friendship, friendship causes pain/It's laughter and it's loving I disdain." If we don't let anybody near us, we get no pain—and no benefit. Only those we allow within our compass— those who allow us within theirs—nourish the priceless gratitude of being.

This is the crucial purpose of church. Church is a container holding affectionate relationship. We preach it, we teach it to our children, we practice it to an astonishingly high degree. Why and how are we able to do that? We are not exempt from the flaws of human nature. We are never spared grief and care and disappointment for very long. None of us qualifies for sainthood in our temperament or a mood of endless good will. Yet here we are, living in amazement. It is the most important gift of our church.

We accomplish no perfection, but we start with the understanding it isn't going to happen and it isn't supposed to. This is important. Remember—*realistic expectations*. We hold them of ourselves and of each other. We start also with the crucial insight of Unitarian Universalist faith: Belief is not central to church or even to religious life. Of course we all believe things—and we should. But we never affirm any one religious belief as the core purpose of our community, let alone the common affirmation. What do Unitarian Universalists believe? The bad old answer is, "whatever we want to."

But wait—maybe it is not so bad. Maybe a re-phasing will work. How about, "a belief is not what we gather to uphold." Call it an "elevator sentence." You have noticed our "Congregational Greetings" takes place within our worship. Why? It is not a social function, but a sacred one. To greet wholeheartedly all who come is our religious opportunity and obligation. It belongs inside our sacred space—our sanctuary. It belongs within our sacred time—within the service, not peripheral to it but at the heart.

Likewise, we place our shared Joys and Sorrows at the heart of our worship. Who matters more than those present with us today—and those we care about? We cannot care for the world unless we first care for each other. It is our great affection—for which we strive and sometimes struggle—that unites us, that makes us a special community, that unleashes what is good in our souls and what good we can do beyond these walls.

"Affectionately yours"—may it always be true.

Amen. Blessed Be. Shalom. Salaam.

The Ritual of Renewal

26 Nov 2017

This might be called the "in-or-out" season. Are we still in something like early fall or is it really early winter? If you are inside there is one answer. Outside there may be another. The contrast between sunshine and freezing rain is usually pretty stark in this neck of the woods. We've had both. Are you in the holiday frenzy—already got the list and prepared to check it twice? Or is that you with small and stubborn hope digging your heels in, clinging to a shrinking patch somewhere outside the impending deluge?

I have been clearing the garden for the winter, which is much easier before everything freezes to the ground. Whether warmish or coldish or even wettish—in-or-out, remember?—the light has changed. It is a subtle but powerful signal the seasons are moving on. My attention has changed as well. In the full light of day, I concentrate on completing a large task before winter sets in. That winter is coming is no longer a "later-on" abstraction, but a concrete arrival. My eyes are quite literally on all the garden debris that needs to be cleared—soon, not some indefinite time in the future.

Life is like this, yes? We plow along through the routines, resolutely or not on any given day. We construct over time—we hope—more lasting projects. We hold a job or build a career. We plait interlocking relationships. They spiral from centrally intimate partnerships all the way out to neighbors we wave at without knowing their names. We build homes and families—and gardens, or stamp collections, or watercolor technique or associations of community from church to the Scouts to the Rotary.

Only once in a while does the fog blow away and leave us staring out at the ocean. It is suddenly eternal more than immediate. The waves disappear into the vastness, the cycle of the tides declares itself and the barrier yields to connection with those on other shores and to some striking part of the universal and the transcendent.

The door of each heart, as Howard Thurman says, opens in these moments. Now is a time to create such an opening. That nature does it is an amazing gift; that we can do it ourselves is an affirmation we too are partners with the universe and the divine. Right now, between Thanksgiving and New Year's, the portal is open to who we really are, and to how things really should be. In the moments most crowded with people, with memories and expectations, with tasks and travel, with events and epiphanies small or great, we are headed home. Like the Magi, we are called to journey by another road to that place, and thus can safely proceed past all danger and delay and despair.

You will note I end every sermon with "Amen." It is not for closure, but for opening, to accept this gift of life we carry with all that exists. I say "Blessed Be" and "Salaam" likewise to express not just the movement of mere objects or beings, but also movement that is truly All. This is the movement of the divine, the self-that-is-no-self.

The fourth word I speak is *shalom*. It appears again and again in the Hebrew Scriptures. It is a place and a ground of being. It is an expression of the will to come forth both as what is and also what is meant to be. It is both movement and stillness. It is both all that exists and each particle of that existence. Jews have understood themselves for thousands of years to be at the core engaged in the eternal project of *shalom*, of the world as the divine wishes it to be and which we too desire. It is what is both good and right. Shalom is the wish. It is the hope. It is also a particular kind of responsibility. It is an essential human project—we are partners, not recipients.

It is no accident that Unitarianism and Universalism are rooted in the Hebrew prophets—in Amos and Hosea and Jeremiah and Isaiah. Those were messengers to troubled times, but they spoke of ultimate strength to overcome tragedy, betrayal and loss. William Ellery Channing and Hosea Ballou, the founders, respectively, of Unitarianism and Universalism, are our great prophets of their troubled times. Both declared everlasting strength was accessible to humans as partners working alongside the divine—not to be objects, subjects or victims. Dr. Martin Luther King, Jr., in our dark days, declared from those same Biblical prophets that our mortal powers are less, but they are not invisible. Every day we are called to affirm just how capacious they are.

Now we come into Advent, also rooted in the Hebrew Scriptures. Dec. 2 is the first Sunday of special liturgical time for both waiting and approach. For Christians, it is Christ who approaches, but that is a graft onto a much older tradition naming the one who is coming as Emmanuel. The prophet Habakkuk proclaimed that shalom will surely come, but it will come in its own duly appointed time—"Let this be read and understood by he who is running." *He who is running*—that would be us.

Begin your renewal by asking: What are you really sorry for? How sincerely do you wish to make right what you have done—or failed to do? How have you fallen short—of what you intended or should have intended, of who you meant to be or should have meant to be, of what you should have said or kept silent? You may not have understood then, but now do. We often don't understand but that is the point. If you truly open your heart, you surely understand now. Now is the time to repair that for which you are responsible. Don't worry; it will come to you. I assure you the list will be long enough.

For what are we responsible? At the heart of all is relationship—and it is the core of our responsibility. Birds flock together and fish swim in schools, but only humankind has any conception of the full fabric of relationship. We live in it even as we create it; we weave it even as we rend it asunder; we dream of it even as we struggle for it. We are conscious of the past and the future and what is beyond our senses and instincts.

We are called to make whole. Thurman invites us to the most obvious repair for which we are obligated, the repair of our relationship with others. What angry words have you spoken? It is not about whether you were wrong or right—it is about the anger you now regret. What petty grudges have you carried? It is not about how justified you have been, but about your willingness to lay the burden down. What part of your days was spent being selfish, small-minded, inconsiderate? How much were you *unloving*—in every sense of the word—of family, friends and strangers alike? How many times have you assumed the worst of intentions, of those you know and those you do not?

If I were Heloise, I could give you hints, but somehow, I believe you know what you must do to accomplish the repair. Perfection is never required, only genuine effort.

Do not forget the other aspects of repair that call out to us. You must take time to repair your relationship with *you*. Identify, regret and apologize to yourself—surely you have not been as kind and considerate and forgiving as you must be to have any chance of treating other people that way. This is not letting yourself off the hook—if it was bad it was bad, but you will do better. You will devoutly promise to be fully human this year.

Take time to repair your relationship with the creation. Yes, the earth is given as a garden and we have dug where we shouldn't and poisoned what was living and harvested what should have been left for others who will come. Will you do better?

Take time to repair, finally, your relationship with first and last—with God, the divine, the transcendent. The word does not matter. The concept is infinitely malleable to culture and conscience. The mystery is profound— "there are more things in heaven and earth, Horatio, than is dreamt of in your philosophy." Surely this is what we know.

Amen. Blessed Be. Shalom. Salaam.

Groundhog Day-after

04 Feb 2018

"Think globally, act locally" works for me when it comes to marmot weather forecasting. Time Magazine informed me about various groundhog reports—some say this; some say that on the "early spring" or "six more weeks of winter" alternatives. As the saying goes, "for amusement purposes only." I can tell you from experience nobody in Madison, Wisconsin—where they look to "Sun Prairie Jimmy"—is ever so foolish to think we are *not* going to get six more weeks of something strongly resembling winter.

At least Jimmy was only five miles away, so some possibility existed of a certain conformity between his instinct and actual conditions. "Punxsutawney Phil," on the other hand, lives northeast of Pittsburgh and that's a long way off, even from Philadelphia. In Philadelphia a decisive break in the weather is actually possible before March 1, but nobody from Pittsburgh has any credibility in Philly, including Phil.

People in Connecticut swore in their own official groundhog this past Friday. He peed on his handlers. Phil has been known to bite but he looked pretty baffled in the TV footage. In Maine I believe we have the right attitude. The change of seasons is going to be what it is going to be, so don't get obsessed about the matter. Previews are a relief, but they are still previews. We had one this week. Spring isn't any closer, or not.

The day that matters, I think, is the day *after* Groundhog Day. If it is going to be what it is going to be—an ultimately sensible view of life if used in moderation, as all things should be—that is the day it will begin. Again.

That was the point of the movie "Groundhog Day," which is 25 years old this year. The circumstance of the humor was broad, even slapstick. TV reporter Bill Murray broadcasts from Punxsutawney, PA, squabbles with Andie McDowell, his producer, and wakes up the next day—and it is Groundhog Day again. He's trapped. No matter what he does on Groundhog Day, it is always Groundhog Day again the next morning. My favorite of the many ways he tests this existential cage is the kidnapping of Punxsutawney Phil (who in the movie is virtually homicidal). A high-speed car chase follows and then a spectacular suicidal crash. Next morning it is Groundhog Day all over again.

We laugh because the sensation is exaggerated to be sure, but also all too familiar. Sometimes "Groundhog Day all over again" does seem to be the way life works.

We come to sympathize—eventually—with how life works between Murray and MacDowell. Murray is a full-bore jerk to begin, and clings to that.

Given new daily opportunities by fate, he burns them all. He tries to get her goat; he tries to get her into bed. I'm sorry for the vulgarity but it is what he does, because he is still a jerk—interested only in himself. Then he tries to get her to love him. That doesn't work either, and then it does, but even after they fall asleep cuddling it is still Groundhog Day.

Anything else would let Murray off the hook far too easily. He must understand—and so must we—that love indeed offers satisfaction but it only *lasts* if started and sustained as an opportunity for relationship. Some days relationships yield immediate satisfaction; some days they don't. The relationship must be nourished regardless. That way, and only that way, do those involved find the deepest satisfaction. Groundhog Day all over again? Never mind—at the deep level it is still good. Life itself is just that way.

Murray escapes the endless cycle of rebirth—yes, that is what is happening—by genuinely changing who he *is*. He trudges along from scornful and sarcastic, to bitter and lost, to loving but only with an object in mind. What finally saves him is to love *without* any object or even an objective. He finally encounters love in everyone. Buddhists might call him a *bodhisattva*—enlightened to his ability to save others. Hindus might say he is dipping into the divine *allness* of Atman. Our Universalist Father Ballou would say he has become the all-forgiving essence of the Divine. In the Unitarianism of Dr. Channing he has ascended to ultimate partnership with God.

And he gets the girl. He gets her not as a trophy, not as a love object, not as an indulgence, but as a companion—a real person with whom to share a life. It's romantic, but no longer just romance. There will surely be ups and downs—but it is finally Feb. 3. Life is still filled with good and bad, but it is at last ready to move on.

How will you and I handle the day after Groundhog Day? I'm going to send our granddaughter a Valentine's Day card. She lives in California, which is way too far away, but it will be her first Valentine's Day and that is plenty of reason to celebrate. I will send a card also to my mother. Her first Valentine's Day was in 1921 but she has never failed to thank me for remembering her. The card doesn't have to be clever or sophisticated—which makes it a lot easier to find one. I will happily choose a simple one to provide a blessed relief from the demoralizing complexity of her everyday circumstances. Her moods are erratic but I think this will be a blessing she can use.

Distance creeps into our relationships; fuzziness comes over who we really are to each other. In this day and age it is all too easy to become "virtual" people, defined more and more by what we broadcast and less and less by our concrete presence. That is the fashionable complaint of our age—it used to be the fault of e-mail. Now it's the fault of Facebook. How then to account for the timeless shortcoming of taking for granted those in your immediate vicinity—the people you see more or less every day, day in and day out? When she lived in Philadelphia, our daughter Kate used to urge me—via e-mail—to ask a little less often *what* she is doing and a little more often *how* she is doing. You would think now that we live in the same house that problem would be solved. I can see what she is doing, and I can surmise the *how*—but that is still not the same as asking her. The loving of adult children can suffer from mission creep into what you can or cannot do to help them, when what is more sorely needed is to listen and be patient while they work it out. I have to do better and the day after Groundhog Day is as good as any to get started with even the smallest step. I know what will happen if I don't—this cycle will repeat over and over for years to come. We will both be trapped.

February 14 is a Wednesday this year, which means I will be here in Medfield and not at home with Sally in Maine. This has happened before and it is—to coin a phrase—not the end of the world for two people who have been together coming up on 43 years. On the other hand, we will miss each other. We always do. What a fool I would be not to remind her that I do miss her even when we are apart for a few days. The people we are closest to are usually the people we are counting on the most. I don't do big fussy things, but I can thank her and I recommend the same to you for someone nearby.

So you see, this is not a plug for Hallmark or a particular holiday. It is some specific and timely examples to represent what I hope you hear as a broader point. How will you live the day after Groundhog Day? What about the day after that and the day after that? There are only so many days for any of us—nobody knows how many. Sometimes we do need to make drastic changes; no one should underestimate them. But most of the time most of us just need to make small changes in attitude and action. Every morning we get another chance. Any day we take it is a good one in a crucial way.

Any day we step away from complacency, from evasion, from withholding—that is a good day. Somebody near you needs—like you—to escape that damn groundhog.

Amen. Blessed Be. Shalom. Salaam.

Asking for Help

06 May 2018

Sally and Kate dug around in some boxes from my mother's house and came up with something I must have given her a very long time ago. It's a picture of me in full Cub Scout uniform, smiling in earnest salute. The frame is carefully assembled of popsicle sticks—just the kind of thing a mother would save all these years.

Obviously, there are many things I did not know as a 10 or 11-year old. One thing I did know was how to pray with my family, no church affiliation necessary. More than five decades ago my younger brother and I knelt in prayer every night before bed. We would take turns—one night at the side of his bed, one night at the side of mine.

We would alternate the Lord's Prayer with "Now I Lay Me Down to Sleep." I am pretty sure the nightly ritual began after our summer at Jubilee Ranch when I was seven. There was a lot of praying there, and we had some extra reason to be grateful. You may remember how I was almost killed by a runaway car that summer.

The praying continued after the following summer, which we spent at Camp Deerfield. I'm sure we didn't use those two prayers—it was a Jewish camp after all—but I know there was a bedtime ritual. The camp had an official "yenta"—a surrogate Jewish mother who tucked the campers in every night and hugged us at every chance.

Except for a brief ascetic period in my mid-teens, prayer disappeared from my life after those years. The family ritual faded away and I came to believe nobody was listening—which eventually became a conviction there was nobody who could be listening, let alone responding. None of us realized how much it mattered that my *parents* stopped listening. "Prayer Changes Things"— it's a famous gospel song, a set piece for the great female soloists like Mahalia Jackson, Marion Williams and Shirley Caesar. Like many people, you might say I loved the music but mumbled the words.

Well, life changes things, too. The lightning bolts of misfortune strike more often around us and sooner or later we get nailed as well. With every day gained it seems inevitable we have more and more to lose. We are witnesses to the resilience of love and life, but equally exposed to their fragility. We probably grow in gladness but also—too often—in fear. We get more philosophical and happier—but we also hear the bell toll.

Been very sick? Been very desperate? Been very sad? I suggest asking for help.

The first and possibly the greatest barrier may be your embarrassment. What am I doing? I am a responsible adult, I live in the 21st century, I have a good education, I don't do that mumbo jumbo with the wafer—I became a Unitarian Universalist to get away from all that nonsense. You may even be shocked, shocked! to find there is gambling going on in this casino, but the truth is, UUs do pray. Some call it that; some do not. Whatever—who's going to see you? Who has to know? Why would you care?

Is it a nagging resistance to admitting the truth of despair and the need for hope? There can't be anything wrong with asking to get well if you are sick, with asking for a path if you are at a dead end, with asking that grief be assuaged. We might be more willing to do this for others, but for ourselves also we should let go of guilt. Why should we not want these things? It is not selfish and it is not superstition. It is human need.

When you bring yourself to ask, who or what are you asking? Asking for help from beyond the human sphere reveals one aspect of the genius and possibility of our religion. Reason and faith are not in opposition or incompatible. They are in fact equally necessary in the world and in our lives. Ours is a holistic understanding. Faith and reason necessarily complement each other and we must and should rely on both.

So, who's out there to listen? Here's another big plus, if we are willing to seize upon it: *Whoever you want is out there.* Whoever or whatever you call divine is out there. Whoever or whatever you need or want is out there. You have only to envision him, her, it or them. If you see Buddha in a cowboy hat, that works! If you see the Goddess in a Ferrari, that works! If a star or a rock or a redwood tree comes into view, that works! Let us be the joyful pragmatists we are at our best. If it works, go with it.

Rest on certainty: Whatever is transcendent is beyond the human sphere and perhaps beyond human understanding, but whatever you believe is there is there, and is connected to you. "Transcendent" can never be properly defined as "indifferent." Time and space separate us from those we love; they are never remote in our hearts.

Again, this is an example of the strength of our religion. We know by science, from Einstein to quarks, that distances of time and space are not fixed. This is good, solid reason. The essence of that which is transcendent we know by experience—by good solid intuition. Great powers and bountiful opportunities and transformative energy are in both modes of being. We are most alive engaging both mind and spirit.

Each one of us has the courage to believe. Why would we not use our strength?

There is no reason why you should not believe the who or the what you are addressing is personally interested in you. There is no book on a "Spirit of Life" that is not inextricably intertwined with your life, and mine. "What is plaited cannot be unplaited," says the poet May Sarton. A force that is the energy of life has to be about life in all its multitude, but that multitude in every species is a congeries of individuals. A force of creation creates in amplitude, in abundance and in variety—yet each is definably unique. There can't be absolute anonymity in this universe; the interdependent web must see each of us and touch each of us as a distinct entity.

No point on that web can be out of touch or out of sympathy with any of the others. All must be in relationship. Again, we know this by science, and we feel it by our own experience. We are in relationship with all the people around us—with family, with friends, with those we encounter and those we do not. We are in relationship to the community of this First Parish. We are affected by and therefore in relationship with that famous butterfly in China. We are in relationship with all that lives, with all that exists or has ever existed. We must be in relationship with all that will exist. We must therefore be connected to eternity, to nothingness and to infinity as well. We must be connected to the divine.

Prayer is asking for help through the certainty of relationship. We let go of our pride and accept our vulnerability and need. We can do this. We envision the divine. We directly address by our entire being the force at the center of the universe, and its synapses as well. We can do this. We declare the courage of belief. We celebrate the timeless human knowledge that what we address, however we envision it, has the power to do what we ask. We can do this. To pray is to transform sickness to healing, to calm desperation, to apply the balm of consolation to our sorrows. To pray is to affirm we are alive and that we truly believe in the power of life. It is to understand its mechanism, which is relationship. It is to renew our own resilience by recognizing the resilience that is all around us. Prayer changes nothing—except us, and that is all that matters.

We can do it. We may not be so good on the "getting down on our knees" part. Yet this is only a way of cracking the shell of our normal posture in the world. Sitting very still works just as well, as does any of an infinite variety of practices by which humankind aligns to the beyond. Take heart, take hold—and unwrap this great gift.

Amen. Blessed Be. Shalom. Salaam.

Believing Eve

25 Nov 2018

Nobody expects the snake. In Genesis, God creates the animals and Adam names them. The snake we presume was included, but no species are identified. All are created from the earth, like Adam himself, as the Hebrew *adamah* is meant to convey.

But there is, as you remember, no companion for Adam. God pulls a rib to get the job done, and Adam names her woman—*ishshah,* as he is *ish*—man. She is called a helper, and the translator's note says the sense is not at all of a subordinate but of a partner. The terms reflect this, and so does the unique creation. They are one flesh.

Nobody expects the snake. The one I'm holding up has been perched in the avocado tree in the Vestry for several weeks. I wondered if anybody would notice, but apparently not. Or at least, nobody said anything—and my snake doesn't talk at all.

The famous Monty Python routine is, "NO-body expects the Spanish Inquisition." It regularly spoils the day of whatever sketch characters are suddenly reminded of this unpleasant reality. The snake spoils the entire Creation. The woman will not be honored as a partner in full. Repeat through human history. It seems that believing Eve was not something anybody especially wanted to do, from the very beginning. "The serpent tricked me," she says, but that answer is never quite good enough.

Maybe we should consider with more charity what she claims. Remember, nobody expects the snake—certainly not a devious talking snake with its own agenda.

This is the First Story—the origin of human life and circumstance. It is filled with mystery. Consider the verses I read today as Opening Words: The man and the woman hear God *walking around.* What do they do? They *hide among the trees.* God has to call out—*where are you?* What kind of God makes noise walking around like you and me? What kind of God can you hide from by getting behind a tree? What kind of God has to holler after you in the transparent frustration so familiar to all parents—*where are you, you little rascals?*

There's more: This particular God has to ask what has happened, and the man has to explain—after, I guess, emerging from the shrubbery. *Who told you that you were naked?* This God doesn't know. *Have you eaten of the tree from which I commanded you not to eat?* Not only does this God not know, but this God also issues commands that are promptly ignored by his own special being—created, you recall, in his own image. What a bring-down that must have been! Maybe it still is.

Certainly Adam is no paragon of taking responsibility when things go wrong. He blames her—and God. *The woman whom you gave to be with me*, he says, just so we don't think it might be any of the other women wandering around Eden, and also so we are very clear where she came from and maybe there should be some kind of warranty claim. She didn't just tell him it was okay— she *gave him the fruit*. Of course he ate it. What else was he going to do? Good thing she didn't hand him that romaine salad with Thanksgiving dinner. God could certainly have pointed out that these are bonehead excuses, but maybe the embarrassment was just too great. God turns instead to the woman, and she blames the snake—*the serpent tricked me, and I ate.*

Who would believe a talking snake? Who would eat something because a talking snake said it was okay? In fairness to Eve—fairness is a good place to start a better conversation on her behalf—everything is brand new, so anything is possible—talking snakes, flying bears, fish that play the harmonica. She just got here; there's some dude standing there looking wasted from having to come up with all the names and also, he's been under anesthesia, but he's *really happy* to see her. Of course, he's not good at feelings or small talk, so she chats with the first thing that chats with her. As far as she can tell, the talking snake is perfectly normal.

Next thing she knows, they are hiding in the bushes and this other dude is yelling at her and he does *not* look happy.

Bad luck—this snake is not normal at all but perfectly diabolical. We've already been told, in verse one, *the serpent was more crafty than any other wild animal that the Lord God had made.* Nobody expects the snake. This snake is not just a creature that does bad stuff; it is a creature that figures out what bad stuff there *should be*, and then talks somebody else into doing it. Remember—it is all new. There is no "good and evil" except in the essence of the tree, which they are not even supposed to touch, let alone eat from. They don't know anything about the very concept—and shouldn't.

Or so we would like it to have been.

But it is hard to argue with a crafty snake. He knows the way to subvert people is not to openly oppose them, but to first to question them. "Help me out here. I don't understand—*did God say not any tree?*" Of course, she is now in the snake's noose.

You can tell because she gives him a perfectly reasonable answer—as if he has asked a perfectly reasonable question. We can eat, she responds, but not from that particular tree, right there in the middle. Very bad stuff will happen if we even touch it.

Pretty cut and dried, but put yourself in Eve's place. "Die" doesn't exist— there is no death in all the Creation. Just as she has no idea what good and evil are, she could hardly have any idea what death is. The snake declares they will not die. He seems quite sure on the subject, and he has inside information on why God is keeping her in the dark. God is jealous they will become like him. Apparently that concept does exist—class-consciousness, I guess the Marxists would tell us. *I'm God and you are not.* Actually, the better translation is *Gods*—plural. This story is older than monotheism. You must not become *like us.*

Oh—what kind of God is this? This is the God of the "J" source. This is the God who walks in the garden in the cool of the day, who can't see everything, doesn't know everything, who calls out and talks face-to-face with the man and the woman. This is not the Big Creator God who gets it all done in six days. This is the God identified as YHWH, pronounced "Yahweh" but spoken or read as *Adonai*—Lord. The J voice is the oldest in the Bible—three thousand years old. Oh, and it may be the voice of a woman.

Nobody can be sure, but the case made by some scholars is in the text. "J" is, for instance, rich with just the kind of personal encounter we see in these verses. "J" likes face-to-face. More telling perhaps, "J" clearly understands the woman's world. The "J" passages are filled with artifacts and social interactions of women, quite unlike the other narrators. We are reading the story told by someone who believes Eve is important.

And she is. She sees the tree is food, that it delights the eye, and that it can make one wise. Of course, she eats the fruit. What human being would not? This is the point, made most famously by feminist theologian Phyllis Tribble: Eve makes the decisions that made us fully human—not only creatures but also our own creators. She observes; she reasons; she decides; she acts. She also shares. She gives some to Adam, and he eats. It is all laid out quite clearly in the final verse.

We should also note she accepts the consequences of her actions. This is humanity also, at our core. What we do, we must own. Eve does—just as much as Adam—forever. It's beyond our story, but Eve triggers history. We should believe her.

Amen. Blessed Be. Shalom. Salaam.

No Wings, No Worries?

09 Dec 2018

They looked like grownups. They had to be in their late 20s—a good five years older than me. He had a real job, as a TA in the Mathematics Department. She had a six- or seven-year-old son. They had a decent car, which was important when setting out for the West Coast. We all piled in one day in Madison and headed for Las Vegas.

They told me their plan. He'd taught himself card counting—*mathematics TA*, remember? They'd saved five or six hundred dollars, and they were off to make their fortune. He'd count the cards showing on the table, bet smarter and beat the house.

I did not have the heart to insist on how deeply deluded this was. I tried. I mentioned the cameras, and the watchers behind the mirrors, and the pit bosses. Casinos munch on card counters. They were going to get bounced quicker than you could say, "Robert De Niro." When they dropped me at the bus for San Francisco and vanished down the Strip, I wished them luck. I hoped they would only be ejected.

In the "detached from reality" department we have of course Exhibit A in the President of the United States. But I am more worried about you and me. Somehow it is the persistent human affliction to take off from the second floor with only a bath towel as a cape. We do it willingly and in some ways even knowingly, even though we are still nursing bruises from prior encounters with *terra firma*. The hard ground is, after all, always waiting there for us. We even call it "the school of hard knocks."

In the holiday season the movie "It's a Wonderful Life" is always playing somewhere. You remember: The angel Clarence explains that every time a bell rings, an angel is getting wings. And we know Tinker Bell flies only if everybody believes. These are dangerous images imprinted on our subconscious. Just because angels get wings, it doesn't mean we do. In fact, I would state without hesitation that God doesn't give out wings, and so we should not assume they will sprout at our initiative. And Tinker Bell does fly, but it is only because *everybody believes*. That means it's not just in her head.

In *our* heads, unfortunately, is a capacious echo chamber of both simple and complex calculation of what we would like to believe is true. That little engine is always running. Part of this is literally about the wiring. Our brains receive so much sensory input we would quickly drown in stimuli if we didn't also possess ferocious editing capacity. We don't think about this at all; we just do it. At the lowest levels of function, our brains are always on hyper alert for the lion in the underbrush. "Does something out there want to eat me" is the first question of any being that wants to go on being.

But the vast structure and function of our brains is layered above the primordial. We are social creatures. By instinct, by experience, by intelligence and by cunning—both low and high—we are furiously paddling to secure advantage in relation to others. The others are of course doing the same. We aren't just receiving, we are continuously presenting—as are they. Whether we like it or not, we are as energetically buying and selling as any Cal Worthington Auto Superstore ever did.

The malignant possibilities are wide. One of them I call "death by anecdote." The climate can't be changing—didn't we just have a big snowstorm? Don't laugh too hard—you and I do it too. Maybe not that one, but there is no question people trust what they have directly experienced over the science any day in every way. That brings us to "confirmation bias," one of a family of terms that all include the same cloudy reasoning—we see what we want to see. Republicans said the economy stank. After the 2016 election, Republicans said the economy is great—even before the Inauguration! Democrats of course flip just as drastically—and just as free of tangibility—on other issues. People have always had lemming instincts—"the madness of crowds" in market economies is studied back to 1700 and seen again every time there is some new diet.

But my story wasn't about society. It was about a very small number of people—a couple, their child and a reluctant bystander. They needed a dream. We all do. The kid needed a family. He doesn't have a lot of agency, but his very existence solicits recognition of this need, and their dream is certainly at least partially in response. They not only made a plan; they worked at it. It was not an impulsive gamble—it was a calculated gamble. They expected to win. They had tilted the odds in their favor. In fact, they had lost sight, for all intents and purposes, of the "gamble" aspect of the plan.

I needed a ride to San Francisco. Truth to tell, I also needed to sell myself as a man of the world, at least next to the naïfs. But I needed a conscience, so I tried to split the difference—caution them, yes, but not in any insistent way that might spoil the ride. And of course, sincerely wish them the best as they set off into the deep and dark forest.

As I write, it occurs to me what a perfect representation this is of the dilemmas of parish ministry—it is embedded in every day. But we will leave that for another time.

For now, I draw you back to something I said last week: Our core identity is *human*. Whatever other identities we have, however important they are—and they will surely need and deserve to be very important—we must not forget our core identity.

We must not forget it because, as I have already stated, we must not forget that being human, we have an intense need to have things be the way we want them to be—including who we are in the world. Reinhold Niebuhr's famous aphorism was that we are never so virtuous in the eyes of others as we are in our own. My not-so-famous aphorism is that God didn't give anybody wings, and that includes you and me. We are never so deluded as when we think we are just about to draw to an inside straight. We launch repeatedly with no wings and no worries—and sooner or later pay for that.

So does everybody else. The core identity of human-and-everybody-has-that means everybody is just as fundamentally vulnerable and confused. In any moment, everybody is just as in over his or her head, just as likely to be rocking down the highway blasting rock and roll, just as likely to be deeply at peace as we are—all, some or none of the above. Do you go around showing the real you? This is a rhetorical question only. You don't need to speak the answer, because it is always some degree of "no." When you react to other people, are you really reacting to them, or to whom you think they are (with their help a lot of the time). The best we can do is be more real than not. That is not a small thing. It is the coin of human happiness in relationship with others. The folding money comes when we are able to allow others to be more real than not.

"This is the reason of cities, of homes, of assemblies in the houses of worship," said the late Kenneth Patton. It is also the reason of all the relationships we encounter.

The irreducible reality is that some of those relationships are going to bruise us—maybe many of them, or at least on a bad day it will seem that way. Consider the alternative—if you can't feel pain and disappointment and even anger, what else can you feel? Nobody should get out of jail free, but all of us deserve to be considered human, with all our faults. Remember Hosea Ballou's most important thesis: There is no need for Hell in the hereafter. We all get more than adequately punished here. We call it life.

And there are the wings. They don't come from the divine. They come from us. They come from people you trust. They come from people you care about. They come from people who care about you. They come from trusting yourself—all human always.

Amen. Blessed Be. Shalom. Salaam.

The Faraway Nearby

17 Feb 2019

After my mother died last year, I got a very nice letter from my cousin Linda. She expressed regret that we have never communicated very much. The last time I saw Linda was 1973. She wondered if this happened, "because our mothers for some reason did not get along very well."

My parents said my Aunt Doris talked a bit too much, drank a bit too much and married too many times. The truth may be that Doris was six years older. As a teenager, she had her own car, a large wardrobe and a set of flashy friends. The Great Depression hit and my mother's high school years were spent with boarders in the house her parents finally lost, along with everything else. My mother never forgave Doris.

In family systems this kind of relationship is called a "cut-off." You can see some classic elements. The presented "cause" is transparent deflection—Doris did not bankrupt the family, but in fact "she got stuff that I didn't." That indictment cannot be answered. Years of on-going resentment are justified by personality differences hardened into petty fault finding. The estrangement is nourished for decades without resolution, and—most sadly and characteristically—carried into the next generation.

The pattern is probably familiar to you, because almost every family carries some permutation of this fault line. It may be more or less acute. I have been surprised in ministry to hear how many families have somebody "we haven't seen in years." Then there is the other version—"I haven't seen *them* in years." That's the acute version. More common is the estrangement—the Black Sheep label. Somebody in the family just doesn't act like the rest of us, or quite get along with us, or stay in any regular touch. Your own wool may be light or dark, but you know how they vote, right? It's not good.

The essayist Rebecca Solnit calls this the "faraway nearby." It wonderfully describes the essence of such relationships. These people are indeed in your life, but they are kind of like too much Indian food—your stomach is stubbornly unsettled. The "faraway" part is an emotional gulf not related to physical distance at all, although it is sometimes manifest by literally moving away. It also isn't directly contingent on blood ties, although people very close to us are clearly the ones most capable of injuring us. Surprisingly often, it's people not close who jump up to bite us. We don't expect it. We famously use Thanksgivings for these ambushes—or weddings, or funerals, or even the family "reunion." It happens when vaguely related people are hopefully included and then prove to be just the so-and-so you always knew they were. They're *family*, after all.

The actual phrase, "the faraway nearby," is one Solnit borrows from the artist Georgia O'Keeffe, who used it in her letters from New Mexico to her friends and relations mostly on the east coast. O'Keeffe's life was itself a series of cut-offs, in her case pilgrimages she argued were made repeatedly into new wellsprings for her inspiration and subject matter. Maybe that was worth it, but it is a pernicious excuse. Solnit's perspective is more honest. *The Faraway Nearby*, which was published in 2013, is a collection of essays with a connecting thread. It is about getting away—from people, places and circumstances. It is also about how those do not actually go away.

The thread is the emphasis Solnit places on Story, with a capital "S." Story is the narrative, that thing all of us use to make sense of the world, that theme we reenact in our lives, that way of viewing the world distinctive enough to be our calling card in company. Besides being a central organizing principle, the narrative we hold is also always under construction. Most notoriously, the things we think we remember—the events of our lives—are continuously snipped and shaped. Our memories are not just entangled with our identities. They are symbiotic—we *are* what we "remember."

There is no moral failing in this. Neuroscience is now quite sure the outcome is baked into the physiological process of memory—it is literally how the brain works. Except in special training, like memorizing your violin part for Beethoven's Fifth, we only remember at all because it makes sense to our story—our narrative—to do so. The purpose of human life is to construct human life. Our genes reproduce. Our identities arise, flourish under our constant attention, and eventually pass on in some very similar ways. Every time there is a "celebration of life," we assure ourselves this is quite true.

Solnit is best known for the essay, "Men Explain Things to Me," which is in some ways a hilarious depiction of how this process can distort the entire social order. Men know stuff—they assume—and thoughtfully share with women, who apparently don't. Not to get off track, and I am not speaking for Solnit, but I see a pretty striking thematic relationship. Constructing reality has consequences and most of us hit them sooner or later. In Solnit's case, you can read about her leaving her lover, her career leap, her move from home and community, and her body struggling to get past cancer—all part of the pressing need to secure new narrative. Mostly you will read about the apricots—the pile on her bedroom floor that is dumped from her mother's apricot tree. Solnit's mother has passed on, but the apricots remain. So does a moving and insightful account of a long and tortured relationship. Mom was difficult—but in all the ordinary ways.

Which brings us back to my mother and my aunt. Nobody pulled a knife on anybody. They were just different people—who can know how that actually happened? It is easy to see from outside that my mother mostly battled an image she constructed. She needed her sister to play a role in the perceived lack of attention from her parents and the collapse of the family finances. None of it was really awful. All of it helped my mother stubbornly succeed in many areas of her life. It was an incentive and it worked, just as Georgia O'Keeffe's remove to the country and then the desert worked for her art.

The price of cut-off relationships is high, however. Almost no matter how they happen or how they play out over the years, they extract anguish from us in the end. Sometimes the anguish comes long before the end, like a cold drip, drip, drip of disappointment. Things just aren't right. We are often baffled as to what exactly is happening. We often suspect or even admit our own complicity in arriving at the dark part of the forest. Of course, no one likes complicity much at all. I recommend a modest self-analysis—or, actually, a modest *system* analysis. Look at your family system.

Get some paper and start drawing boxes—one for each family member. Arrange them in generational tiers just like the royal family. Be sure you have all your siblings, your parents and all their siblings. Add at least your grandparents or your adult children. Three generations is the minimum. And add in spouses or partners—and former spouses or partners. This gets you to the fun part. It's a basic genogram. Did you remember everybody—all the names, in the right birth and relationship order? Who was Aunt Edie's first husband? Can you see an outlier in each generation—somebody who is more or less successful, happy or lucky than the norm in your family? Can you see which relatives are or were close to each other—or noticeably not? Explain your genogram to your significant other, and, if possible, have that person do one and explain it to you. Discuss—it will be worth it. Welcome to The Faraway Nearby.

We all live there. Each of us is a mystery to the people around us. Each of us is a story. It's okay—just don't be too stuck in yours. And I have to write back to my cousin.

Amen. Blessed Be. Shalom. Salaam.

A Darker Mask

17 Mar 2019

I was not very surprised that debt collectors were cited in the article as early adopters of a new research angle on the potentially "constructive" uses of interpersonal anger. In fact, according to *The Atlantic* Online, they have been at it for some years ahead of anybody else. In the North Woods, we know that black flies will get through any screen, no matter how fine. Debt collectors no doubt have similar talents.

Apparently at least some had discovered that if they were angry on the phone with the debtor—not just wheedling or demanding, but angry—the debtors became much more likely to pay. The trick was to push it just far enough so the debtor would pony up and actually feel relieved of the emotional static. One collector yelled into the phone *and then hung up* before the debtor could say a word. In a few minutes he would call back and politely request payment. He claimed people pushed the money on him.

Well maybe and maybe not. In any event, as was pointed out, nobody answers the phone any more so that's that. Unfortunately, anger is more and more the currency of our age. It seems almost quaint that a stranger would yell at you on the phone. We have worse, far worse, and every one of us has adjusted our emotional landscape to fit. There is, without question, an "anger-industrial complex," and it is pervasive. It used to be the peasants who ran around with the torches and pitchforks. Now—observed in the broad political realm—it is exactly the people we might think least likely. Repeated studies have demonstrated the major outrage culprits are the most educated, the best informed and the most heavily involved. Generally speaking, that would be us, you and me. We reliably poll as the most partisan, the most vociferous, the most suspicious and the most unwilling to compromise—or accept anybody else doing so.

At the meta level this poses a troubling challenge to the Unitarian Universalist version of the human project. As traditionally conceived, UUs are the "worth and dignity" people, but more practically we are the people who swear by education, reason, the integrity and improvability of the individual conscience, and the truth as something comfortably flexible to meet our enlightened needs. But it may be we are wrong. The arc might bend somewhere else than justice, at least in our time. Or maybe "justice" is a whole lot closer to what used to be called "Biblical" than we want to acknowledge.

On this larger subject, stay tuned. You and I are formulating the answer. The upstate returns are not in and the graveyard is getting voted as we speak.

But I am more concerned today with the personal. What does it do to us to be swimming in a sea of anger? Leave aside for a moment any consideration of how justified anger might be, in a million ways. In the end, it is anger. It is rooted in the brain—literally in the base of the brain and in the lower level functions least accessible to our cognition. It is only a half step above the instinctive—like responding to physical danger, to the chance to eat or the need to flee, to the search for shelter or sex. Like Shakespeare's Caliban, it is a servant in search of a master: "Get a new master, be a new man." Or woman, as may be.

Who might that master be—between us? The gist of the study being reported on was that appropriate anger between two people—not society-wide, but just one-to-one—might actually be helpful. Under experiment, participants reported feeling "more heard" after what looked like a burst of testiness. They reported feeling better understood by the other person—and more valued. Anger under these circumstances seemed to function like a time-out, like a vital moment that interrupted the routine to make a recalibration possible. A recalibration in a relationship is the portal to improvement in relationship—or at least the possibility. *Now you are really paying attention to me, to us, to who we are and where we might be going.* Worth noting—no matter which party was the one with the outburst of feeling, they each felt benefits.

Use with caution, of course. Do not exploit emotions to collect overdue bills—it's against the law. I'm not a social scientist and I am not testifying to the rigor of any academic research—I wouldn't know how. I am instead working with an idea about relationships, drawing on my own experience and observation to make a larger point. Two people who are in any way close for any period of time are going to have anger. Life just works that way. People just are that way. Consider it a darker mask if you will, but ignore anger at your peril. If it isn't there, this is probably not a really authentic relationship. It isn't deep enough yet; it isn't honest enough yet; it isn't tested enough yet. You want me to officiate at your wedding? Come back when you are past the Prince and Princess phase. I have a professional responsibility. This is, I might add, just as true for Prince and Prince and for Princess and Princess. It has been quite fascinating to see that affirmed. A relationship that doesn't include some anger is highly likely to be missing some other essential parts. Friction happens. You can't get there from here.

This is important: There are rules. Stay within the boundaries. The expression of the anger needs to be spontaneous. Lightning is okay—sometimes there needs to be a trigger and that can be something we agree on. But ambushes are out. If you're planning it or setting it up, take a step back and consider what might really be happening. Ambushes usually mean malice is in the neighborhood and that's not okay.

The anger needs to be proportionate. Please do not set your partner's car on fire. Throwing his clothes out the second-floor window may be a classic but it has some obvious issues with demonstrating beyond what is probably necessary. Threats or intimidation is also absolutely off the board. Again, it signals malice and it means you are not in a place for a frank exchange of views but one requiring a trained counselor. Watch your language. Bad words are not out of bounds but name-calling is, and we draw the line at "you always" characterizations as well. Nobody is guilty of any "you always" except maybe breathing, and a spat isn't the right setting for what would have to be called a grudge, not a fit of pique. I wish I didn't have to say this but I do: No rough stuff. Under no circumstances is that remotely acceptable. No breaking things either. Breaking things is deeply traumatic—it implies violence and we have to know that.

Let's turn off "The Honeymooners" and reach for a deeper meaning. Every one of us makes a singular journey every day. It is a journey into the unfamiliar. "Today is the first day of the rest of your life" also means tomorrow may be the first day of your life you do not recognize, no matter how we try to pretend otherwise. The darker mask is a face we turn to what is unfamiliar, because the unfamiliar is scary. Most of the time, what we present as anger is really fear. It is often pain or sadness. We quite naturally don't want others to see this. Few people like being exposed. All of us have our worst moments and we are stubbornly unwilling to let even those closest to us see them. Our unwillingness can even shade into being unable to let those closest see us limping badly.

If a stranger expresses anger, try hard to let it go. Why should it matter? If it's somebody you care about, try to remember you do care about this person. When there is a relationship, remember that. When we help somebody through a bumpy spot, we are helping ourselves. Stifling the urge to strike back may be just the thing needed to recalibrate for mutual growth. A pressure valve is meant to go off before the machinery is damaged. We too need a safety valve— or we will never get through here in one piece.

Amen. Blessed Be. Shalom. Salaam.

Made for Goodness

21 Apr 2019

The picture used to pop up every year somewhere around this time—the traditional bright yellow baby chicks of Easter all dyed blazing new colors of red and blue and green. It looked like what we used to call "a Kodachrome moment."

Of course, Kodachrome and its moments are long gone. The days are also gone when you could dye fluffy baby birds without getting the animal rights people in your face, which is probably all to the good for the birds and for us.

I always feel a little guilty because one fond childhood memory is getting both chicks and rabbits for Easter. That was the mid-1950s and we know now it is not right. I don't remember what we did with the chicks, although we did not raise them. The rabbits we did raise. We had a hutch in the back yard. I remember feeding and watering them. I quite vividly remember standing on the lawn at Swarthmore College the bright sunny day my mother donated them to science. She got tired of rounding up renegade rabbits from the flower garden of Mr. Black, who lived up the block.

Somehow that was also the day I nailed my brother with a garden trowel. He still has a small scar on his forehead. I did graduate from high school with Mr. Black's grandson. He'd heard about the rabbits. During World War II, when my mother and older brother lived with him, Grandfather Chandler kept a menagerie in his back yard—including rabbits. I wonder if this is why my father went along with our having them.

So that is the nature of memory—moments entangled and entwined and enmeshed with people and places and their happenstance of intersection. The mind remembers what it thinks it experienced. The colors may be too bright, the actions or words may be regrettable, the subtle relationships may unfold years later—or not. And on this day, it is the progress and dynamic and possibility of life that we celebrate—the memories making new in every moment. Who knows where and how they will return?

There are both theological and philosophical answers to that question—how return?—and no shred of consensus. In fact, there sometimes seems only discord.

None of us, however, has to be disputatious, and certainly not in an abstruse intellectual way. None of us has to work out Fermat's Last Theorem. We can answer simply and straightforwardly. We can say *yes* or *no* and smile as benignly as we can manage.

We know, after all, why chicks and baby rabbits and decorated eggs exist for this ancient holiday, whatever it is we consider ourselves to be celebrating. Add chocolate and children to the mix and it is crystal clear what we believe and what we are doing.

Chicks are tiny and fluffy and chirp adorably. Who doesn't want to hold one? Who isn't delighted by a clutch of them? Baby rabbits are small and soft and they make little noises also. They are irresistible. Eggs are—well, they are eggs. They are the start of life—for us also. Chocolate—who does not feel its uniquely pleasurable taste at the very mention of the word?

All these things are made for goodness. They are made to remind us of that truth.

Chicks become chickens, of course—nasty tempers all of them. Rabbits breed into pests. Eggs give birth to creatures good or bad—or they molder away in an awful stink. Chocolate puts on the pounds. Thinking about it sometimes appears to have that effect.

But all that is *outcomes*, not *opportunities*. It is Fate, not Creation. It is what *happens*, not what *is*. It is the shroud of pessimism instead of the beacon of possibility.

And children? No matter how related to us—or even not related at all— why are they central to what we actually do on this day? We may not put it this way, but they are the same. Every child is made for goodness. It doesn't matter who or where or why—every child arrives innately qualified in that way. Humans are never perfect in body or mind. We well know how every one of us who arrives as a child embarks on a lifetime of exploring ways to sometimes be and do what is less than perfect. Some of us start very early, and some of us will go very far. Remember that is Fate. It is not Creation.

But here is what we believe and how we put it: "The inherent worth and dignity of every person." It is the First Principle, the foundation of all that comes after (see page iii). All six principles that follow—everything that follows—is a product of human effort, even if only the effort of understanding and connecting. "Made for goodness," on the other hand, is not an effort. It is the alpha and the omega—there at the start and there at the end, and there at every moment in between. It is a quality intrinsic to every human.

It is a quality intrinsic to everything living. Beset by evil and by ill fortune we must remember—all contrary evidence notwithstanding—*we are made for goodness*. It is Creation, not Fate. Life is made for goodness. So is every element of the universe, now living or once living or someday maybe living. It is all good—we can be certain.

Amen. Blessed Be. Shalom. Salaam.

Ministry Is A Team Sport

Who Goes There?

18 Sep 2016

Minister jokes begin in seminary: "What do they call a divinity student who graduates with an A average? *Reverend.* What do they call a divinity student who graduates with a C average? *Reverend.*"

Ministers warn each other not to become "four feet above contradiction." The power of the pulpit is persuasive. Sometimes it must be prophetic, but it always pulls in harness with the power of the pew. Let us pull together and use our power wisely.

Every minister laughs at this story, no matter how many years or in what setting: The great religious writer Frederick Buechner recalls his youthful self telling a New York socialite he was studying for the ministry. "Is this your own decision," she replied. "Or have you been poorly advised?"

These jokes are the rites of passage and reassurance common to all human endeavors. They must be both true and fabulous. I am using "fabulous" in its archaic meaning—not dazzling and wonderful, but having to do with *fable.* Fables are stories we tell to epitomize not facts or objectivity, but rather the truth of our inner selves and our intuitive wisdom. They help us understand not how the world functions, but how it *is.* They tell us not so much what we should do, but who we are.

In religion, fables are called "parables." In culture they are "myths," and in literature, "allegories." In counseling they are often known as "stories." Whatever term is used, "fabulous" invites us to answer the question, "Who goes there?" in an out-of-the-ordinary way. We do not give a prearranged password. We do not provide mere description—"five foot two, eyes of blue," as in the song. The real answer must be in the *encounter.* It is a place of change for all parties through their inescapable interaction.

"Who goes there?" In most languages the phrase translates as, "Who comes?" This is better wording. The answer must include what is, what has been and what is yet to be. "Yet to be," is of course not known. That is the nature of encounter—a moment in which the direction of things goes off in a new way, and we feel that movement, without any intellectual process. Remember the beginning of "Hamlet"? The ghost of the king—Hamlet's murdered father—stalks the battlements, but will not speak or respond to the watchmen. A wild tale surely must unfold. Shakespeare knew how to hook an audience.

Ministry has its fables, stories that help make some sense about how it is lived. In seminary it was important to remember ministers are "formed" through experience and reflection, not through classroom instruction. In the parish it is critical to practice good ministry by being authentic, not authoritarian. When we laugh about being "poorly advised," we renew our commitment to ministry as a vigorous calling, not a job. For me, that calling is to serve the people of this congregation—to serve you above all.

The glass slipper does not always fit on the correct foot and ministry fables too are regularly bruised by hard reality. That's how fables are—some days you eat the bear and some days not. But authentic fables—good parables, allegories, myths or stories—are only extenuated by adversity. Their essence is not truly diminished. They continue to connect our workaday lives with ultimate reality, and thereby we are truly saved.

Once upon a time there was a small boy. In the photo he stands solemnly in front of a white frame cabin. You can tell it is a long time ago because the picture is in the brownish tones of the 1950s, and the boy has buzz cut hair and wears a belt-length jacket and corduroy pants and what appear to be sneakers—probably Keds. Behind the boy's right shoulder, the side of the cabin looks smashed in.

Late one night in the summer of 1957, a car careened out of control across a clearing until it slammed head-on into the wooden wall of that cabin. The boy was sleeping in an iron cot against the inside of that unfinished wall. His counselor woke up, pulled the chain on the light bulb, and felt a moment of sick dread. The boy's head was under the front wheel of the car. Then that boy sat up and began to cry.

All I remember is falling out of bed, hitting the floor and being scared by the commotion. Of course, you have guessed the boy is me. I say "is," not "was," because this is my fable, my touchstone of ultimate reality. It has shaped my life.

Who goes there? I must answer—a fabulist comes, telling parables and seeking stories. I do not mean to be oblique or deceptive, but strike through encounter into the heart of ultimate reality. Mere causality is not enough. Who goes there? We must answer—*here is my story.* We remember every bit but honestly cannot say exactly why or how or when. It happened just that way— we think. What we have done and who we are and what we will do the rest of our days—all are deeply rooted in timeworn fable.

My fabulous happenstance begins with the obvious—I did not die. I could not have become a minister—or anything else—if I had died. There is no good reason I did not. Another picture shows my cot bent in two like a paper clip -- somehow the spindly cot threw me just far enough. That explanation does not answer the big question, why?

As a child the "why" was a simple miracle of an individual kind. God had a special purpose for me and for my life. Since the incident took place in a camp called Jubilee Ranch, run by an evangelical radio preacher named Reverend Bob Anderson, you will appreciate this perspective was strongly encouraged. There are, however, timeless words: "When I was a child, I spake as a child, I understood as a child, I thought as a child: but when I became a man, I put away childish things." No further miracles occurred; no special purpose seemed evident. After putting away childish things, I assumed the delightful role of religious debunker.

Near-death experiences are usually indelible. Mine, however, had no perception of death. I suffered no fear or resignation, had no time to contemplate or bargain. It just happened—bang! Perhaps that's why the power of the experience faded, subsumed under many other layers of incident and understanding.

It seemed to mean nothing, yet remember this is a fable. It is not a story of circumstance but of wisdom, not an explanation but an insight—an Intuition, as the Transcendentalists earnestly proclaimed, the source of capital "T" Truth. Human beings stubbornly insist on meaning and purpose in our lives. We are determined against letting it drain away. In our stories we sum it and spend it and share it again and again. Look carefully at your story—at anybody's story—and you will find right at the nub, the always-asked question, why? Why, indeed? Every story ultimately reveals the answer.

One Sunday afternoon some years ago I happened to look out at the pond behind the country house where I was staying. I saw a most fabulous thing. The first golden leaves of autumn had scattered across the surface, where the water almost perfectly mirrored the dark green fir trees lining the far shore and the bright sky around and above them. The surface of the water was so clear and the light itself so golden the leaves seemed to float in space, each of them an independent glittering point. They drifted almost imperceptibly on a gentle breeze, each one distinct and fully embodied, and yet visible as a swaying constellation all in mystic harmony at the same instant.

This is how my fable has returned. I was able to see what I needed to know, through a small window that opened on eternity and the cosmic wholeness. A God who sits in his bathrobe in some distant heaven did not especially save *me*. Something knit into the matter of the universe saves us *all*. The energy of being, a living encounter with all possibilities, reaches out continuously to enfold every one of us in divinity. This beyond is always in our midst. I have come to see myself gifted with a life that might not have been. The road can be hard but the gift is no burden. No need to worry about *why me?* We are all recipients of this gift, all included in ultimate reality. There is no good reason for us to be here. Or maybe there is. We don't know. But we can, in better moments at least, appreciate in our hearts how incomparably fortunate we are to be here at all. Our hands can affirm this reality and extend it in the world. Our stories add to the timeless narrative, line by line, in good will and witness. It is all in encounter.

It does sound a little fabulous, but I affirm it just the same. I welcome the fable you and I are already creating. May it unfold and unfurl as we go forth together.

Amen. Blessed Be. Shalom. Salaam.

Who's on First?—Locating Interim Ministry, Part I

25 Sep 2016

We were sitting around the table, enjoying a very convivial conversation after a fabulous potluck dinner, when the talk turned to backyard farm animals—chickens, horses, goats, cows, geese. These are not household pets but not exactly agricultural either. Well, wait a minute—my wife Sally's family did have a pet pig. Of course, it got too big for the house, and it sounds like it also got too ornery as well. Goodbye, pig.

And I remembered "Musings of a Pig Herder," which you have just heard. All the new UU Interim Ministers had to read this story as part of our training—I wonder why? Do you imagine the UUA was trying to tell us something? I wonder what it might be?

"Leading Unitarian Universalists" can be considered an oxymoron, like "Army intelligence." Earnest but futile as such attempts may be, they have long been described as "herding cats." This is unfair to cats. Somehow, I don't think the change in metaphor is in support of the farm-to-table movement. The transparent point is to understand pigs—I mean, people. They need time. People need time to understand change, time to consider its merits or lack of them, time to move ourselves along as and if we choose.

The more important point is that pigs can indeed move as a group. This is not the nature of cats, no matter what you try. The new metaphor is more optimistic. You might even borrow some of our traditional language and call it a version of "the larger hope." A group of people—call it a congregation—can move together if they go about it the right way. Even the freest of free associations can locate direction and momentum. You have done interim ministry in the not-too-distant past, so maybe this is already a clear possibility in your minds. We will revisit it because interim ministry does evolve.

The right way will certainly start with patience. There is no such thing as a church emergency, unless the fire alarm goes off. But the second "p" word is also necessary—persistence. Milling around for a bit is okay, but at the end of the day we must decide, and we must move. The Committee of the Whole must commit.

The third motivating word is purpose. We consider change because we want to get somewhere. We go ahead with it because our purpose currently feels incomplete or unfulfilled, and therefore unsatisfactory. We are compelled to move. Better yet, we conceive a purpose not previously seen—we move because we are inspired.

Best of all worlds—people moving because they are inspired. Inspired by the destination is good. Inspired by the journey itself is better. It is closer to the lesson of life itself. How you go is more important than where you get to, and the getting to is actually a continuous arrival—a day-by-day pilgrimage into the riches of experience.

"Who's on first—what's on second"—you know the routine. It could be the Red Sox, but it's not. It is a timeless metaphor of confusion and miscommunication. What prevents congregations from being inspired to movement? They will tell you—and each other—it is a lack of resources. Experts are unanimous: This is almost never the real reason. A church spending a million dollars a year will swear it lacks resources. A church holding a million-dollar endowment will swear it lacks resources. It is baloney—and just as much for a church a tenth that size. Been there, done that, got the t-shirt.

The whiteboard tribe—you know these folks—will pronounce "lack of vision." People do spend hours and hours in one technique or another, one workshop after another, "clarifying our mission and vision." This can be another form of milling around—with bullet points and boxes and arrows, and a camel is a horse by committee. It is very good news you have carried this uncertain process through to a most productive conclusion. We must continue to remember mission statements require to be lived, and visions may be captured in words, but do not announce themselves that way.

Don't get me wrong. Resource constraints are real. Planning and discussion are essential. What I am targeting here is the alpha and omega of useless, energy draining, and disingenuous excuses. There are always obstacles. What human endeavor does not include them? The truth is, human beings thrive on obstacles. We go through, we go around, we go over, and we go under. Obstacles? Our evolutionary genius is to prevail.

The real culprit, the stuck-in-the-muck, the rope binding our feet, is confusion and miscommunication. We are rich in resources—of dedication, caring, experience and even (sssh) money—but we are confused about what these are for. Confused, I mean, not at all in the sense of ignorance but in a broader compass—lack of clarity. This is an entanglement through miscommunication. Is our purpose clear? Is it the right one? Are we applying our resources to it? Are we getting results? If not, are we clear about how to change course and what to try next?

You will note there are never final and everlasting answers to these questions. That would, among other things, be insufferably dull. An organization that is confused and miscommunicating can be one with everybody running off in different directions at high speed—like the pigs. It can also be an organization that is resolute in its complacency. That is the existential challenge facing most UU churches. It's the Charge of the Light Brigade without the thrilling ride or all the bloodshed, but just as fatally lacking in true direction or impact. You will remember they got the wrong orders.

An organization that is unconfused may buzz with activity, but everybody knows what everybody else is doing, even if not directly involved. That is the quality of good communication. An organization that is unconfused may be a solid phalanx of unified initiative, busy getting there in good march step, not confined but powerfully acting as one. That is another quality of good communication. An unconfused organization apprehends both obstacles and opportunities, engages them fully in a continuous feedback of action and evaluation and renewed action. There is no rush, but rather a calmness of humming vitality, the essential dynamic of every particle of the universe.

Apparently, the proper way to herd pigs is with a stick, ticking them on the shoulder as indication of the desired direction—or so my dinner companions advised. Here is where we leave the metaphor behind, perhaps a little the worse for being stretched already too far. You are not pigs. I am not a pig herder. No kidding.

On the other hand, it is the responsibility of every minister, even an Interim Minister, to tick you on the shoulder when necessary. We use words, not sticks. We use "inside voice"—as we tell the kids. In an interim ministry the judgment about when that might be "necessary" is deliberately more circumspect than in a settled ministry. It is constrained by a strict time limit. It is rooted by informed consent. We all agree this work belongs to you, this interim process. We agree you are fully capable. You will seek with your own good judgment and move at your own chosen pace.

We also agree on a matter of common sense—it is a good idea to get some help. I am here to care for you, and to help. It is my job to listen more than talk, to suggest more than propose, to offer skills that might be useful—but not too often. It is proper for me to initiate some changes, if only to underline your ability to live with change. I will offer opinions, but not too often and—as noted—not too loud. I assume you too are willing to listen. I am looking forward to a very fulfilling relationship with you all.

Who's on first? Your minister is, of course. We are here together.

Amen. Blessed Be. Shalom. Salaam.

What's on Second?—Locating Interim Ministry, Part II

02 Oct 2016

In the days of old, New England churches often paid their ministers at least partly in firewood. Even now this is no modest favor. Imagine what it meant when all the work was by hand and harness, and the fireplace was the only source of heat—if one could call it "heat." Changes in the Land is a classic environmental history of early New England. Author William Cronon calculates thirty to forty cords of wood burned per household per year—blazing fires in every room and shortages within a few decades.

The late Conrad Wright, a famous historian of New England religion—including Unitarianism and Universalism—reminds us the "firewood option" gave congregations ample opportunity to convey to the minister their satisfaction—or lack thereof. If he—they were all "he" in those days—found the wood in the dooryard, that was good. If it was neatly split and stacked—take a bow, pastor! If, on the other hand, no wood—that was not so good. Other recorded expressions of disfavor included uncut logs in a heap, or even whole trees just dragged in and dumped. Good luck with those good folks, Rev.

We might be tempted to call this "acting out," but it is never helpful to impose contemporary standards of behavior on people and places far removed from our time. Let's give them the benefit of the doubt and focus our own effort to avoid the confusion and miscommunication I spoke about last week in Part I. This is especially important during interim ministry. To reiterate, our time is limited. We have only two years, and mine is a two-thirds-time position. To repeat another important point, our relationship has a special purpose. I am and intend to be your minister in full. By this I mean to give both the professional and—most important—the personal support you need during this time. I am a minister first. I was and am called to that role. Even though you have hired me to this pulpit, not called me, I must hold our relationship in that same vessel.

But I must also be something else—a kind of organizational development consultant. I am not to form long-term bonds with you. A ministry of the heart? Yes, but not forever. That will be hard on us both, but it is required. I am not to initiate programs or activities outside your own initiatives. I am not to "fix" things. These two statements clarify my role is to assist you in being and becoming who you want to be. Inspiration? I hope so. Aid and support? Absolutely, but it is your proper place to lead.

Is this clear as mud? Perhaps. Let me reassure you. There is no escaping change, as I have already said. There is a certain element of risk and thus a legitimate anxiety always lurking. There is also a plan. We do not head into the dark woods without a flashlight—and spare batteries. And it is okay to hold hands—a trust walk.

Here is the plan:

We will pay attention in various ways and at various times to five Focus Points. They are: 1) Heritage, 2) Leadership, 3) Mission, 4) Connections, and 5) Future. Aren't you glad you came to worship today? Now you know the whole agenda! No, you don't have to scribble these down on your Order of Service. I will explain them and you will start seeing them in use. There will be lots of reminders and lots of opportunities.

Remember first the mantra we spoke at the beginning of our time: Where do we come from? Who are we? Where are we going? Still true—the lodestar, if you will. The five Focus Points are tools for answering those questions, especially making sure we explore them fully. It is so tempting to rush on to the Next Big Thing, the shiny prize, the Christmas presents we snuck down to see at 3 AM. Careful—we can end up with all manure and no pony. Patience, persistence and purpose—keep those attributes handy.

So, "Heritage." It is simply stated: How has this congregation been shaped and formed? By what path have we come? What do we remember—and what does it mean?

Is the narrative a full and complete one, or have parts been downplayed or denied?

"Leadership," then. No organization, from a tribe to a nation, goes anywhere without good leadership. Who are our leaders now? Who will lead us in this time of transition? These are not necessarily the same people, though equally honored. How do we raise up our leaders, individually and as a group? Who will lead us in time to come?

"Mission"—words can be too easy to invoke but hard to embody. What is our purpose? What is our authentic purpose—not demonstrated by inspiring words but by our everyday actions? Why should this congregation continue to exist, and for whom? Whom do we serve and why—what values do we seek to uphold by living them?

For whom, is a very important question indeed. "Connections" reminds us we are in relationship with each other, with our faith and its constituent parts—with other congregations, I mean. How are we relating? To what other communities are we related—other faiths, other organizations, the places and the people with whom we live, work and socialize outside this church? The world is there for us—are we there for it?

Finally, the point of all this: "Future." There is an old saying that does make a good point: "You can watch things happen; you can make things happen; or you can wonder what the hell happened." That would be the essential challenge of the future, yes? The future is also ahead of us. And it belongs to the children, etc.

"It's hard to make predictions, especially about the future." This pearl of wisdom is from St. Yogi of Berra. Getting to the best future does require predictions, no matter how much guesswork is also indisputably involved. The critical difference is between good guesswork and bad guesswork. The Focus Points are to improve the quality of your inevitable guesswork. You sit with the questions. You talk about them, using the framework for clarity, thoroughness and—most of all—safety. Everyone has to feel safe in order for everyone to be heard. Only if everyone is heard is everything heard.

Wash, rinse and repeat. These are not one-time activities, not a list to be checked off as each "task" is complete. That's a big reason why the Center for Congregational Health uses these one-word terms instead of the "Developmental Tasks of Interim Ministry," as they are still called by the UUA. These are all processes, not individual steps. I draw the analogy of our Seven Principles, which are also presented as a list (see page iii). Read closely however, and you will quickly see they rise through levels of relationship from personal to cosmic, and are actually circular. The Seventh Principle continually leads back to the First Principle. This is a vital understanding of what we hold as truth.

As everything is heard, decisions become sounder and—this is crucial—owned more broadly. New decisions lead to new experience, which leads to new discussion, new vision and new actions. This is a "virtuous circle." There will never be any pure consensus. We wouldn't want one—the church would grind to a halt. The goal is something more vital and more promising: It is the process of framing and making decisions. The process defines us. It is who we are and how we appear in the world. It is how we encounter the world, with all its beauty and ugliness, how we engage life, with all its ups and downs, how we embrace each other, with all our gifts and foibles.

What's on second? It's the Future. It's dynamic, shaped by what we know and what we don't, includes what we welcome and what we dread, begins with what we do and what we do not do. "I got to light out for the Territory ahead of the rest" is what Huck Finn reckoned. It is dangerous but filled with possibility. We will do the same.

Amen. Blessed Be. Shalom. Salaam.

And Quit Show Business?

23 Oct 2016

You have likely heard the joke. The guy on the barstool is going on about hating his job. He works in the circus, cleaning up after the elephants. The bartender nods: Yeah—the stench, the drudgery, the lousy pay, the menial status—I get it. Finally, he says, why don't you walk? "What, and quit show business?" is the indignant reply.

The fashionable term is "framing"—how do we choose to ask a question, how do we articulate our options, how do we understand the narrative of our lives? These all play a most crucial role in our decisions, large and small. Are we in show business, or are we spending way too much time shoveling you-know-what?

In church there is always a little of both, as anywhere in life. Any congregation is a self-identified group of people with some sense of shared purpose in the world. The immediate tasks necessary to maintain both the church structure and the community social network do often qualify as drudgery. Sometimes they even stink—at least metaphorically. How does it feel if you find someone in your church to be insanely irritating, or insensitive, or even insulting? Of course, it stinks. We are only human.

Whether it is washing the dishes or mediating annoyance, the challenge is never-ending. The answer is always the same: Find some way to reframe what you are doing. As a church community, we reframe even menial tasks—coffee making, dishwashing, weeding the garden—as personal spiritual discipline. They are a commitment to greater good. It works. Other activities and programs hinge on our social bond—the groups carrying out organizational tasks feed on our pleasure in doing things together. The engine of ministry is often deeply personal but the mechanism is communal. To do good in the world requires an enlarged capacity only present when people will work together to inspire, organize and manage the tasks. This is church. It is practice. Many people say they are "spiritual but not religious." This sharing is what they miss out on.

There is as well a deeper spiritual agenda. In community we need people who are more than just friendly. We need people who support us at a deeper and more personal level than affable acquaintance. We need people who will risk for us, people who will risk knowing and being known, not just being polite. We need friends here who will be who they are and invite us to be the same—prepared to risk real relationship with us.

Churches—even UU churches—have a tendency to waver on this central purpose, although we hate to admit it. I remember vividly how much time, effort and emotional energy my mentoring minister in Harrisburg devoted to keeping the church at least tolerant of the one avowed Republican in the congregation. The scuff wasn't his political positions, which were moderate. It was his stubborn insistence on who he was.

Humans are always tribal, but as UUs we are obliged to openness and affirmation of a broader variety of people. We are constantly challenged not just to admit, but also to invite, not just to nod along to the superficial but also to risk the deeper places of joy and sorrow—and the deep discord of most human experience. Real people must be our tribe. Real people are fraught with opportunities for friction—that is, after all, how you know they are being real. If they don't exist prior to coming here, the congregational experience—the collective search for spiritual growth, for social justice, for genuine care and concern for each other—ought to be causing them. You heard right—a church is a place where a certain level of contention should be not only expected but encouraged.

Call it shoveling or call it show business, it is our best claim to authentic human community, distinct from others. We are the church that promises first of all to affirm and promote "the inherent worth and dignity" of every person. Of course it is hard, but that must matter. Noble intentions are a dime a dozen. Words are important—even revelatory—but only embodying them in practice shines our own light in all dark places.

I had the good fortune a few years ago to spend a ministers' chapter retreat with several dozen colleagues and Rev. Dr. Forrest Church, Senior Minister of All Souls, New York City, and writer of many popular books on the intersection of American history and liberal religion. Church was certainly the most famous contemporary UU minister. We were there to learn from him, knowing even then he was terminally ill with cancer.

He emphasized a particular story from his early years at All Souls. One Sunday, Church told us, he noticed a new person in the pews, a woman of middle age and ordinary appearance. She looked deeply distressed, but he had already begun the worship service. At the beginning of his sermon, she began to sob. Halfway through, she got up and walked out. She was gone when the service ended.

He never saw her again. After decades of successful ministry, Church's heart still anguished. How had his words not reached her? Why had he not stopped the sermon to console her? Why had he believed in that crucial moment somebody would go after her, somebody would know her, or how to find her? Why had he assumed she would come back next week, next month, next year? How had he—and his church—fallen short?

This interim period will include many hours of effort to renew your vision of what you most want your church to be. Speaking and listening are critical—

who are you, why did you come and why choose to stay? What is personally valuable in this community? A reimagined and clarified mission is possible, as is renewed purpose and promise. You can have a more focused and effective organization. The good can indeed be greater.

I do suggest it is nonetheless true you will spend the most energy on spending. The devil is in the details! I recommend: Keep calm and carry on. To choose between two good things, advancing one and setting another aside—this is normal. The right to decide is actually a great gift of community. Who would we be without our choices?

I believe you should anchor in the lesson Forrest Church drew for us on an April evening in Lewes, Delaware. "Remember," he said, "In every moment of your community's life there is someone among you who is giving your church one last chance. It may be the first chance you have been given, and the only one you will get. Life is not fair. As a minister—as a congregation—you must engage every minute with what is wanted and what is needed, and by whom." Success, Church pointed out, is never going to be guaranteed and never going to be complete. It is still our obligation to seek it out.

Human needs are endless and diffuse and difficult to discern. Sometimes they are most difficult when they seem most obvious—and the truth is hidden in that very distraction. I believe you owe each other the willingness to be revealed in the places where you are needy. You have and must protect a quality of esteem for each other. It is not enough to "love" each other, whatever that means. You must trust each other. The discipline is to assume good intentions as the foundation of relationship, no matter how garbled or annoying the immediate static may be.

Whatever "size" the church, it must be large enough in numbers, in spirit and in energy to meet authentic needs. It must do so for enough people in enough ways and with enough impact to actually matter in the world. No one ever got there by an easy road. The specifics of what you choose to have or want are not as crucial as taking the leap of faith—beyond ordinary priorities, customary attitudes, thoroughly mediated daily lives. That is the only way to really build anew. Do bring a shovel; we will need it.

Amen. Blessed Be. Shalom. Salaam.

Too Soon Old

07 May 2017

Four years ago, a few months before I got my new hip, Sally and I had one of those "aha" moments of mortality in the surgeon's waiting room. A joint replacement clinic is quite obviously filled with people limping badly. It was not hard to overhear how many were back for the third or fourth procedure. After I shuffled back from X-ray and sat down, Sally leaned over and said, "I'm not sure I like the long-term direction of this." I agreed. The blessing of modern medicine—*we can fix that*—was concretely accompanied by the enduring reality of the human body—*something else will break.*

From his deathbed, W. C. Fields is supposed to have muttered, "On the whole, I'd rather be in Philadelphia." Me, too. Yet this most profound wisdom is easily stated: Yes, the very end will come, but until then every moment presents options. Take firm hold of the best one available. Facing a firing squad? What the hell—drag on the cigar and spurn the blindfold. Taunt the Federales. Yell Viva Zapata! Be your own legend.

"Too soon old; too late smart," is an aphorism of the Pennsylvania Dutch. My father's mother was "Dutch" as they say, so I learned this pithy observation for all-purpose application. Anyone living life without learning anything was a fool, no matter how high-flying. Hard experience is guaranteed to all of us— no options on that. Some people live in denial, but that tends to set up a worse takedown. It is better to accept smaller doses to immunize the system, and not incite the animosity of the Fates. It is likewise better to grasp this essential quality: Life cannot be made entirely safe.

Experience is inherently dangerous. Without risk, there is no reward. Without failure, there is no success. Nothing truly worth having is going to come easy or cheap. To expect otherwise is exactly the Sin of Pride as long understood—of thinking you are exempted from laundry duty, elevated above common humanity. It is to be special more in your self-regard than your self-worth. It is to live without the corresponding virtue, Humility. To grow old before realizing this truth is always too soon, no matter what your age. It is always too late to be "smart"—no matter how many your years—if you aren't avoiding at least a few mistakes because you did make them before. Here are three ways to become old instantly: Avoid love because it won't last forever, integrity because it only irritates people, and other people because they only irritate you.

Today in our Opening Words the poet Rilke tells us how important it is to plumb what he calls, "the days of my life, already lived." He "finds" them he says, as tangible articles, like "old letters," and they can be held "like a legend, and understood." In "The Man Who Shot Liberty Valance," director John Ford works the same vein in the opening scene. Riding the train into town, the editor of the Shinbone Star tells Senator Jimmy Stewart—whose success began as that long-ago man—"This is the West, sir. When the facts become a legend, print the legend!" What Rilke called "the dark hours of my being" and Ford's sagebrush shoot-out could hardly be more unlike each other—except for the central point about the legend. That might mean there is something to it.

I told you some weeks ago about my first ride on a freight train and what I learned in the most dangerous way. Here is what I learned on our next attempt to get to Pittsburgh by illegal rail. First, we hitchhiked to the Enola Yard outside Harrisburg, where trains really depart for Pittsburgh, thus markedly improving our chances of getting on one. The second lesson was to accept help. After we snuck into the yard, we were startled in the middle of our dinner of cheese sandwiches. A railroad worker politely inquired where we were heading, and then pointed out a train about to leave.

The third lesson came this way: Most of the train was empty coal hopper cars, so we climbed into one and settled—somewhat uneasily—on the cold steel slope. The train was already gathering speed when another trainman popped his head over the side. "You can't stay here," he shouted. "You'll freeze to death in the mountains, and those hopper doors pop open. You'll slide right out the bottom." Oh—who knew?

Wait, there's more. He instructed us to stay in the car for the moment. The train would stop at the yard limit. We should then get out and run up to the cab of the third locomotive. "Just don't let the Tower Operator see you," he said as he disappeared. The journey was unforgettable. We arrived in Pittsburgh in the misty dawn next morning.

Why did the first trainman not have us arrested for trespassing, let alone point out the train we needed? What caused the crew to keep an eye out and the second man to risk his own safety by coming back for us? Why in heaven's name, stuck with such obvious blockheads, did they then conspire to put us into the cab? I suspect they did it for the bravado of their own legend. Railroad workers have always been hard men with dangerous jobs, great pride in their skill, and tight bonds with each other—and always cocking a snoot at petty authority. Now they are women too—and still like that.

So how are things in your personal legend? How are you feeling about your particular story? Who belongs in it with you—and who does not? Where is it heading? Is that the direction you want? If not, will this be the day you change course? If you're really not sure—an honest and illuminating admission to make to yourself—what will you do about that? Are you reaching into your gut for the strength to stay on the horse—to steer through the fog—to suffer the dark without despair, knowing light must follow?

If held like a legend, as Rilke says, and you do understand it, your life might be headed in a promising direction. It might not—the understanding and the attitude are essential—but here is the promise as he proposes: "I can open to another life that is wide and timeless." Legends give birth to that possibility. The danger of life is also the opportunity for its great reward. To live beyond the everyday round is what we are always capable of. It is how we get smart through experience, good and bad. Our bodies get older hour by hour, but we do not have to—if we will to take it on those terms.

Church is a great place to nourish that conviction. It is a place to set aside distractions. A distraction is anything that holds you back from living and learning your own legend. Church is a place to be present with your heart and your inmost spirit. It is a place designed to encourage thinking and feeling, joy and sadness, courage and comfort. It is a place meant to be safe first of all in who you really are. It is okay to be that person, in all the flawed gallantry and the stumbling prima ballerina that is you. We don't mind—if only because we make a promise not to, and because we remember we are just the same. The shoes we wear may not look like yours, but they all have stones in them. We are all limping, visibly or not—and all is visible sooner or later.

We know you don't belong here and are looking for a train. Over here—we'll show you. We know it will be cold down the line, the ride will be fast and bumpy and treacherous at speed over uneven paths. We are watching so you don't go the wrong way. We will put you into a better conveyance, if you are willing, and we don't mind ruffling feathers to do it. We will see you get there, across the miles and the mountains, through the darkness to the finer day that is coming. We will all enjoy the ride.

And finally, not ever too late no matter how long, everyone gets smart because you are us. Everyone here is everyone here. We are all us, and all of us are together. This is a plan, connected to how things are and should be. It's been known to work.

Amen. Blessed Be. Shalom. Salaam.

Nice People Do

24 Sep 2017

It should have been a straightforward memorial service—if there ever truthfully is such a thing. The man who died had lived a long and very full life, filled with accomplishments, adventures, family and friends. The death had been expected.

He had made some specific intentions known to his daughters—something all too rare in my experience. A word to the wise here—tell people what you want. It makes circumstances a lot easier. Please—you will not be "volunteering" to depart.

Even more unusual, he did—speaking to me through those two daughters—clearly understand and firmly believe he would be welcomed on the other side by his family and friends, who had gone before. He named those he would see again.

Why then, had this family of strangers come to my door? Well, one of the intentions of the deceased was to be cremated, and they had promptly done so. Upon hearing this, the church of his heritage refused to allow a service. Their theology was clear: No body meant the ultimate resurrection into eternal life was in no way possible.

Olympia Brown, whose words we have just recited [Singing the Living Tradition, #569], speaks of a "great message." What is the "great true principle" which she asks us to stand for, to work and sacrifice for? With what are we "entrusted," infused by its power with the strength and joy to live in active faith, "without counting the cost"?

Her great message was universal salvation—eternal life a certainty, body or no body, good person or bad, religious or not—all comers welcome. Saving us all is not by human decision, or even by divine decision. It is the immutable nature of eternal God.

Olympia Brown was a Universalist—the first formally ordained female minister in the United States. She organized the willing, the curious and the wary into new, small town Universalist congregations. Her world of the late 1800s may sound familiar. Industrial capitalism was seizing the first national markets; federal and state governments were venal and ineffective. Large numbers of immigrants flooded onto farms and into factories. Wall Street speculators manipulated the currency. The new mass economy gave prodigiously but very unevenly. It periodically collapsed into what were called "Panics." They often caused several long years of pervasive misery.

What links the perambulating memorial service to our UU history, expressed in the words of Olympia Brown? Knowing what was her great message, what is ours? It is likely not universal salvation, but the answer—some answer—is as critical now as it was then, as important to us as it was to her and her listeners. To look for it, to think about it, to speak of it—this is to live as vision-seeking people. It is one of the incomparable rewards of religious community. No matter how halting or uncertain the progress toward a vision, it is still progress. Any movement at all—as opposed to no movement—is every bit as significant as the distinction between the quick and the dead.

We can establish we do not care if there is a body available for our memorial services. Rev. David will bury you sitting in your Prius wearing a bowling shirt if that is what you asked for. I will solemnly recite the 23rd Psalm and "Do Not Stand at My Grave and Weep." I will tap my foot to Mozart or Justin Bieber if that's what your family says you liked. I will speak fondly and with at least a breath of candor about you, even if it is mostly second hand. Your family will guide me—in words or not.

Rev. David will pray for you, silently or not. I will ask the blessings of God, Jesus (although not "Our Lord Jesus Christ"), of Buddha and the Goddess, of reason and religion alike. I will wish sincerely for your safe journey to wherever you are going, or already are. I will do my best to heal those you leave behind. Sometimes it even helps.

I do this because my entire call to ministry is anchored in the absolute faith that, as each human is born with inherent worth and dignity, so each of us must die into the same state. We traverse our meadow of mortality searching for this final reconciliation. It must and will be fulfilled, to the end of eternity.

This "great message" of mine doesn't have to be yours, but you need a minister who can present one. Not all can. This is crucial: Ministry must root in deep values—the minister's and yours. Relationship in community is the power to believe and to accomplish what is almost always beyond us as individuals. A minister is embedded in your community—and this is where the word "congregation" acquires its real significance. You inspire and challenge your minister to live deep values. You call your minister to inspire and challenge you in turn, as individuals and as a people gathered under a covenant. The word means "sacred promise," which matters. Ministers can be personable, pastoral, thoughtful and inspiring, but there must also be covenantal steel.

Keep always in mind your First Parish must be a promise you make first and foremost to each other. Your minister will walk the same highway you are traveling, but it matters most how you treat and think of each other, before and after any particular minister shuffles across the stage. Think hard: Where else in our world is there such a priority—how we treat and think about each other? Where else would you go to be among such people? Your vision, however you come to phrase it, must reflect your loyalty as Brown names it, loyalty to a faith primarily in each other. She believed in "one God which ever lives and loves." So do I, but you get to make your own free choice.

However, you must believe in yourselves. You must believe every day in joyous, loving, fulfilled and grateful as qualities accessible to and even foreordained to you here in this sacred place. You must accept the evidence of your eyes and ears even despite the evidence of your eyes and ears. What? What did he just say? Wake up, there!

Yes, it's true. This is what "universal salvation" means. It means we belong here—here on this earth, here in this universe, here in this all-encompassing scheme of things—even if no scheme of things is ever evident to us. Each one of us belongs in this time and this place—here now. It means we can never be anything but an integral part of the eternal. We may be everlasting souls or angels working on our wings. We may be only molecules left over from the Big Bang—we are that. We are entangled in love for each other. It has been shrewdly observed the great historic strength of Universalists was their commitment to live the reality of love, embracing and bettering each other's lives. The world would improve for all through relationship, and they made it happen hands-on to an amazing degree in their congregations and their communities.

Who does this now? It is still a great message. Everywhere are people conflicted, aggravated, frustrated and despairing at least some of the time. Everywhere in our world are promises to grow a soul in the privacy of your living room. It will never be complete without sharing relationship. Everywhere in our world are hucksters selling love as a commodity. Our hearts will never be truly gratified. Everywhere in our world are communities of people being nice to each other—polite, civil, smiling, shallow, withholding. No one can be continually nice without a heaping tablespoon of withholding—the truth is, no human has ever lived without darkness and clutter inside.

Being human means real relationship cannot be easy. Every inch of genuine spiritual growth is gained in adversity. Every ounce of true enlightenment is paid for in humiliation. How rare and precious to even try. Tell the world you are people who will.

Amen. Blessed Be. Shalom. Salaam.

Being Crazy for Love

22 Oct 2017

Do you remember *Catch 22*, the famous 1960s novel by Joseph Heller—and the later film by Mike Nichols? The protagonist—Yossarian—was in an exceptionally dangerous line of work, bombing Italy from the air during World War II.

You could get out of the duty—you could claim insanity. But if you made this plea, you were obviously aware combat flying often proved fatal. You had reached a perfectly rational conclusion—which proved you were not insane. Bingo—"Catch 22."

Searching for a new settled minister is very much a "mission"—and it can have a certain surreal quality. There is, first of all, the sad truth: The phone company has a mission. Goldman Sachs has a mission. So does Bank of America. None of us is so foolish as to believe a word they say. They are certainly not in it for us.

Religious communities are different. Still, we too stumble over cultural blind spots. Corporations are profit-driven and hierarchical. They say stuff that is phony. Churches are loving and egalitarian. We tend to say stuff that is nice but vague.

Any statement on which everybody agrees is likely to be weak tea. But the stronger and more specific the brew, the greater is the likely dissent. The devil is always in the details. Grumbling may be noisy during the search process and silent afterward, or the other way around. Either way we are all too aware a small volunteer-driven organization, which means every single Unitarian Universalist congregation in the United States, is unlikely to have any chance of making an impact without the energy of whole-hearted endorsement by everybody. This is one version of Catch 22.

Still, there are powerful reasons to proceed. Whole-hearted endorsement unlocks a tremendous vitality we are scarcely aware of unless we really seek it out. Small groups who do get headed in the same direction can by that cohesion develop a tremendous momentum. From small things done well, with vision and passion, the great accomplishments in the human world are built, and always have been. As a religious community we also stand to reap tremendous spiritual rewards from acting on our understanding of every human soul as a work under continuous construction. Laying up the individual bricks, day-by-day, is honorable spiritual practice, and who knows—it may be one of the great cathedrals we are erecting. Or not—and that's perfectly okay.

When it comes to ministry, "mission" must be pursued as both mantra and menu. To be successful, we must seek inspiration. Our goals must be large enough to be worthy of serious effort, to stir up real visions of how things will indeed be better. "My ideas were few but grand," said the radical Florentine monk Savonarola. "Life, liberty and the pursuit of happiness," says our Declaration of Independence. "To form a more perfect union," says the Preamble to our Constitution. This is the "mantra" component. The words may look idealistic, but they root in the world as it is and as we intend it to be. The dynamic resonance is precisely how things aren't—but we plan to alter them.

Don't forget the menu component. Congregations and ministers must "govern in prose," as the saying has it. We need to share the particulars together. Without priorities, without plans, the poetry of mission is crippled as to actual value. Without specifics, the proclamation of mission has no actual function except maybe public relations—we're the church that raises the dead! No—more likely we make a high-minded declaration that conspicuously lacks any mode of concrete implementation.

The bugbear for you and your prospective minister is choice. No choice—no chance, is the iron maxim. But choice is scary. We are choice-making creatures—fight or flight? Friend or foe? Good-to-eat or maybe not? As individuals, we are haunted by our choices—what if I chose wrong? As social creatures we dread making choices in obvious conflict with the choices of others in any group we wish to remain part of—so we don't. We go along with the acceptable rather than risk the possible.

You may remember I offered the process of discernment as a religious path to overcome the disturbance of latent conflict. I hope you recall it hinges on intentional reassurance. Everyone is safe in the relationship; all will be valued and heard even if they are not being agreed with. Good so far, but here is another hard law: All of us react badly—and by almost uncontrollable instinct—when we perceive we are being exposed. We can't help it. For a hundred thousand years being exposed put you out of the tribe, and you died. All of us—each and every one—have buried triggers to that primal fear.

To find a minister, you must be exposed. It is that kind of relationship. Your minister must be likewise exposed. This vulnerability is the crucial Catch 22—Ernest Hemingway's "true grit." What is the truth about us, about me, about our heart's desire?

Remember the ministry menu, the specifics of the mission and the relationship. The menu items are not meant to be permanent. Nobody loses forever because every choice can be unchosen, or at least rechosen. There is no success in tacking back and forth like a will-o-the-wisp, but any group unwilling to change course is headed for failure. What have we in our world but a torrent of change? What is our biggest resource for coping with change? It is not money—surprise! It is all our people. It is every one of us as alert, pragmatic and motivated people determined, as church consultant Dan Hotchkiss puts it, to envision and make real a "mission to the future."

It requires ministry that is responsive, innovative, flexible, intuitive and experimental. Its most important focus must be on who will be coming to church next month, next year and ten years from now. The opportunity of change must be continuously embraced. Plans are made, but they are always evaluated and adjusted. The right goal is important, but equally critical is the process by which the community perceives direction and perpetuates motion. Like any organism, people who feel truly part of something living are much more truly engaged. Tomorrow always beckons them.

Who will our activities benefit? What will those activities be? What will we commit to carry out those activities effectively? This is all a way of uncovering the key question—what difference are we prepared to make, and for whom? For ourselves, of course—every community must nourish itself before it can call others forth. But mission fully embodied is to understand ministry too focused on those already here will never really be enough. Having a real impact on the community cannot be properly defined as winkling out a dozen people more or less just like us who will agree to be adopted. The payoff for the shared vulnerability is the sharing of deep purpose.

"Being crazy for love," is what I call it. What thing is it you and your new minister will be and do that is not who you are now, not that nice comfortable place you snuggle into every day, but someplace new and different—so inspired you forget to be scared or embarrassed? What will get you out on the dance floor? Remember the Hare Krishna? Orange robes, bare feet, shaven heads, chanting in the airport—nothing embarrassed those people. "Go thou and do likewise"?—well, no. No reason to get merely weird.

On the other hand, there is a critical lesson: True ministry is what you will do when everybody is looking, what you will be that is more than what you are, what you will sacrifice from what you have to get something more that you really want. It drives out complacency and timidity. Follow your strength of heart. Your minister should too.

Amen. Blessed Be. Shalom. Salaam.

All Hat (and No Cattle)

11 Feb 2018

J.R. Ewing used it as a putdown in "Dallas," but it is the 1956 movie "Giant" that best unpacks the phrase, "all hat and no cattle." James Dean at his sneering zenith (his last movie), Elizabeth Taylor and Rock Hudson in their prime, husband and wife with their ranch house interior by time-lapse slowly encrusting with pastel colors, drapes and wall-to-wall carpet—and miles and miles of Texas cattle country becoming oil country.

Thus a Technicolor flood of shiny cars and stainless Stetsons and nothing on fancy hand-tooled boots but a little dust—none of the real muck of what real Texans once considered real work. By extension, it reminds us not to fall for image or fast talk.

Your Search Committee is looking now for someone who will do real work in your pulpit, so it seems okay to lend my perspective about ministers. Of course, these are strictly my own observations, from the other end of the telescope as it were. Take these thoughts—if you take them at all—only for what you may find them to be worth.

In every congregation I have somebody ask me if ministers keep confidential what is told us. I always say yes, we do, and—as I was trained to do—also mention two key exceptions. They are threat of imminent harm to oneself or others, or information about child abuse. It's very possible this question always comes up not really as a question but as a way to share something to stay between us—checking the ground.

Nonetheless, it always reminds me of one major learning in 13 years as an ordained minister, which is this: People—even intelligent people regularly present in smart congregations like yours—may not know, at least in any specific sense, what ministers actually do. Folks, it does not mean what you think we do is necessarily wrong, but they did move the cheese. There is always a challenge of disconnect.

Two generations ago UU ministers were all male, mostly married, almost all white and at least presenting as straight. None of these things is true now. Most ministers worked or were on duty/on call 24/7. This was expected and just to make sure, most lived in a parsonage to which congregants had unfettered access. Mrs. Minister usually spent most of her time as unpaid all-purpose church support. You don't want to know what this did to the Preacher Kids. It was often not good. Many ministers moved every few years—you can still read these obituaries in the UU World.

This spin down memory lane is not about demographics. Two generations ago the academic, legal, bureaucratic concept of "confidentiality" did not exist. The implications I am sure you see: Privacy and discretion relied on individuals; now it is a system. There are rules and training, legal and professional protocols—and sanctions. A minister's work has changed in this way in virtually every area. Once—for better and worse—a minister did mostly whatever he thought best. Ministers today are very much better trained—more empowered, if you will—but also very much more constrained.

To illustrate this paradox: Can any former minister come visit? There are rules, in fact. We do wiggle around them, but cannot defy them. There are reasons for the rules, but—somewhat exaggerating for humor—we do now work for the Post Office.

Some UU congregations do have to be reminded of the new demographics, especially the ones where ministers have stayed for decades. You do not. My point however, is more nuanced: The functional architecture of the job has changed. The systems and procedures a minister has to internalize—and somehow make visible—are much more complicated and extensive than the old days. To sneak back to my opening metaphor, it is like going from free-range cattle ranching to barbwire everywhere.

This is definitely not all bad. Competence is much better assured. Breadth of knowledge is significantly enhanced. Professional behavior is both clearer and better supported both positively and—when necessary—negatively. Quality control is much better. There is general agreement on that. What is also widely observed is that we seem to be less inspired—less idiosyncratic, less charismatic, less "risky." No wonder.

The system of "formation," as it's called, does not at all encourage those qualities. We are allowed to be inspiring, but only if all the required boxes are properly checked first.

Here is good news. An amazingly high number of ministers thread this needle. Somehow, many of my colleagues get there. It will take some luck, but you can find one.

It will help to talk about what you mean by "inspired." I see three broad categories. One would be inspired in doing the work—your average saint, for example. Another would be inspired in the creative expressions of the work— say, somebody who preaches great sermons. Now, a "great" sermon can mean it's moving, challenging, surprising or clarifying. Not every Sunday, but triples are enough. A third category would be inspiring to you—particularly to you as a congregation. You may not know how it is you are motivated—it could be any quality—but you will be sure you are.

It is wise to consider which of these modes of inspiration is your preference or your priority. Please understand you will not get all of these in one person. You will not likely get even two of these qualities in an individual. They are learned behavior that is honed with experience, but they are also innate qualities of temperament, outlook and the passions of the soul. Remember, while we are talking about ministers, all of us are like this in our own ways. "As the twig is bent, the tree's inclined," and all that. It is backed up by extensive social science. We shape ourselves; we cannot escape ourselves.

Here is where I remind you about "all hat and no cattle." You do take concrete steps to strengthen your congregation's organization, operations and finances. Nothing reduces any minister to walking dead status quicker than chronic dysfunction in these.

Count on competence from those you are considering, but check just to be sure. You do think about your preferences and priorities—and then you must open yourself to leaving them behind if inspiration and emotional connection flairs, as it so often does, in some form you did not anticipate. Keep your head in the game, but go with your gut. A good minister, the minister you want your relationship with, does exactly the same.

Why this path? It is crucial. The heart of the relationship is caring. Nothing else comes close. Think about someone you really care about—it takes your heart and your head, doesn't it? It takes, in fact, everything you have, especially as time unfolds.

I will note that ministers can be quite charming. That has not changed. We are very strongly predisposed to want you to like us and extensively trained in getting you there without being too obvious. I hope this is not shocking. I hope you realize that in the end, being liked is the only coin we have to spend for things you want and expect. Please be assured we are also carefully screened not to abuse this skill, and that too is one of the advantages over the old ways— because it mostly works, although not always.

All this stuff is essentially the herd of cattle the right person will bring. Do be careful about the hat. Keep in mind it is possible to like a minister too much, to bathe your relationship in agreeableness. Ministers must say and do things you do not like. It is our calling. Be wary of anyone unable or unwilling to be unpopular in the short run for a clear reason. Be wary of anyone who speaks no contrarian points of principle and purpose. Demand the unorthodox. Make sure there is some real muck on those boots. Be sure you put some on your own boots—it is how successful ministry has to happen.

Amen. Blessed Be. Shalom. Salaam.

Of Time and the Reverend

30 Sep 2018

Here is an important question: How long does it take to write a sermon?

I have 18 years of experience, as student, candidate and ordained professional. As a settled, interim and guest minister, I've written on average three to four sermons a month over thirteen church years. How long does it take? My answer is this: True.

However long you might think it takes, that's how long it takes. There is no clear or complete answer. The ambiguity is inherent in any creative act, which is what sermon writing is. The ambiguity is also inherent in ministry.

Like baseball, there is no game clock in ministry. We play until the last out—it may be two hours or ten hours but that is just how long it takes. That essential ambiguity makes "how long does it take" an important question. It is also important because under most circumstances in a congregation the sermon is the central act of ministry. It is the pillar of the worship service. It is the most sustained and intensive expression of the minister's voice. Good sermons are almost always the number one quality congregational surveys say churches are looking for in a new minister.

Of time and the reverend? The central agreement between you and your minister will be how many sermons you want preached in a normal month of church. How much time that takes thus determines how much time is left for everything else.

Does anybody remember reading Thomas Wolfe's *Of Time and the River*? It is a very long book and filled to bursting with avalanching words and phrases—and that is after editor Maxwell Perkins chucked about half of it. It is not a good model for sermons, except of course for the willingness to chuck about half of what you start with.

The mossy joke about ministers is we have it pretty easy—only an hour of work a week. Here is the rule of thumb for sermons: One hour of preparation for every minute of spoken presentation. The normal sermon slot in a UU service is 15-20 minutes. You can do the math. In a preaching week, preparing the sermon is almost a halftime job. The writing is, I assure you, very hard work. It is intellectually challenging—there must be some coherent ideas in there. It is emotionally challenging—there must be the breathing human presence of the author. It is physically challenging—sitting in a chair concentrating intensely for long periods of time is always draining and often grueling.

UU congregations of course demand intellectually challenging sermons. We always have. Increasingly, we also demand authentic emotional connection in a sermon. That these two qualities are in a certain inevitable tension with each other is a small act of rabbit-out-of-the-hat we tend to just assume our minister will know how to pull off. It isn't the only one, but I will avoid digression on that topic, at least for today.

I will point out that writing is an intensely solitary activity. It must be quiet because I am hearing the phrases in my head as I type them, choosing alternatives of words and structure and, like a chess game, also scoping out where this is all trying to go. Ask Sally how ornery I can get when I am writing at the kitchen table and she insists on using the microwave or the coffeemaker. Well, maybe you should just take my word.

The thing about "intensely solitary" is it is not the only thing the minister is doing this week. All the normal responsibilities are going on—the meetings, the administration, the service preparation, the pastoral concerns. The schedule is full—always. The days of the old boy locking himself in his study and having the church secretary run the show until it's time to type it all up are as dead as the carbon paper and the mimeograph.

Add in the very firm and public deadline to show teacher your work. Add in also the need to do the whole thing again next week, and again for nine months at a stretch.

I was a freelance writer long before I was a minister, and I wrote for daily newspaper deadlines where "get-what-you-can-and-go-with-what-you-got" was the trade motto. Most ministers do not have this background. Thus, you have our favorite Facebook group—the "Saturday Night Sermonators." In too many cases, it is Sunday morning—right after midnight up to right before the service.

Most of the time the problem is an inability to get to the point, and—more deeply—a failure to comprehend the challenge. To write one interesting sentence after another, you have to let go and just do it. A contributing problem is trying to put way too much in there. I had a lot of that problem when I started as a student minister—way too many ideas. I had to cut back to get inside 20 minutes, and my first year as a called minister I cut back to 15 minutes. This helped me keep from overloading the listener and also gave the worship service itself more time to breathe.

As sermon listeners you take a critical role in making this effort worthwhile. Most important, always remember and remind your minister regularly that a sermon is a dialogue. No one sermon is going to be carved on my tombstone. They are never actually finished. They are a dialogue with you, the listeners. They are a dialogue with those who may read them somewhere down the line. They are a dialogue between the past and the future—a present flair of what Emerson called the "fire of thought"—but always evolving to some future moment of inflammation. Preaching is a process, not an end-state.

Our deepest understanding is primarily by accrual. There are epiphanies, but they too are part of a process. This is a core value of our theology as a "free church"—free to experience and reason and develop our conscience and our comprehension.

As a practical matter, that means the sermon before me today is the one that must be finished today—and having done that, I let it go. There are central ideas and problems I am wrestling with—in the world, in the congregation, in my own life and in yours. I come back to those problems again and again—and I'm sure will always do so. After all, they don't get solved. Of course, right there is a perennial problem that deeply engages me—are there ever real answers, or are the deepest problems of human life so entangled in our essential nature as to be beyond anything more than reconciliation?

That will preach, as we declared in seminary, back when we didn't seem to have enough ideas for sermon topics. Who can imagine such a state of innocence?

The late Forrest Church recalled arriving at his first pulpit with three sermons. "All of them were about Thomas Jefferson," he confessed. Church learned how to be a very popular preacher and writer. Your minister will, too. It may take a year for a new minister to secure the voice appropriate for your congregation. I urge you to be patient. I encourage you absolutely to offer feedback. I hope you will focus on what you liked, even if that is scant. I remind you what you heard is often not what the minister intended—and that is perfectly okay. We must learn to thank you no matter what.

Two last thoughts: First, remember there are five essential roles a minister fills in church life. If the sermons are not outstanding, it may be that worship is, or teaching, or pastoral care, or even keeping things organized. Look for the gifts and embrace them.

Second, try to embrace each sermon. Enjoy the journey. Go where the minister is trying to take you. Listen to the end, talk about it, take it home and let it sit for a while. We are so indulged in a consumer culture with exactly what we want. A church is also about what you need. As pages must be blank and minutes available for a sermon, we must provide some open space for our needs to be spoken to. You will not regret it.

Amen. Blessed Be. Shalom. Salaam.

Making Worship Worthy

04 Nov 2018

The film is more than fifteen years old. It's probably floating around somewhere on YouTube by this time. It shows a large room with rather poor lighting and a whole bunch of people jumping around to driving, polyrhythmic, drum-heavy Afro-Caribbean music. The better dancers have elaborate costumes on, each in a color theme—blue, red, yellow, green. The not-so-good dancers look a lot like my seminary class, because that's who it is—in Havana, Cuba, in January of 2003. I'm the tall guy in the middle, waving his arms to sprinkle the crowd with blessings. Yes, it is quite amusing.

But it is what I was supposed to be doing. The spirit of the River—the *Orisha*—had given me her wand and I was way into it—the energy was surging through me.

Worship, you say? Yes, in the style of Santeria, the distinctive blend of Yoruba African religion with Catholic saints and Caribbean rhythms, created under the noses of the Spanish masters some 500 years ago. I do add that no chickens were harmed in our service, which is one way the rituals were toned down just a bit.

Worship, you say? Yes, because it worked—for me and for many others, as was freely admitted, even by the Presbyterians. Yes, because it was the collective creation of the community of worshippers—those trained in its ritual practices, those willing to join together in the moment, those living within its culture in the past and carrying that into the future, keeping it connected and responsive to recognizable needs in their lives.

Nothing else is required to worship, except these: It must be communal, and it must work. What the community specifically decides is what makes worship pass muster as Catholic or Muslim or Baptist, but those are varieties of worship, not the essence. They are choices, not requirements—unless you accept them as boundaries.

Unitarian Universalists have no requirements. There are none, zip, nada. Chalice lighting? Only in the past 25 years. Prayer? Oh my, no. Learned address? Nope. Scripture reading? Only Mary Oliver. Music—what did you have in mind? Silence? Well, on this, being talkers, we prefer as little as possible. Dancing around? Not likely. Hand clapping? Are you trying to start a fight?

Somebody asked me after a recent sermon why I refer to UUs as "living on a volcano." This is another way we do. We are free to do what we wish. We are simultaneously burdened with having to figure out what the heck that might actually be.

One-third through this sermon I remind you we are all of us hurting in these days, in many ways. I will ask you to respond by caring for each other in all ways.

Please note that, having figured out a worship that works for us, we then have to do it again the following week, and the following week. We have to maintain continuity—nobody likes "shake-the-box"—and also changes— nobody likes the same-old, same-old. We have to speak well, move well, play and sing well and share well. We gather 50 or so people and open our hearts, souls, bodies and minds—each of us unique and in only one short space of time, a little more than half a percent of our week. In other words, our widely varying needs, wants and longings are inescapable.

Do you better understand the volcano analogy? Earlier this year—one of those stifling hot and sticky days—I spent four hours staring at the Order of Service for the coming Sunday. I could not get it to work. I shuffled hymns in and out, I shuffled readings in and out—they did not work. I got up and paced around. That did not work. I swore. That did not work. I had a sermon in mind, although not yet written, and I could not get the rest of the service to cohere with what I expected to say. Oh yes, that small requirement of coherence we do expect to be met, and we should.

Keep in mind I have been doing this for twenty years. I have been trained in the art and science of worship planning. I get paid. I am, in other words, a professional. Almost every week it all comes together just fine—in fact it is a lot of fun. But I do remind you this is a benefit of aptitude (some aptitude) and a fair amount of experience. And, more important, it is a benefit of how you respond to worship. It is your part that matters. I made this same point about the preaching of the sermon. You've heard the expression, "falling on deaf ears." You may know that Jesus was, famously, "a prophet without honor in his own land," after he went home and was rejected by his family. If you arrive not yet ready and willing to worship, it is reasonable to expect the service itself to help you into the frame of mind. That is a crucial goal of any worship service.

On the other hand, if you maintain a heart of stone—as the Bible puts it—if you resist or pick at everything—which is worse—even the second figure of the Trinity is not going to raise your spirit. Neither is Buddha. This is the same point I made about the sermon, now extended to the whole kit-and- caboodle. You are not going to get Jesus or Buddha in your pulpit. You are going to get a human being. If you truly understand yourselves to be a people on a journey of life with a chosen company, you surely must understand that your feet are going to be stepped on occasionally—just as you will step on the feet of others. Did you ever travel anywhere significant without a wrong turn?

Two-thirds through this sermon I remind you we are all of us hurting in these days, in many ways. I will ask you to respond by caring for each other in all ways.

So, worship always has a strong element of uncertainty. It is, after all, the unknowable we are seeking. It is the transcendent we are attempting to connect to. It is our humanity on display. Let me emphasize that being receptive to worship does not mean you should sit there and be mere recipients. It is not entertainment, nor is it didactic—although I did once sit through a history of the Fairmount Waterworks, and tendentious lectures still happen way too often in what is supposed to be sacred space and sacred time. As a congregation you have the right to shape the worship you want. It is your expression, and the ways you do it must be ones that are effective for most of you most of the time, and all of you at least some of the time.

Remember your worship leaders can see how you are reacting. If you are smiling or staring intently or gazing vacantly into space, we see that. We see you checking your phones, too. We feel the energy in the room—high, medium, or "get-me-out-of-here." Any of these reactions is absolutely okay—it is you, and it is your day and your time. I only remind you not to assume we can't tell, not to forget we have feelings, too. Any experienced minister has had great worship services flop or simply fall short. He or she has likewise had services that were on paper "a-wing-and-a-prayer" but lifted in person to amazing heights, because the people in the pews wanted them to. You have that gift.

You also have the crucial gift of patience. Many of your worship services will and must be led by guests or by lay people, volunteers who do this because they want to. If you hear or see something you do not like, I do not urge silence and I do not urge acquiescence to mediocrity. I do ask you to keep in mind the longer view. Worship is a dialogue, and most likely what you have heard or seen is a mistake, a misunderstanding, or that most UU of all circumstances, a legitimate difference of opinion. Do give feedback, but do give it mindful of your shared community. We choose each other.

At the close of this sermon I remind you we are all of us hurting in these days, in many ways. I will ask you to respond by caring for each other in all ways.

Amen. Blessed Be. Shalom. Salaam.

Searching Out Believing

A Matter of Degree

16 Oct 2016

"Mary Don't You Weep"—it's an old song known in the world of black gospel music as a "house-wrecker." Get it on a live recording if you can— Marion Williams with organ and gospel choir in her home church, Aretha Franklin on her "Amazing Grace" album from 1972—also in a packed church. They do bring the house down.

Bruce Springsteen's version on "Seeger Sessions" is fiddles and guitars, drawing on the folk music settings invigorated by the Civil Rights era. He nails the chorus:

O, Mary, don't you weep, don't mourn,
O, Mary, don't you weep, don't mourn.
Pharaoh's army got drownded.
O, Mary, don't you weep.

"Pharaoh's army got drownded"—it's not Standard English, but it is far easier to sing this way—to drag the "drown" and then nail that hard and emphatic "dead."

"Dead," is what Pharaoh's army got—not their feet wet or their clothes muddy. The Red Sea crashed over them. They were swept away and utterly destroyed.

Or so the story tells us. Is it true? To modern, science-oriented people truth or fiction seems the ultimate question. "True" or "not true" looks like a binary proposition—if one, then not the other. Yes or no. But why does that really matter—for a story?

We can now understand truth and falsehood, like good and evil, to lie along a spectrum, to travel around a circle that inextricably links them, making them at times difficult to distinguish. Truth and falsehood are relative, a matter of context and perspective. Some people loudly proclaim this "relativism" to be the end of morality, a terminal corrosion of standards of right or wrong. It is not. It is a morality not of yes or no, but of multiple choices. We do make them. We are responsible to make the best choices we can, to weigh alternatives and their consequences on all those affected. We make mistakes but we learn from our choices to make better decisions in the future.

This, I suggest, is core Unitarian Universalism. No required specifics of belief or practice, but there are essential values—choices, human agency and accountability to experience. We have a central object: The robust exercise of individual conscience.

It is a matter of degree how far along this path any of us may be at any time, but not a confusion about the goal. Here is where faith enters in: We believe human beings discern the good, and act upon it. In fact, much of history casts serious doubt on this proposition, and so do many philosophers. Ralph Waldo Emerson was famously dismissive. "No better men live today than ever lived," he argued in his classic essay "Self-Reliance." Emerson championed progress as a possibility, but he disdained complacent assumption of its inevitability. To cultivate self-reliance was to assume individual responsibility for a better life and a better world. We must do the same.

So we believe: There is no tide of history, but only you and I. We do the best we can. Our hope and faith are a world made better by our commitment to make it so.

Pharaoh's army got drownded. It doesn't matter if it actually happened. This story has been retold for at least three thousand years. People have believed not in every detail, but in the story itself. The Parting of the Red Sea, and the Exodus narrative in which it is one episode, lie at the heart of Judaism and, through the Abrahamic heritage, the heart of Christianity and Islam as well. All three traditions agree on a core confession: God is powerful and indeed does intervene against evil.

Who needs these traditions? African Americans used the Exodus story to endure and subvert and transcend their bondage. It inspired Liberation Theology, the "preferential option for the poor" that continues—despite implacable opposition by religious and political hierarchies—to be a global faith of the poor and powerless.

Along the spectrum of truth and falsehood then, it is the story that is truth. It has flourished against thousands of other stories that did not. A powerful and protective God—a God who fights for us—meets a compelling human need. You and I may not need a God like that one, with a personal and superior place in the cosmic order. Lucky us—maybe. I suggest we do hold another need ultimately just as crucial. We need to know evil can be stopped. It is essential for that to be true—by whatever mechanism.

Remember the famous photo of the man outside Tiananmen Square, holding up a column of tanks by standing in front of them? The power of those tanks was the power of evil. Yet what else could that man have believed, even if unconsciously, but that evil could be stopped? And what else could have happened except that the men in those tanks agreed, at least momentarily, not to do evil but to honor the good? It is a matter of degree—he was an absolute hero no matter what his sense of the situation, but the tank crews also made his heroism possible by acquiescing, no matter their motivation. Pharaoh's army got drowned because Pharaoh wavered in honoring the good.

He agreed to let the People go out of bondage, and reneged. His people suffered the plagues and he agreed again. And then, as the Bible famously phrases it, Pharaoh's "heart was hardened" and he led his army after the

Israelites. Put yourself there. You are trapped against the Red Sea. You spy the clouds of dust. You cannot flee or fight. Your family is all around. The least awful possibility is returning to slavery, but the People had no good reason to believe they would not suffer rape, mutilation and death. No outrage was impossible. No constraints were enforceable. Pharaoh's will be done.

Instead, those who had that absolute power of destruction were themselves utterly destroyed. No one knows exactly why or how. The People may not have known themselves, but they knew evil was stopped. Evil has never left the human world, and never will. Is it really any wonder this story has not left us either?

Jews have just observed Rosh Hashanah and Yom Kippur, renewing themselves as a People in a special relationship with their God. You will notice that, although the Egyptian gods of Pharaoh are known, no one is in relationship with them. It is the stories of the God of Israel that have prevailed. Atonement trumps arrogance and bellicosity and mendacity. I have used a verb here to call your attention to this: It matters which God we follow home but it matters very much more which stories we allow to prevail. Millions of people in our country and elsewhere are in thrall to malicious stories—of fear and anger and even violence directed at strangers. Any God can easily take care of God's self, but it is up to us to take care of our humanity—all of it.

The grief caused by evil is perpetual in human life. It is a matter of degree how much we suffer at any moment, but we always need stories that tell us suffering can end. Oh Mary, don't you weep, don't mourn—Mary of Bethany is in agony for her dead brother, Lazarus. Why should she not be inundated in despair? Because Pharaoh's army got drownded in the story from her childhood: Evil absolute and overwhelming was utterly destroyed. In her horror and grief, Mary can still believe this about unconquerable evil and unmitigated suffering: It is not forever. And her own story in the Gospel of John is about to take wings—Jesus will raise her brother from the dead.

Is it true? Remember the stories are about us. Our truth is unambiguous. When we act for good, overthrowing evil and relieving pain, we hold the power over despair and even death. Helped by powerful stories, we can do this. We must be willing to try.

Amen. Blessed Be. Shalom. Salaam.

In Us We Trust?

22 Jan 2017

The first time I hopped a ride on a freight train, I made two rookie mistakes. My buddy and I wanted a train going to Pittsburgh. We got on the wrong railroad and the wrong train. It was outbound from Philadelphia, but not to Pittsburgh.

Two long days of hitchhiking were required to correct this cluelessness, but I could have paid far more dearly for the second error. I ended up sitting on the air compressor in the end framework of a cement hopper—rather comfortable, out of the wind and with a strut to hang onto as we rocked and rattled into the long night.

The long night—of course I inevitably dozed off, then startled awake in terror. Dozing off is bad enough when you are behind the wheel of a car. In my position a drowsy bounce or a slip would have put me instantly under the wheels of a freight train.

Some time later, I learned hoboes and boomers never "rode the rails" without a rope or a sturdy belt to tie them in place against just such a possibility.

Who knew? Not me, not my friend who had hopped a lot of trains but only for short distances. We were males in our late teens. This is not a group known for conspicuously good—or even minimally adequate—evaluation of life or death risk.

In recent years I am struck more and more by how much we all tend to live this way. Our cognitive capacity matures, but we continue way too prone to follow personal judgment, to overweight our own capacity, to mistakenly and sometimes bizarrely credit our own motivations. Human beings want what we want, pursue it relentlessly and make up fierce and elaborate narratives about why it is the right thing for all concerned.

Alongside this incontrovertible fact is another—we come to church at least partially to counteract this self-interest and self-justification. The countervailing force is not "the church" as such, but religion itself, in all its myriad expressions. "In God We Trust," it says on the coins in your pocket. Every church defines its own gods, but the common coin represents an understanding shared throughout history and cultures. Humans persist in seeking something—no matter how named or pictured or prayed to—that is larger than us, and can be trusted. Any faith tradition is an explicit way of living this truth—this need to trust more largely. A great faith leader—Gandhi, Dr. Martin Luther King, Jr., and even Pope Francis—can become everybody's leader.

This puts Unitarian Universalists in an intriguing position. What exactly is our faith tradition? We have no held-in-common concept of the divine, let alone any God. We explicitly reject "creeds" and dogma and required religious rituals. It is said of the Irish you only need one to start an argument. The Irish say that about themselves. So do Jews. So do UUs. Each group is proud of this pugnacious quality: We are prepared to insist on the very personal settlement of right order in things from the quotidian to the cosmic, and we do. In God we trust? Not without a very vigorous argument.

We hold fast to our own ground. The good news is this creedal reliance on individual conscience doesn't have to leave UU churches incapable of rich spiritual life. Without a religious roadmap, however, it can be a puzzle whether to believe at all. Yet we often do—eclectically, conscientiously, skeptically and even disputatiously. There we journey, skittish to the edge of faith—and sometimes find very deep faith indeed.

Still we lack obvious cues, so we must navigate in community. In us we trust—we must care for each other. We cannot merely show up and go through the motions. We have no body and blood of Christ, no prayer wheel, no Beloved Ancestors. There is no salvation on order. Heaven cannot be filled with UUs. We might get there but can't count on it. To save ourselves we must learn to trust—not God but each other. Our congregation is gathered around that vision. It is our intention of highest purpose.

UUs are usually scornful of conventional miracles, of the Virgin Birth, raising-the-dead and "Touchdown Jesus" kind. We suspect anything that smacks of carnival tricks and tend—as people do—to overlook our own commitment to the mechanism of the miraculous. We are nice people, we say. How can we not be a nice community? We are smiling and welcoming and friendly and we use good table manners and largely courteous speech and social interaction. How is that not truthful trust in action?

Let me count the ways—some other time. Now, however—during an interim ministry—is the time to realize believing good things will "just happen" in a human community, even this wonderful First Parish, is every bit as much of magical thinking as expecting to walk on water. It has the same effect—you can't get there from here. The desired state may appear but it never approaches, unless we accept we have to do the walking. To arrive anywhere at all, we must take the risks inherent in movement.

Speaking honestly, speaking openly, speaking directly—saying what we feel and sharing what we believe—this is the behavior of trusting. It is proper conscience, which surpasses individual settlement to establish collective well-being. It is deliberate before instinctive, learned before habit, reinforced before standing strong. That's why we try to bring along a rope or a sturdy belt. Trusting, like prophecy, is not for the faint of heart.

This question first and last: Do you trust yourself? Look in the mirror, rest in your favorite chair, take a walk in the woods or just pause the TV. Think it over. If you ask, do I trust myself, what is your compelling answer?

Don't be misled by "perfect" or anything near it. Nobody is or ever will be. Perfection is for divinities and we are human beings. Don't be distracted by the hint of tooting your own horn—or the false piety of staying silent in modest expectation of applause. We are all vain creatures, every one of us in our own way. We like to pretend other people don't know this about us, but of course they do. Step up to the plate, then. Ask and answer—if you don't trust yourself, how can anybody else trust you? The heck with believing in God—do you believe in you?

If being UU means anything, it has to mean believing in us. We belong here. We are worthy—if not in all our actions at least in most of our intentions. We accept responsibility when we fall short because we believe we can and will do better. Each of us is interconnected but every one of us is sovereign, not ever to be without innate dignity and value equal to all others—and never to have it unreasonably withheld.

What does this mean in your congregation? It means your feelings are your own and no one should be allowed to take them away from you. It means you are free to be sad or glad or anxious or joyful—and these are safe to express because everybody else guards that safety and you guard it for them. No one is ever made to feel small.

Your opinions are your own and no one should be allowed to silence them. Please don't confuse this with everybody agreeing with you, because we all have our own opinions also. What I mean is, nobody should be allowed to make you feel wrong just because you speak up for what you believe to be right. No one should ever be unheard.

Trust in yourself and in what you feel—if each of us does, all of us can. Believe in yourself and in what you think—if each of us does, all of us can. Does it actually work this way? No. Could it actually work this way? Yes. What we commit to each other is to live intentionally in the in-between place—never accepting the "no," even if we never entirely accomplish the "yes." In us we trust—and so we must. It is who we are.

Amen. Blessed Be. Shalom. Salaam.

Expecting Miracles

26 Feb 2017

"Good Luck, New Jersey"—it sounds like a joke told by people from New York or Pennsylvania, or maybe the grimy setting of a song by Bruce Springsteen. The Boss is from New Jersey, and he knows what he is talking about.

But Good Luck is a real place—in New Jersey and in the history of our faith. It is the spot on Cranberry Inlet where John Murray, the first actual Universalist minister, came ashore in 1770. His ship, on the journey from England to Philadelphia, had run aground on a sandbar, and could not get off without just the right wind and tide.

What happened next is in the nature of the miraculous: Murray was expected. A farmer named Thomas Potter had in that very place built a chapel a few years prior. Potter hoped what he called "a true minister of God" would come to occupy it.

Murray was a badly failed minister of God. The Universalist preaching of James Relly had converted him from Methodist but Murray's call seemed in vain. His congregations dissolved; his wife and child died; he went bankrupt and was put in debtor's prison. He swore to minister no more and headed across the sea to a new start.

Thomas Potter was a persuasive man. He wheedled an agreement: If the ship were still stranded Murray would preach in the chapel Sunday. It was and he did and the people came. Murray did go on to Philadelphia, but he never again lost his call. You will find his church in Gloucester, MA. You will find his words in our hymnal: "Give the people something of your new vision…give them not hell, but hope and courage."

Those words invoke a sturdy belief—in belief. Hope and courage are qualities of sturdy resistance against all appearances to the contrary. UUs sometimes forget the mechanism. Unitarians rejected the miracles of Jesus: They could not be enough to prove his divinity. The place of miracles was their central dispute with the orthodox, and their quarrel continued with Transcendentalists and spiritualists as recently as 100 years ago. Remember that Emerson, despite his famous evocation of "self-reliance" and his protean invention of capital "R" Reason, understood both these concepts clearly in the context of an Oversoul and the spectacularly miraculous nature of the entire cosmos.

But not for us the midrash—the rabbinical teaching—that says the Red Sea did not part to save the fleeing Israelites until they walked out into it—

some say as deep as their noses. They had no earthly alternative to expecting the miraculous. UUs are cozier with Fate. Our delegation will carry signs berating Pharaoh on behalf of the 99%.

Still we retain a certain characteristic magical thinking. At a District meeting a member said his congregation was suddenly bursting with young families. They thought it was because of the sign put on the highway to identify the church—finally. Expecting miracles—us? We all laughed at the UU chestnut about the congregation that met in the public library and wondered why nobody new came, until realizing they were gathering behind a door with a sign saying, "Emergency Exit Only—Do Not Open."

Then there is our version of manna from heaven—how the money appears. Every UU congregation I have never been in or even heard of clearly holds it as the essential act of resolute faith—church funding will just appear. Presto! Every year, everywhere, the canvassers—the people who try to make it appear—get the same questions: Why do we have to talk about money? Why do we have to ask for it? Why should we publicly thank those who contribute? Why do we have to work at this?

I'm not starting any debate, but my observation is: We are expecting miracles when we expect money to "just appear." It will not.

It is true we do sometimes get money in odd ways. One church I was in received a bequest of $335,000. They had no idea it was coming. A far-sighted member was the estate lawyer. A probate judge did agree the bequest was legitimate. If this seems odd to us, and possibly unethical, please note a widely held explanation of why people so often used to leave money to churches is that people used to die at home. The minister was highly likely to be holding at least one hand—probably the signature hand.

Only in some quite alternative universe does money for religious communities just appear. And it is simply a fact the most economically-challenged congregations give the most. There is a widely accepted explanation: Those who need most, give most.

New members and necessary funding are manifestations of the miraculous in community. If we are or ever hope to be who we say we are, they should not be out of our reach. This is important. UUs don't endorse divine intervention, but we are commonly found expecting another, very characteristic miracle: We expect people to be nice. More to the point, we expect people to behave because they choose to, not because they must. That this is contrary to all human history and universal human experience doesn't seem to faze us in the least. We are good people, are we not? We are free of ignorant superstition so prevalent in every other faith…we say. We tend to be highly educated and do "behave yourself" kinds of work—as opposed to roofing or coal mining.

Somehow people inevitably don't behave the way we think they should. We inevitably don't behave the way others think we should—and we are then "shocked, shocked, to learn there is gambling in Casablanca."

David Brooks of the New York Times once called this the "Pretty Good Person Construct." Americans believe we are pretty good people. We know because we act pretty good—at least most of the time. Of course, as he delighted in pointing out, when judging ourselves we use a very forgiving curve. Social scientists have run multiple experiments proving human beings will behave badly when given the opportunity. What people will not do—even if cued—is behave too badly. They will act to maintain the self-image they are "pretty good people" and they will judge that good enough.

My favorite example is the taxi drivers caught by researchers taking tourists for a lengthy whirl. They didn't do that when the person was blind. That was just too blatant.

Unitarian Universalist theology—both intrinsic and in action—is rooted in human goodness. Thus, we may be the only ones who have a real excuse, but this belief is just as deluded as raising the dead. We must live the truth we know: Individuals can never be anything but self-interested. Only communities can be good—by working at it.

Miracles by their nature take place wherever you may happen to find them. Ours must take place in community, not in who we are as if castaway on some desert isle, but in who we are with each other, caring for each other and responsible for the good of all.

You have to expect a miracle to get one. You have to understand them as available, even constant; you have to feel yourself in the presence of the possibility. Does this seem preposterous? I remind you how all of us experience falling in love. It is not there—and then suddenly it is. It may come when we least expect, but it never comes when we give up hope. It finds us only when we are truly willing to be found.

Miracles are like love: They are interactive, a change in relationship, a new dynamic, bending what has been into what now can be. Doesn't every romance you have ever heard about or experienced turn on somebody being pried into giving in to love? Doesn't every one involve some drama of belated recognition—of true revelation?

Like Thomas Potter, our chapel is for new vision, and so it will surely be revealed.

Amen. Blessed Be. Shalom. Salaam.

Mind the Gap

26 Mar 2017

I walked two blocks to get a hamburger and, on the way back, detoured across the front lawn of a campus building. The cop shouted, "Halt," and ran toward me waving his billy club. I halted. Yes sir, I was at Burger Chef, a block that way. Yes sir, I live a block that way. No sir, I do not know who just firebombed the drugstore in between.

I was a college freshman and it was my first riot. I would never be so trusting again. Where I grew up, police officers were public servants. They did not whack people over the head. The reality for black and brown people I had seen on TV but it was not mine. Welcome to the club, longhairs—pun intended. I believe those who came of age in the pervasive civil violence between 1963 and 1975—assassinations, riots, and lawless repression—were deeply scarred as people. I'm not eager for any kind of "do-over."

"Mind the Gap," as you may know, originally meant, "Don't get your foot caught between the platform and the train"—caught in the gap, in other words. It may seem less consequential than many other dangers, but there is some "mind the gap" quite pertinent to Unitarian Universalists. To be the people we are, in the place in which we find ourselves, might be a higher good than attempting to be somebody else.

Many of the gaps now riven through American society—gaps that face-slap us 24 hours a day—are the distance between seriously differing values. Taking other people not seriously at all—as people, I mean—has become contagious. Any time the word "stupid" floats into your head—or comes out of your mouth—and you apply it to a group of people without differentiation, you are not taking those people seriously as fellow human beings. Or maybe we are taking them too seriously in all the wrong ways.

As UUs, we should also think in larger terms—if only because we cannot be sure anyone else will, at least not in the same way. The central gap in American society—the most dangerous chasm—is economic. The long-term hollowing out is of the working middle class, the continuing loss of almost every job in between the highly educated and skilled and the less educated and low-skilled. These middle-class jobs are the ones most Americans hold. They are going away. They will continue to go away.

That means us. Unitarian Universalism is and always has been a middle-class religion—not just demographically but congregationally and theologically. Who will be the UUs if there are fewer middle-class people and economic pressures squeeze their time and resources? We already struggle with that challenge, including here in your congregation. "Free association" is a thoroughly middle-class invention. How will we be in community if fewer people understand it, seek it, practice it—and have the collective resolve to sustain it? Free associations are withering everywhere in American life and so are many congregations.

Theologically, every one of our Seven Principles is an expression of a middle class ideal, from individual worth, to conscience, to democratic process, to educated worry about the environment (see page iii). These ideals rose among the intellectual elite in the 1700s, but they had no broad weight until the rise of the middle class—the bourgeoisie as we used to say. A middle class less prosperous—let along smaller—does not turn more liberal. In every society where prosperity has waned, the result is exactly the opposite. If the past 30 years has been painful for our values, how bad will the next 30 years be?

That is not about numbers and elections, but about values. Are we successfully making the case for our values—and our church—among our peers in education and employment? If not, we are going to fall into a deadly gap. They will not come. They will not care. Are we connecting and communicating with all the people in our communities—the ones not so educated and well-employed? If we do not, if we act as if 100 UUs is all our church needs or wants thank you, what real voice, what significant impact, what genuine service can we provide for the many neighbors not exactly us? What are we really doing for those residents? More important, what are we doing with those residents? It is a deadly gap—a shortfall of vision and practice.

To successfully be the people we are, in the place where we find ourselves, mind this gap especially: What distance between our church only adequate—content to be average and pre-occupied with survival—and our church that might be outstanding? This is the essential challenge. Every "church-good-enough" is really only buying time. Circumstances well beyond our control are shortening the time we can buy, and may significantly degrade its quality. You know the famous analogy of the frog in the pot is false. The frog will jump out well before the water boils. Is the average UU as smart as the average frog—and as sensitive to ambient temperature? The jury is out.

Fortunately, you are not, by a long jump, average UUs. First Parish people, and their congregation, are clearly outstanding in many ways. Will they be the right ways? First you need to be able and willing to ask that question. You need to hear each other, not just listen. You need also to grasp the difference between goals—things you want and will work for in any area of church life—and values. Values define who you are trying to be, as individuals and a community. I can't stress enough that goals are meant to be accomplished—or not. You can't succeed at them without being willing to fail, but in success or failure, they are always means, not ends. They are meant to be under continuous review and revision.

What might it mean to focus on excellence in our goals, as something we already are in some ways and could be in others? What might it mean to go after a wide vision, an expanding capacity, a larger presence? What might it mean to gather our energy for the challenge to create the best future for those who will be here next year, in five or even fifty years. Hard? Yes. Impossible? No—obviously not. Churches have more lives than cats, and this church has had more lives than most. You don't get to more than 350 years by failing the continuous tests of time and circumstance.

You have a great advantage if you will take it. You know for certain somebody figured it out—over and over again across all those years. They figured out the correct goals—probably by swinging the hammer as many times as needed to drive the nail. Remember no one goal can possibly define this diverse community, so keep the courage to set and discard them as you freely choose. They figured out the correct values. They did their choosing in community, in relationship to each other and to those around them. Put relationship at the center and tend it vigilantly and everything else becomes properly proportionate. There is nothing human beings need more than other people who care about us. There is no gap more bitter and destructive than feeling unwanted, unheard, unmarked when you are here and unmissed when you are gone. Mind that gap and you fill a need that never wanes. Mind that gap in what you do and say, what you will seek to make happen in the world, and your energy will never go to waste.

Emerson famously asserted that no better people ever lived than live now. Those before us proved adequate to the tasks they faced. Not perfect, but adequate. Those before us had not more or fewer resources than we do. They had themselves, and they had within them the strength of spirit to survive the bad places and celebrate the good ones. So do we. Mind that gap then—summon your spirit and put it to work.

Amen. Blessed Be. Shalom. Salaam.

Practicing for Our Own God

04 Jun 2017

April 13 was Mr. Jefferson's birthday. In 2015 Sally and I observed the day by driving to Jefferson, NH for a wonderful view of the White Mountains from the north. During his lifetime Thomas Jefferson, our third president, was an egalitarian "Mr." to friends and political supporters, and he still is. We share the same birthday, so I qualify.

Mr. Jefferson created one of the most amazing artifacts of American religious life. In 2011 the Smithsonian Institution—through its National Museum of American History—completed a painstaking restoration of the "Jefferson Bible." It cost almost a quarter-million dollars of public and private funds, before going back on public exhibit.

On the title page, in Thomas Jefferson's own serviceable handwriting, is the full title of his work: *The Life and Morals of Jesus of Nazareth: Extracted Textually from the Gospels, in Greek, Latin, French & English.* It is a fascinating work in many ways.

The original is 86 pages and dates from 1820, long after Jefferson had retired to Monticello and only a few years before his death. He was very serious and scholarly about the project. Although it is wrong to call him a Unitarian—he never went to church—Jefferson strongly identified with a central cause of our forebears. He too wanted to rescue Jesus of Nazareth from what they judged to be the claptrap of centuries of accumulated distortions by the organized Christian church.

Jefferson was fluent in Biblical languages as well as French and German, so he gathered the best texts and commentaries he could find in those languages as well as English. Then he set about constructing the Jesus in whom he wanted to believe. He marked all the passages in which Jesus actually spoke, and then the passages of narrative he believed authentic and historic—or likely to be. He took a large pair of scissors and cut out those passages in the four books of the New Testament. He then reached for the paste pot and assembled them in scrapbook style—and in chronological order, which of course is a radical change from the way they appear in the Bible.

Jefferson also eliminated the many alternative and conflicting versions of the words and actions of Jesus. He discarded every one of the miracles attributed to Jesus.

This is our history: For Unitarians, the intellectual endeavor. For Universalists, Jesus of Nazareth the loving teacher. No, to orthodox Christianity. Not for them a God who walks the earth in fully human form, mysteriously both flesh in every way but without any sin whatsoever, joined in unimaginable but perfect unity with a cosmic creator God and also a mysterious indwelling infusion of spirit. Please, no Trinity.

This is our practice: We go forth in search of our own God.

Our God may not be the Enlightenment divinity Jefferson and his peers envisioned. On the other hand, we almost certainly have the same need Jefferson did—without the paste pot probably, but driven to answers for the same questions: Where is God? What is God? How is God present? If in doubt, take your mental scissors and slice out that word "God." Glue in small-d "divinity," or "transcendent," understanding those words to stand for what human beings certainly cannot make happen and maybe cannot even comprehend.

If God is far away, does God care about us? If God is nearby, how do we know? Is our God cosmic, or personal—above and beyond, or able to hear and see each one of us? Does God understand what is hidden in our hearts, or hurl bolts of lightning—or both? You will recognize these are questions with no provably true answer. All of them are possible, and all of them have vigorous adherents in the spectrum of religious belief and thought. There is no one right answer to any of these questions—except this one: TRUE. That is, TRUE if you find it so—all, some, or none of the above. If you find yourself wondering what Unitarian Universalists believe, we believe TRUE is possible, but nobody else gets to decide it for you.

We may find TRUE to be far afield from God questions. Maybe it is "god" without the capital letter. Maybe it is the mystery of mathematics, which—rather like the law of gravity—seems to work in the real and theoretical worlds without any clarity about exactly why and how. Maybe it is the intricate wonder of our local or global ecology. Maybe we seek the divinity of the Enlightenment, as Jefferson and many of his peers did. Some were Deists, generally thinking God may have started it all, but as we say with Elvis, subsequently "left the building." Velvet paintings, anyone?

It turns out Jefferson's Bible was not his first "cut and paste." He did something similar in 1804, while president. In that shorter version he apparently organized the moral teachings of Jesus by topics, but it has been lost. The Bible we have was in his family until bought for the public in 1895. Here's another sign of our fallen civilization: The 1904 printing authorized by Congress lasted well into the middle of the twentieth century—and a copy was given to every incoming United States Senator. Can you imagine that happening today? I wonder how many wouldn't even risk touching it.

But we can. The Smithsonian Institution has published a facsimile version, and the standard volume has never been out of print. You can get versions in paperback or hardback, in Kindle or "modern" English or illustrated or spoken word. This is happier news than the state of the Senate. It means Jefferson's protean idea—God belongs to us, not the other way around—is alive and well and on Amazon. It lives in our hearts and our minds and even in the crowded marketplace of our culture.

As all humans have, through all time and in all places, we practice for our own God in tangible but different ways. Some of us instinctively crave silence, that we might practice the God who speaks to us in the hush of contemplation. Some of us are most invigorated by celebration, by singing and speaking straight from the heart. Some of us have a rigorous hunger for understanding, for history and ideas and good order. Some of us long to lay our hands on the remaking of the world, or on supporting those who do.

I hope we know all of these practices are right. All of them are necessary. All of them are God. Whichever one you favor—and almost everybody favors one ahead of the others—I hope First Parish remains always a place where each is honored, respected—and expressed. I hope we seek answers continually, and practice alone and together.

Where Sally and I pulled off the road that day to take pictures, we had Mt. Starr King behind us. It was Thomas Starr King—first a Universalist and then a Unitarian minister in the Civil War era, whose quip it was that Universalists believed God was too good to send us to Hell and Unitarians believed they were too good to go there. This is a reminder to go about our works with suitable humility, especially when we are right.

And this final thought only a few weeks after Easter. In the Gospel of Mark, the women enter the tomb and look for the body of Jesus. A figure clad in white tells them, "He is not here. He has gone." There the oldest version of the Holy Week story ends, for Jefferson and Bible scholars. Thus, no doctrine of Resurrection is required for us to see that what is divine, what is transcendent, is that beyond death and despair. It is forever and ever, able to renew us in every dark and threatening hour, joyful in every birth and bounty. However we imagine, however we believe, however we worship, what is divine belongs to us. Practicing for our own God? We should not hesitate even a moment.

Amen. Blessed Be. Shalom. Salaam.

Discovery—or Disbelief?

01 Oct 2017

Long ago—40 years ago—I played black gospel music on the radio every Sunday night. It was hair-raising stuff—literally. That's why I did it. I heard from a resident of the state medium security correction facility within range of our signal, who reported this testimonial: "Brother talks too much, but he sure does play the old-time church!"

Another Sunday night I got an excited phone call—and that fan showed up right after the show. He and his girlfriend picked me up in his Cadillac and we all went out to dinner in a very nice downtown restaurant. I had unknowingly played songs he had not heard since his poor-white childhood. Almost a decade later we met again and I learned he was the owner of one of the largest manufacturers of office accessories in the US.

I still talk a lot. I still find perpetual amazement in "doing church." The first time I heard the great Marion Williams singing "It Is Well with My Soul"— courtesy of a live album from her Philadelphia church—I got goose bumps. I feel the same when we sing "Spirit of Life." Intellectual detachment is whisked away, and never regretted. How much more we all need becomes obvious— and how much more is available.

Of course, we have to be at least willing to let it happen. At best, we need to be willing to hunt for it—to take stock, to take note, to take risks, to "read the signs of the times." We have to be willing to enter into community and reach within ourselves in a spirit of discovery. We have to crack the hard shell of disillusionment and disbelief.

Unitarian Universalists are too often encouraged to treat disillusion and disbelief as precious possessions. We confuse them with conscience. We misidentify them as the search for truth and meaning. We mutter darkly about religion in the nugatory—all too emphatic on what we don't believe and dismissive about what we have escaped, thank God. Well—maybe not quite that way, but you probably recognize the sentiment.

Some 80 years ago the American Unitarian Association's Commission on Appraisal evaluated worship in our liberal churches. They found "monotony and vacuity"—which they attributed to pleasing critics, at the cost of authentic worship. They listed "things rejected"—historic language, prayer, ritual, the Bible—but not replaced. That failure to replace, they said, had swallowed the movement of the Spirit.

It was this same Commission that in 1936 worked out the road map by which our denomination survived the heavy church losses of the Great

Depression. The Great War—we call it World War I—killed the ideal of inevitable human progress. The Commission revived what could be saved into the liberal internationalism of the 1940s and 1950s. They showed the way for Unitarians and Universalists to finally join in 1961. That date marked the middle of the only two decades of sustained growth in our denominations since 1845.

Today, after years of the feeblest gain, the annual increase of adult Unitarian Universalists hovers around zero. It might be good to consider some received wisdom.

The Commissioners were certainly not interested in restoring Christianity to a central position—many were passionate Humanists. They were rather pointing to the cost of hollowing out spiritual life and community experience, instead of enriching it with deeper and more diverse faith and practice. They saw our churches becoming places where belief no longer deserved a place in the pew.

They were concerned especially about the fatal instability of this "worship lite"—the utter reliance on the sermon to carry all the weight of meaning. It was—and is—an impossible task. The sermon wobbles into—these are their words—"useful discussion, a forum, a social experiment, an aesthetic experience." All these are good and proper things they concluded—but none are the unique task of the church. None will long nourish the life of a people gathered in religious community.

Some years ago, I was one of the local clergy appearing at the Interfaith Fair on the University of New England campus in Biddeford, ME. One student told me how she had studied religions of all kinds. She knew her stuff. I asked if she was a religion major. No, I'm only a sophomore, she said, but I've been reading about it since middle school.

It was an eerie conversation—so much learning, so little of what Powell Davies might have pointed to as "lived experience." What little religion she actually remembered was Pentecostal, when she was only seven. UUs should have more churches down South, she said. I agreed. We also agreed the world can be very puzzling and human experience very unsettling. It is absolutely best to keep an open mind.

Another young woman rushed across the room to my table. "Are you the local Unitarian Universalist church?" "Yes, we are." "Do you have Sunday services? Can I come?" "Yes, we do—and we'd be glad to see you." "Wow, that's great. I always wanted to go to a UU church."

I drove home thinking who am I to argue with the enthusiasm of youth? Whether guarded or exuberant, calibrated or explosive, it is one of the natural wonders of creation. I was reminded, and I take this moment to remind you, it very much matters that First Parish is here. It matters who we declare ourselves to be. It matters how we carry out that promise. There are people all around looking for this church.

"As for me, I know nothing but miracles," said Walt Whitman. What will we offer if not the miracles to which we are witnesses? What have we to give except the miracles we are part of creating? What kind of miracles might those be?

As we enter into autumn, what kind of miracles are you prepared to find? This is a time of gathering in the bounty of the summer, but also of putting up and laying by what will carry us through the winter to come. As we renew our community in this season, what kind of miracles are you prepared to make together?

The great Process theologian Henry Nelson Wieman put it bluntly in a 1979 pamphlet he wrote for the UUA: The question is, in what way will you be different, not how other people will change. This is the central question of all varieties of religious life, answerable only by the belief we can be different and it matters that we make the effort.

Yom Kippur ended at sunset yesterday. It is usually translated as the "Day of Atonement." The popular gloss is that Jews are sorry for the wrong things they have said and done the previous year, and start the new one fresh by saying this. But the true acknowledgement of our wrongdoing is much more profound. Wrongdoing must be properly understood as inextricable in human life, entangled in every moment from first to last. It is universal, but also and always something we can affect by our own action.

Ashura also concluded yesterday at sunset. Sunni Muslims celebrate just these understandings, of humility and culpability, but also of the human power to act rightly and to repair. Mohammed drew on Jewish tradition. This atonement is available to us as well. It is not one of regret or apology or even forgiveness. It is one of faithful belief our relationships can be put right. Our relationship with the divine can be put right, and with the Creation, and with each other. "Putting right" is not perfection, not the erasure of what is past. It is not forgetting, but agreeing and acting to remember in a new way.

May you and I go forth then, in faithful belief we can put right the promise of the future. We are called together to do just this. No other thing is truly necessary.

Amen. Blessed Be. Shalom. Salaam.

A Flexible Certainty

25 Feb 2018

I was updating my overnight call log when the message came in just before 11 PM. A patient on the 8th floor of the Silverstein wing has just been admitted and wants to see a priest. It is a predictable request in a large hospital.

Except there is no priest—there is only me. I am Unitarian Universalist. I have not yet completed seminary. Chaplain—Chaplain Intern, to be exact—is only my summer job. But from 6 PM this evening until 8 AM tomorrow morning, I am the only chaplain in this 850-bed hospital.

"Probably not dying," I think on the way up. But at the door—why do they want a priest when there is one sitting right there? Well, the man who lay quietly in the bed wasn't an ordinary patient who's Catholic. He too was a priest—but not a regular one.

What matters about this encounter is its conclusion—the Monsignor asked me to pray for him. I did and he thanked me. Two days later I stopped by and he asked me to pray for him again. I did and he thanked me. My efforts were modest but sincere, and I didn't doubt the gratitude of this princeling of the church was just the same.

Pope Francis notwithstanding, the Catholic Church is not very flexible on core faith and doctrine. The close of Vatican II was followed by a half century of just the opposite—a concerted and sustained effort to narrow the boundaries of orthodoxy.

But no theology was being debated in that hospital room. Something more important needed to happen and it did, for the man in my spiritual care and for me. We were both flexible about what we believed, about how we practiced our beliefs, about who we were and who we were with. The catchphrase is this: "Good enough for God"—and in that moment we were. We got there by first being good enough for each other.

It is a truism to note how many of us spent at least part of the end-of-the-year holidays with at least some people we do not like very much. We do pretend of course, unless we don't—sometimes because the person we don't like very much is the one we are. Hopefully, between now and spring, all will be forgiven—or at least accepted.

Tolstoy's aphorism about every unhappy family being unhappy in its own way sometimes seems famous precisely because it is not how we experience things. We bump and scrape against our families in precisely the same ways. "Mom always loved you best," as the Smothers Brothers put it. Or, as I once read in Dear Abby, "What do I do about my husband bursting out of his office and yelling at the TV when I am watching the news?" Good luck with that. Good luck as well to the family who were, according to another letter, fighting over whether the vegan teenager had the right to demand only vegan dishes be on the Thanksgiving table of her beleaguered aunt—who didn't care to serve tofu turkey like last year. You couldn't make this stuff-ing up.

How flexible are we about our certainties? How much do we think we know for sure? What happens to our firm beliefs when things are not working out that way?

Some years ago I got a phone call from a woman who told me she had been for some time intending to come to the church. Her story was a narrative of stark tragedy—accident, chronic illness and death. "Who," she asked, "would put this on a family?"

It is a striking memory—one many ministers share. She and I talked for a while. Her pain ebbed and flowed. "I wish I could believe in something," she said again and again. It was clear the "something" desired was some settled and certain answer to her question: Who, indeed, would put this on a family? It is a request perhaps predictable for anyone limping on a difficult path. How do Unitarian Universalists answer that question? How does our church answer that question? How do I answer that question?

There was no priest. There was only me, and I had no answer—and never will. But I believe your congregation does have the answer—except it is not an answer but an action—a response. We hold hands during the scary parts. I don't consider that a simplistic way of putting it. I deeply believe in it as a profound truth. It is a certainty, but of essentially flexible character. I believe this is not at all an inadequate gift, but one of surpassing importance, one well worth seeking and sustaining. The quality of mercy not being strained is a human truth in every age and epoch, everywhere in the world.

This was the operative assumption about the universe and our place in it—about the human family and our place in it—on which the Monsignor and I were in full accord. Our differences of earthly position or eternal destination did not matter.

I tried to explain to the woman steeped in the tragedies of life, as I have tried to explain to others—caught in tragedy or not—that Unitarian Universalists not only don't believe in "something," we can't believe in "something." Our certainty is to have no certainty. What we believe, we choose to believe by our own lights, and no other. Our experience, our conscience, our community—this is what we believe. Whether we make a deliberate choice or not, whether we are aware of the inherent paradox or not, we are willing to embrace ambiguity, uncertainty and even inadequacy—and call it our own.

I met another man in the Trauma Bay during my chaplaincy. He looked like he had gone over Niagara Falls without the barrel. What relief was it for me to tell his family he was alive, to guide his Deacon through the ER so she could pray at his side in the hard, emphatic cadences of their African American

Pentecostal faith? The church had, you see, literally fallen in on him while he and a friend were attempting its repair.

What relief was it for me to lay my hand on his head and pray in that same way more than once in the next few days? We were as flexible as needed to get the job done. He went home in a wheelchair, but he was smiling and I never gave a second thought to how I prayed. That he had a personal savior and I did not—or at least was not willing to accept one—was of no practical consequence whatsoever. We still healed together.

The richness of these encounters did not spring from my virtue. They were rooted in our faith, in a way of believing you and I share, in the enigma of circumstance. A Unitarian Universalist church raised them up as values, as this church does also.

Early Unitarians said this, you know—revelation is not sealed. They did not proclaim revelation impossible. They did not argue it was of marginal importance. They declared it continuous, unfolding always and forever. They believed it to be accessible and amply demonstrated inwardly and all around us. This conviction infuriated orthodox Calvinists. They ejected our forebears from the established church.

We may today believe revelation comes solely by human reason. I only disagree with the "solely" part. I suggest human observation is more than adequate to catalog many things we do not reasonably understand and never will. You make your own call.

"I wish I could believe in something"—I don't think we can do that, or should. We do not know any answers. Whether we set our own boundaries by science or intuition, by nature or creation, by epiphany or mystery—we do not know any answers.

But on this we surely all agree: Truth was and is available to us—to mortal creatures living ordinary lives. The warmth of human relationship is available to us, if we will have it. The beauty of nature and transformative connection to the Divine is available to us, if we will have it. All power of creation is in our hands, if we believe that.

May your late winter days and nights—and all the year—be filled with flexibility.

Amen. Blessed Be. Shalom. Salaam.

My Uncle, Leonardo

03 Jun 2018

This is the black & white original of "The Mummy," starring Boris Karloff. The tomb is dark and dusty. The mummy stands in a sarcophagus propped upright against the wall. His back turned; an archeologist writes by a flickering lamp. The camera cuts to the next room, where the other scientists hear a blood-curdling scream. They rush in just as the last few inches of tape trail out the far doorway. "What happened?" they cry. "He…he went for a little walk," says their colleague, dissolving in maniacal laughter.

Hold those two thoughts—the mummy and the little walk—while our scientists jump-cut to 1999. A Yale statistician demonstrates a mathematical relationship between the size of a population and the number of generations back to a common ancestor. An expert in the 100,000-year history of Homo sapiens eventually hears about the model. They contact an MIT neuroscientist and computer expert, and the three devise a massive computer simulation to re-enact human history. Call it, "Out of Africa."

Input population size, distribution, birth and death rates and patterns of migration. The computer may have hummed, clattered or smoked, but here is what it eventually spit out: Every human being alive today—all 7-and-a-half billion of us—shares a common ancestor. Not very long ago at all—somewhere between 2000 and 5000 years back—there lived a person who can count each one of us as a descendent.

Perhaps equally startling, a little farther back—5000 to 7000 years ago, according to the scientists—the family tree of every one on earth traces back to exactly the same set of ancestors. Looked at from the other end of the telescope, every person alive during that small window of prehistoric time has all the people of today's world as descendants, or has no living descendants at all. "Had you entered any village on earth in around 3000 B.C.," said an Oxford University statistician who commented on the research, "the first person you would have met would probably be your ancestor."

I've mentioned the affiliations of these good folks—Yale, MIT, and Oxford. They presumably did not get their diplomas by mail and they are not affiliated with an online university. But remember what I said about the mummy and the little trip? Well, the mummy gives us a real time frame, although the most likely location of the common ancestor is actually East Asia—somewhere in Taiwan, Malaysia or Siberia according to the article published in Nature. The most obvious part of the mechanism is that some family lines die out—any acquaintance with history demonstrates that. Neither George Washington nor George Armstrong Custer has any direct descendants.

Yet the most important part of the mechanism of mutuality is migration, as suggested by the little walk. The computer model allowed fairly low levels of migration—which produced the date of 5000 B.C.E. for our most recent common ancestor. With higher but still moderate levels of migration, the date came much closer—if we can think of the year 1 as being "close." Recent historians, archeologists and anthropologists dramatically revised estimates upward of how many of our ancestors moved around, how far and how fast. Also revised upward, and increasingly provable by genetic testing, is how willingly and widely our ancestors, shall we say, "entertained the stranger."

In our world, faithful Muslims, Jews and Christians all record the special promise God made to a nomadic shepherd named Abraham—that he would be the father of a great nation. Some claim to be devoted to their patriarch but slaughter others almost anywhere the three religions live side by side. This is both history and current affairs.

Now is a good time for Unitarian Universalists to expect better from human beings. Believing in human beings is the distinctive thing we do in the world. The sense and judgment, experience and inspiration of all people are necessary to the human task. All of us are the everlasting fiber of the cosmos, but insight and opportunity also fill ordinary life. Sometimes the old phrases are best—revelation is not sealed, salvation is available, eternity is universal. Hard times call for hard-earned wisdom and clarity.

There are differences of meaning and mechanism in these truths, but we proclaim them as engines of cultural vitality and distinctiveness, of pragmatism and inspiration, as progenitors of all the rich variety of human experience. We celebrate the hunger for apprehension of the divine, the transcendent—what is lasting instead of what decays and departs—not as something particular but as a shared heritage. In whatever words or concepts they use, all people seek that which fulfills, not that which disappoints. It is our witness that any religious faith offers fulfillment—as do many other ways of understanding and of being, although not best described as "religious."

We spring from the Age of Enlightenment proclamation of human beings as elevated above hopeless depravity, as capable companions to the divine and as beings of improvable conscience. This was the turning point on the path to the modern mind.

No mind is more modern than that of Leonardo da Vinci. Surpassing curiosity, an experimental bent, a genius for innovation, a restless energy, pragmatism and flexibility—these are hallmarks of one of the great entrepreneurial intellects in human history. I call him "Uncle Leonardo," because my uncles always returned like travelers to make strange places comprehensible. Perhaps your uncles were or are the same way. My Uncle Ed liked to sneak off work to shoot a few holes of golf and came back to reload the trucks for the afternoon deliveries. This made him the Chandler-family black sheep—but he taught me how to cut flagstone. My Uncle Jack was a City of Philadelphia Police detective. This is a very foreign world to me, but when we later worked together, he brought donuts every day—Krispy Kremes. My Uncle Don died when I was nine, but he was a top salesman for IBM in the 1950s. Sally's Uncle Jack—my uncle by marriage—retired as a Lieutenant General of the Air Force, and had autographed pictures of all of the Mercury and Gemini astronauts covering an entire wall in his basement.

While we are all related to Leonardo, he had no direct descendants. Our common uncle did not live in the modern world. Neither do we. The modern mind of Leonardo existed before the modern was born. Our minds exist after the modern has died. We live in a post-modern place of ambiguity and subjectivity, of mystery more than certainty. Even our best understanding of science is as process rather than outcome.

Leonardo reminds us to understand the retreat of the modern does not mean giving up our modern minds. He not only dreamt of flight but planned for it, and we too can navigate by our fundamental tools—reason, experience and conscience. We need not apologize for flexibility and should not grow discouraged because human beings and the world are complex and mysterious and too often seem malevolent. Like Leonardo, we must design what cannot yet be built. We too can measure and calculate what the world must be and become, and record sepia lines and words across the paper.

Like him, we may have to write in mirror-reverse to be prudent against those who would do us harm. Like the poor archeologist we can even become temporarily deranged when the mummy gets up and walks. Yes, it's scary. Yet every day, we can also take heart in the strength of character and optimism in the power of the mind. We can accept there are mysteries—why else would the Mona Lisa be smiling?

We do not need to be ignorant or fearful. After all, we have family all around us.

Amen. Blessed Be. Shalom. Salaam.

Six Smooth Stones

21 Oct 2018

As Unitarian Universalists, it is our special religious privilege to live atop a volcano of central paradox. We are not unique in this regard. The Trinitarian paradox is obvious: Jesus is fully human and fully divine, without diminution of either nature. Buddhists famously dwell in both being and non-being, in fundamental equipoise. The Tao asks us to understand the jug and the space within—as does Sufi teaching in Islam.

It should not be surprising that religion engenders paradox—what is more essential to our experience of human life than paradox? We are good and bad, lucky and not, sick and well, happy and sad, loved and shunned, prosperous and pinched. All these happen in a whirling tangle of days against the eternal paradox of alive-but-aware-we-will-die. It is no wonder we look for some way of ducking life's fateful ricochets.

But UUs are special. We are the ones who believe everything. Check the hymnal at your leisure. I guarantee you will find Leviticus, the Bhagavad-Gita, and Black Elk—all riding on the same bus, at least as we have decided they should. And every minister knows the answer to the question, what do Unitarian Universalists believe? Anything you want of course! Ouch. This is either nonsense or genius—maybe some of both. Thank goodness we have a rule: Nobody is allowed to tell anybody else what to believe. That is the first rule. The second rule is that your congregation will get kicked out of the UUA if it violates the first rule too obviously and egregiously, like being segregated. Yes, there were UU churches that were segregated. There were many more churches that balked at the UUA's plan to eject such churches—on philosophical grounds, they said.

I point out that to believe everything (or anything, as the case may be) means you actually believe nothing—at least nothing that convicts, consoles or converts. Like the fabled Flying Dutchman, you wander the sea forever in "free and responsible" search.

But wait! There in the front of the hymnal—which must mean it is important—is our Statement of Principles and Purposes. We will never be saved—we don't believe in it—but we can be rescued. Of course, it is voluntary. It is also only obligatory on congregations, not individuals, and in fact no congregation is exactly required to agree, except to state you are collectively "in harmony" with the Statement. And you only have to do that once, upon application to join the UUA. Nobody ever asks again.

Seven is the number you probably associate with the Principles and Purposes. The Seven Principles (see page iii) are at the top and we do rather vigorously promote them—vigorously for us, anyway. We remain famously diffident in our rooted New England way about intruding on other people's space, but at least this is a huge and notable improvement. Only a few decades ago, scarcely a word was spoken about believing anything—except that there must obviously be an encrustation of atavistic superstition on almost any religious doctrine, language or practice. This often included our own.

Follow me here: James Luther Adams, after witnessing—among other eye-opening events of the 20th century—the callow and quisling response of the Lutheran church in Germany to the rise of the Nazis, formulated what he called "The Five Smooth Stones" of a liberal religion he proposed to be free from coercion but vigorous enough to anchor our lives and our world against such atrocity. The image is from the Biblical account of David picking up the stones to put in his sling and fell the ferocious Goliath.

If you look below the Principles, you will find what is identified as the sources of our "Living Tradition." (see page iii). There are five. Although they did not come directly from Adams, the number is not a coincidence. They are formulating the same ideas. More important, they have the same essential purpose. They are meant to anchor our ethics—our shared understanding of rightness—in qualities across the ages of humanity that still live in the present. These qualities are anchors for authentic belief. They are deeper than the ideals of the Seven Principles. They are not more important, but they do offer robust conviction, consolation and powerful conversion across diverse human cultures.

Who can deny the power of mystery and wonder, or the challenge of prophets, or the wisdom surely accrued in all our varied religious thought? Who would not accept that we are rooted in Jewish and Christian traditions, however far we may journey now from the Hebrew prophets and the parables of Jesus? Who would reject reason and science—most especially when they hang a red warning flare on the idolatries that plague us in every age, that ignorant certainty so corrosive of human well-being?

Well, perhaps you dissent on any of these, or even all of them. Such is your right, and I'm always glad to hear your ideas—but do mind the Void. Words alone don't suit.

I will note that the Statement of Principles and Purposes was passed unanimously by the General Assembly to become a Bylaw in 1985, the second of two years it was approved as is required. Some accounts say there was a single shouted "no" from the back, but do imagine for a magic moment the idea of several thousand UUs agreeing unanimously on anything—absolutely anything—and appreciate what an accomplishment this is for our people and our polity. We do sometimes get big, important, worthwhile things done.

Several years ago, some churches hatched the idea the Principles and Purposes should be overhauled. They were 25 years in place and seemed "too individualistic." The working draft of suggested replacements clunked like an old Dodge, and the idea was shelved for the moment. It will surely be back. If you are interested, you can look up The Eighth Principle Project on the UUA website. It proposes draft language to add "dismantling racism" to the list. Some congregations already use "Eight Principles," although without General Assembly approval this cannot be official. There is also an ongoing debate about whether "inherent worth and dignity" should apply to "all creatures," not just human beings. This year GA did change "prophetic men and women" into "prophetic people." They might better have settled on the core identity of "prophet" and left the gender marker entirely silent as being unnecessary.

It is absolutely true the Principles and Purposes could possibly be improved. The best evidence is, they already were. The Sixth Source is not in your hymnal, because these books were published in 1993. In 1995, by acclamation, this language was added: "Spiritual teachings of Earth-centered traditions which celebrate the sacred circle of life and instruct us to live in harmony with the rhythms of nature."

What words to describe our beliefs has always been fraught. William Ellery Channing held out for "True Christianity," until he didn't. "Unitarian Christianity" then became one of his most famous sermons. "Things commonly believed among us" was a formulation by William Channing Gannett that healed the split between the Eastern churches (read, "Massachusetts") and the Western churches (read, "Ohio Valley") in the late 1800s. The secular humanists and the theistic humanists battled it out in the 1920s and the struggling Statement of Belief came within an eyelash of scuttling the 1961 consolidation of the Unitarian and Universalist denominations. It is a remarkable tribute to the energy and persistence of UU women that the current Principles and Purposes came about through a deliberate and successful process of consensus building.

So, we can tell people what "we" believe, with appropriate qualifications always. We do, after all, still live on top of that volcano. Everything is subject to adjustment.

Amen. Blessed Be. Shalom. Salaam.

Outside Epiphany

03 Feb 2019

My good idea for 2019 so far is to print short passages in the Order of Service to help guide you in the "sermon space." The minister's good ideas must always be handled with caution, but today that passage is the first of our Six Sources (see page iv). These are identified in our gray hymnal as among the "many" that underpin what is declared to be our Living Tradition. You remember there are only five shown in the hymnal; the sixth was approved after the book was printed. "The Six Smooth Stones" is what I called them in an October sermon. Their official role is to complement the Seven Principles enumerated above them (see page iii). They are meant to bolster the strong ethical progression of the Principles with actual roots in the broad history of human moral and religious thinking. They are wide and deep, as inclusive and profound as we would like to be. As a practical matter, they answer an obvious question: "Where did we get this stuff?"

The exact theological term for the faith and practice of Unitarian Universalism is "syncretism," but what it means is simple. We have a lot of stuff in the house of UUs.

We have, as we should, stuff from words and deeds of prophets—many of them. We have stuff from the world's religions, as we are supposed to. We have stuff from Humanism, as befits a very educated polity. We came to acknowledge, rightfully, that earth-based traditions now guide and inspire our spirits and rituals. I asked after that sermon which of the Sources inspires you most, and which might be the most important for our collective belief. All of these got votes.

Jewish and Christian teachings did not, which is no surprise. Most of us hear "church" there—probably all the things we did not or do not like about church in our world. It's okay, because we do at least occasionally revisit and discern the words actually written there, which name an ageless call to justice and mercy. It is that love that underlies our edifice, not details of mechanical procedures. God is at your option.

Speaking of those traditions, you know we have just passed Epiphany, a major observance of both western and eastern Christian churches. Remarkably, they mostly agree on the date—famously not the case with Easter. Epiphany is the Feast of the Three Kings, the commemoration of the revelation of Jesus as the Christ to the Three Magi, who rode their camels to his birthplace and brought gifts one would give a king.

January holds the observance of another famous epiphany, the episode "on the road to Damascus" in which the Pharisee Saul of Tarsus was struck down by a vision of the Christ and a huge voice demanding, "Why do you persecute me?" After three days struck blind, the man history knows as Paul the Apostle saw a new purpose to his life. He would claim status as a Disciple, although, as he later wrote, "one last of all, as one untimely born." Over three decades in the middle of the first century, he would travel and write widely in the Roman world and essentially codify and construct Christianity.

Our lives and perils are thankfully more modest. We are not likely to be shipwrecked and none of us has to face the end of our lives coming at the hands of a Roman executioner, as Paul most likely did. Our responsibilities are smaller as well, but we too have our "epiphany clause." We too have a source of understanding that is larger than us, at least us in our normal compass. We too have a beyond that is at some times, in some places and by some methods not beyond us at all, but present in full. It is not a matter of examples or teachings or traditions of any kind. It is not, in other words, something that can be imitated or learned. This is crucial.

We name it "direct experience." It is the first Source. As is usually the case, "first" means most important, that there is no place further to go without this one being clear and committed in our hearts and minds. See above for the First Principle, the "inherent worth and dignity" principle. Because they are a process, the Seven Principles are best understood as circular, as leading back from the end of the list to the beginning of the list. The Sources are not this way. You can choose one as primary. I would argue however that all of them are necessary. They are a package.

Our small group discussion concluded the first one is what makes all the others possible. It is the engagement. The others use these words: a "challenge," an "inspiration," a "call," a "counsel," an "instruction." They invite us in various ways to various paths, to ways we should know and ways we should live. "Direct experience" is a horse of a different color entirely. It puts us there. It doesn't consider; it does. It is not a possibility; it is. Every one of us has it as inevitably as breathing. It does not admit of maybe or of when I get around to it. It is the stuff and the way the stuff comes to us.

What is the priority stuff yielded by direct experience? This matters. It is "transcending mystery and wonder." What a remarkable claim this is! Let me count at least some of the ways it is so—call it, if you will, do-it-yourself revelation.

What else could it be called when "transcending mystery and wonder" is suddenly apparent to ordinary human beings—when the otherwise hidden springs of the cosmos are revealed to us? It must be our everyday existence that is transcended. The words "mystery" and "wonder" are meant to range outside the mortal limits encompassed by the scientific method. Of course, there are "mysteries of science," but they are by design problems we solve or at least believe we can and will solve by rational experiment. "Experience" is not experiment—it is inherently emotional and intuitive, albeit the results over a lifetime do somewhat have the effects of an experiment. Thus we say, been there, done that—not going to do it again, thank you. We all learn this hard way.

If you think it still might be a science project, that's okay with me, but please note the further fruits of this direct experience. "Renewal of the spirit" and "forces that create and uphold life" may be glimpsed at your local Shaw's, but you can't buy them. They are tangible but they cannot be quantified—3 for a dollar, 99 cents for a pound, buy one/get one free. The spirit and life itself are both infinitely large and infinitely small, and everywhere in between. They encompass us even as we encompass them in our embodiment as mortal creatures. At your option again, they may also be eternal in us.

Compare and contrast to other religions: Unitarian Universalism has offered much prophetic witness and in its time a few people with major beards, but no prophet of the Biblical magnitude. Likewise, we have no savior. Our salvation must be entirely by human effort. Our consolation must come by our companions in community.

Notice also, we have no sacrament—coffee does not count. Nothing in our practice constitutes the body and blood of the divine, either literally or by metaphor. Nowhere in the armada of words we are fond of is there much that qualifies as scripture—again, Mary Oliver notwithstanding. There are good words, but hardly sacred ones.

We are without these ordinary signposts of human culture. We could be lost in the desert or drifting on the ocean or alone in the dark. We could be doomed to a never- ending search for truth and meaning—qualities never to rest entirely in our grasp.

Yet we are not any of these things. We are anchored and we are astonished by the everyday miracle of direct experience. No one goes without. No mediation is necessary. Experience will be more pleasant or not, but it cannot ever be superior or inferior to another's. Each and every one of us lives each day well inside our very own epiphany.

Amen. Blessed Be. Shalom. Salaam.

Wanting What Is Right

The Fire Next Time

06 Nov 2016

In the Spring of 1970, I lived in a 3rd floor studio apartment above a florist and a funeral home. It had a metal balcony smaller than a desktop that hung over the narrow alley. Madison—the home of the University of Wisconsin—was in chaos already, but the strange noise one night was different. I stepped out and peered down, very quietly.

In the darkness below, a phalanx of City police officers trotted past, from the back parking lot toward the avenue, taking the shortcut I used every day to get to class. They were shoulder-to-shoulder, 15 or 20 of them. The distant streetlight glittered off their helmets and face shields. Their nightsticks were at the ready. They were all dressed in black jackets, gray trousers and black leather boots that clattered on the asphalt.

It looked like the end of the world.

"The Fire Next Time" I have borrowed from James Baldwin, who in turn borrowed it from a gospel lyric: "God gave Noah the rainbow sign/No more water, the fire next time." Thanks to seminary, I can tell you the original story comes from the Biblical book of Genesis, after Adam and Eve and the Tower of Babel and before the curse of Ham, youngest son of Noah. Why is Ham cursed? He looks upon the nakedness of his drunken father. In retribution, Ham and all his descendants are to be slaves of his brothers and all their descendants, for all human time. It is God's will.

My story and the Bible story come from my sermon delivered eight years ago, just before Barack Obama, a man of mixed race—commonly referred to as "black"—was elected President of the United States.

I was working my way through a then-new book called *Nixonland*. The author, a historian named Rick Perlstein, chronicled the years 1964 to 1972. He framed them by their presidential elections. In 1964, Lyndon Johnson received just more than 61% of the popular vote. In 1972, Richard Nixon received just less than 61% of the popular vote. Just how we staggered from one extreme landslide to the other was the epic of a rising tide of bitterness, anger and fear. Nixon was wily and driven, but it was the American people who gave in to our darkest selves. We became our own worst enemies.

This must not prevail again. That has become your obligation—and mine.

The call of history is often to difficult times. Our proudest moments as Americans are those times when that call was answered well. Our claim to a compelling vision for the world rests on them. Our shame and our sorrow, at home and abroad, are those times we failed this crucial test.

Ignorant, accusatory and demeaning rhetoric—often driven by electoral hyperventilation—is not now and was not then the primary culprit. The villain, as Perlstein spent almost 800 pages documenting in stomach-knotting detail, was the willingness of more and more Americans to believe the angry words. The center—not just of American politics but of American life—withered into an ineffectual shadow of the immense power it displayed to win World War II, contain Soviet expansion and fuel the greatest burst of prosperity in human history.

Baldwin's book summoned apocalyptic overtones in his indictment of slavery as the American Original Sin, of the blinkered unwillingness of white people to admit pervasive oppression, of complacent middlebrow Christianity and the compliant accommodation of the black church in which he was raised. Yet it was in the end a heartfelt plea for the necessity of changing these narratives. Baldwin praised the breadbasket accomplishments of Elijah Muhammad, but rejected the separatism of Malcolm X, at that time—1962— still a prophet of the Nation of Islam. He wanted us to avoid the fire, for whites and blacks to talk to each other and construct common good.

So, no—what we are living with is not new. In 1970, burning cities and assassinations were not new. There was fresh blood at Kent State and Jackson State, but now, after a lifetime, it is a little puzzling how innocent we still were. Watergate, of course, was still to come and I suspect that is the explanation. What we have today is not an electorate that sloshes back and forth, disconcerting as that was, but an electorate bunkered in and almost entirely unmovable. How richly ironic we Baby Boomers get to have our adult lives bookended by pervasive outbreaks of boiling chaos. We will head out as we came in, aiding and abetting the painful birthing of some kind of new world.

We must remember our faith and affirm our religious identity to hold fast. Every one of our Seven Principles reminds us not to plunge into fear (see page iii). It is not our best selves. It is not even our passable selves, filled with human flaws. We cannot expect to lead people if we forget our human connection, what we envision as the purpose of human community and the means society should use to accomplish its goals. We must live, in short, as people whose vision of a better world springs from our faith, not our platform.

What are we now prepared to believe about each other? Do we subscribe to the best or fear the worst? Here's a quick point of reference: Which of these is your worst nightmare? You find on Nov. 9 that 40% of voters have chosen Trump and Pence. This proves a lot of Americans are misguided idiots. Or is it this—you find on Nov. 9 Trump and Pence have been elected? This proves beyond a shadow of a doubt a truly horrifying number of Americans are malicious idiots. Apocalypse to follow.

In the political game, this technique is known as "push polling"—the question directs the answer. My best guess is the former outcome is most likely, but the latter outcome terrifies us. I was on retreat this week with colleagues from all over New England. Even those of us with little hair left are tearing it out—quietly or not—searching for some way to hold all of you this Sunday and next. We held hands a lot, so we could manage our own anxiety. But our focus on you meant a clear priority was set.

The day after is when the hard work begins, whether it starts with a good cry or a sigh of relief. The fuse half a century ago was lit by a fraudulent consensus. We said we were at peace when we were not, that we were content with our lives when many were forced into the shadows, that economic opportunity was fairly available to all when it certainly was not. Today we harbor no such illusions. We know we are entangled in a debilitating war. We know we are engaged in a long struggle to secure the equal rights of all. We know we are dragged into the whirlpool after historic financial calamity.

We should know that none of these challenges will—or even can—be solved on the 8th of November—or next January. We know more than ever how all of them come with rich and beguiling opportunities for fear—for fear of the future, for fear about our lives and our loved ones, for fear of losing what we have and never getting what we need.

The greatest temptation is still giving in to the fear of others. Other Americans must be idiots—misguided or malicious or worse. Immigrants must be subverting our culture. Foreigners must be implacably hostile and dangerous. What are we prepared to believe about each other—now and in the days to come? Do we subscribe to the best or fear the worst—and can we avoid being either heedless or paralyzed?

The curse of Ham was not the stain of slavery, loathsome though it is. It was the stigma of evasion, of blaming God for something people did—and could undo. Let us stoke a fire of heat and light and not be consumed by flames. This is in our hands.

Amen. Blessed Be. Shalom. Salaam.

Grievous Angels

15 Jan 2017

"I read the news today, oh boy—about a lucky man who made the grade." In Rockville, MD, a Jewish couple gets a Star of David note that says, "Enjoy the mayhem." In Cincinnati, Hebrew Union College gets a swastika on its sign. In Lawrence, KS, Centennial Park's Polaris missile gets a swastika. In Inkster, MI, a Muslim man's car gets swastikas, and the tires slashed. In Zion, IL, the owner of a Dairy Queen uses racial slurs to a customer and admits it to police. In Zion—Dr. King would catch the irony.

"He blew his mind out in a car—he didn't notice that the lights had changed/A crowd of people stood and stared—they'd seen his face before."

The words are John Lennon's, from "A Day in the Life." The stories come from "The Week in Hate," a new feature of the New York Times. The paper-of-a-sad-record.

It was Abraham Lincoln who famously evoked "the better angels of our nature," and he promised they would and must prevail. No 20th century American staked more on Lincoln's beliefs and his promise than Dr. Martin Luther King, Jr. In the movie "Selma," there is a grim scene in which Coretta Scott King mourns the "black cloud of violence" haunting every minute of her life, and his. We may remember it was a stalker who murdered Dr. King. We may forget the earlier attack in which a knife pierced his chest right to the heart. We may not count the number of times his home was bombed, or how many times he was beaten or threatened with beating—in jail and on the street.

Hatred and violence, anger and ignorance, selfishness and despair—these are the grievous angels. They are the dark side of our human nature and they loom over us in these days. It may help to recall they loomed as well over the days of Lincoln—650,000 dead in the Civil War, Americans killing Americans. They loomed over the days of Dr. King. Many of us were there. Americans are "making the grade" handily now. Neither the spirit of our times nor the angels of our nature appear to be on the "better" setting.

Yet, like Lincoln, Dr. King believed in the marrow of his bones there are not good people and bad people. The world, he stated repeatedly, is filled with good people who do bad things, because they are ignorant or confused or frightened or feeling unloved. We do bad things—sometimes appallingly bad things—because we are human beings, because we have free will and to be free in truth must be free in reality to do wrong. As did Lincoln, Dr. King lived with a routine of the terrifying. To preserve the union, to end slavery, to achieve the full promise of human dignity—they were willing to die, and did.

Against "appallingly bad things," Dr. King gave us not despair but the gift of prophetic voice and the sacrifice of prophetic example. Prophecy does not speak with most resonance when times are getting better, but when they are bad and seem to be getting only worse—times like this. Prophets remind us, when in the darkest doubt, there are larger and more lasting promises that bind us to the future and to each other.

Dr. King was not a prophet just for Christians, or religious people, or black people, or poor people—or even "good" people. His vision, abiding faith and compelling community are for all people—all races, all classes, all conditions, all degrees of moral compromise and nobility. He spoke for all Americans, and ultimately the entire world.

The prophets Dr. King called upon himself lived more than 2000 years ago in a small and turbulent land. Amos was the first. He came from nowhere—that is, no power or learning or recognition. He was said to be a shepherd who left his flocks and journeyed to the part of ancient Israel where a new trading economy had made a few very rich and left the rest very poor. He denounced them for their self-serving desertion of the bonds and obligations of the common good—and went back to obscurity.

Jeremiah likewise denounced the rich, but also the priests and the rulers and the self-satisfaction of the people themselves. They had all abandoned the long traditions that routinely provided for the poor and unfortunate not as irresponsible or even victims, but as members still of the community—as people who mattered and still had rights. They were entitled to glean the fields after harvest and to a Jubilee Year—the regular forgiveness of all debts, such that none should fall into perpetual poverty.

"Isaiah" is actually more than one prophet who may or may not have had the same name. One Isaiah called the people to return before it was too late to the humility and responsibility of what we now call "right relationship." This was not primarily for their reward, but because they dared to claim God's preference among all the peoples. God, Isaiah said, was growing angry about their failure to live up to that obligation.

We will read from another Isaiah at the end of this service. His time was the Babylonian Captivity, when the elites of Israelite society were prisoners in a foreign land, forbidden to practice their religion. They were not slaves as in Egypt in the time of Moses long before, but they were not free either. Everything they had built and believed in had been utterly destroyed. The God who spoke reminded them why it happened and how they could repair the trauma. It is this Isaiah who Christians believe foreshadows Jesus. The message is of repentance, sacrifice and hope. The hope of Isaiah rested above all in a new kind of God—not violent and vindictive but a deity of enduring love for a troubled humanity. Paul preached that God across the turbulent Roman world.

Does any of this sound relevant in our world of recent months? I suggest it does—and that should give us heart. First, Unitarians and Universalists all the way back to our roots were equally passionate about these same ancient prophets, and for much the same reason as Dr. King. Second, the call is made to all the people to the hard work of a social compact that includes all the people. Progress will always be hard and painful. No bogeyman is to blame for who we have become. We are the responsible parties.

Dr. King stood on the ground of abiding Christian faith in a living God. As UUs, we stand on faith as well. We trust human beings to make the world better. We hold stubbornly to a belief that human beings will, somehow, someway, prove equal to this responsibility. As is often the case in human history, the evidence seems currently to be running strongly against Lincoln and Dr. King. What about Theodore Parker's famous "arc of the Universe"? Of course, it "bends toward justice"—if you push the endpoint out far enough it could bend anywhere. "Justice" may indeed be getting no closer.

If the current runs against us, what then do we truly believe? None can be blind to the reality of evil, in the world and in us. None can fail to feel the pain and the peril, but we must have the courage not just to avoid giving up, but also to keep working to build the good. Dr. King spoke always about the deep urge to do right, to live with dignity and grant it to others, to be part of a society that plays fair. Time and again he drew the critical distinction between evil action and evil nature—denouncing the former and denying the latter, except as persistent human weakness. He called out the corrosive power of fear and the designs of all those who would fan it and feed it.

Prophecy is not for the faint of heart. Now maybe more than in years, we must hold close the promise to "carve out of a mountain of despair, the stone of hope." In these troubled times, in this difficult year, you and I are being put to the test.

Where will we shed the despair and loneliness of human life? The same place as Dr. King—in community and hope. Right here is our deep well of love and courage.

Amen. Blessed Be. Shalom. Salaam.

Rockets' Red Glare

12 Nov 2017

Every Sunday morning, I drove through the western mountains of Maine, on the way from my home in Saco to my church in central New Hampshire. A Confederate flag always flew from the signpost of the Ossipee Mountain Tattoo Company in Waterboro. I more or less ignored it for a year, but a few weeks after a white supremacist shot nine people to death during a prayer meeting in a black church in Charleston, South Carolina, I wondered if the tattoo parlor had not yet gotten the memo. I thought about stopping in to… Well, I'm not exactly sure what I thought—very briefly—about stopping in to actually do. Complain about the flag? See the owner in the decorated flesh? Get a tattoo as a trade for taking it down? Discuss the relative merits of heritage and symbolism in contemporary culture and politics? Ask for the nearest klavern?

"None of the above" seemed the most sensible answer, so I drove on by. It was a rather faded flag, maybe there for years, and a little forlorn really. It was the Confederate battle flag, the "Southern Cross." On long-ago battlefields clouded with black powder smoke the actual flag of the Confederacy, the "Stars and Bars," looked too much like the Stars and Stripes, thus the purpose-driven redesign for special use.

In my childhood that flag was an ensign of Jim Crow intransigence, in my youth it was put to jingoistic waving from pickup trucks everywhere, and in my adult life it was cash-register-qualified by country music and NASCAR. After Charlottesville, we see what purpose-driven special use it now serves, one that is both ugly and dangerous.

Flags have practical purposes, of course, but they are far more useful as symbols. Flags since ancient times have been very powerful symbols—powerful because of the meaning we attach to them, because of the values and heritage they seem to represent. They declare history not as facts, but as myth. Myths are motivating and threatening alike, triggers of compelling loyalty—which means we will fight to define what the proper myth is. Who gets control of the narrative? Whose myth are we enlisting in?

Undoubtedly the most famous American flag is the one that inspired our national anthem. Allow me to point out that Francis Scott Key did not see the Star-Spangled Banner waving over Fort McHenry during the battle, by the "rockets' red glare," or any other way. He was downriver, it was raining hard and the famous flag wasn't flying during the actual bombardment. "At the dawn's early light," when told the British were withdrawing, the fort commander lowered the smaller "storm ensign" and triumphantly hoisted the garrison flag. It was huge—30 feet tall and 42 feet broad, quite visible to Key eight miles away. He did write the first lyrics on the back of an envelope.

Here are two little "heritage" points about that flag, which you can view today at the Smithsonian Institution. It had 15 stripes, one for each state. Only in 1818 did Congress decree 13 stripes for all time. It has a star cut out, and eight feet off the end. The commander's family had for some years clipped away pieces for souvenirs and gifts.

Surprised? So was I. I knew the flag was tattered—with battle damage, I assumed. What were they thinking? The Smithsonian is rather kind; pointing out this activity was widespread, egalitarian and meant to honor the givers and the recipients. The world of 200 years ago is, mysteriously enough, not our world. Many of the actual fragments—but not the star—are on display, alongside the flag although not part of it.

We could also ask how they came to own a public icon—the receipt still exists—but that too would only point out the gulf. It reminds me of the farmer using Monticello as a hay barn. What was he thinking? Probably he just wanted to keep his forage dry.

No individual conscience interfered, which is my point. Nobody's moral compass began spinning. No ethical warning light started flashing. Social sentiment snipped away pieces of the most important flag in our history. Pragmatic utilitarianism turned Jefferson's peerless masterpiece into a glorified shed. No conscience said not to.

In fairness, we have these artifacts because conscience did eventually intervene. The flag family stopped cutting and eventually donated it to the government. An idealist acquired and preserved Monticello. Children's nickels later bought it for all Americans.

But what about the proprietor of that Confederate tattoo parlor? What about his or her individual conscience? Maine and New Hampshire are the whitest states in the Union, so not likely to be a lot of pushback from customers. Maybe it is deliberately racist. Maybe it marks the home of a dedicated re-enactor. Maybe it advertises a particularly popular tattoo. Whatever the answer, we would have to concede a difficult point. It is a symbol—of what is a matter of conscience. Here is where it gets painful.

"The right of conscience" is the fifth of the Seven Principles (see page iii). I became a UU because of that principle, as well as—equally—the Fourth Principle, the "search for truth and meaning." I responded, as I'm sure many of you did also, to the "free-range" religious concept—to find what you will where you will all through history and around the world. And, of course, only your individual conscience decides if it is "right" or not. Being UU looked deeply absorbing and completely safe. It is a powerful combination.

Powerful delusions may also arise. If everybody follows what only individual conscience dictates, we become comic-book libertarians. We risk being both testy and compliant. We risk failing tough real-world tests and tasks. We are indeed failing now.

How does this happen? Libertarians do no harm—as they alone decide. Somebody insistent on his or her point of view is almost inevitably testy, or at least disharmonious. Rand Paul just got reminded of this. Most of us avoid disruption by sometimes going along with things we should not. We invoke "dialogue" and "education." If only people would talk to each other, we say— if only they were better educated. These are the faith-healings of liberal piety. The truth is, we don't agree—"we," I mean, as in the whole body politic. That means accommodation will be hard-won. There are no shortcuts. "Agonism" is the current term. It means we are going to have to thrash it out, not pretend everybody has the same myth, let alone the right one.

Some good news: Human beings need relationship. "Conscience" requires a context. This is the difference between tolerance and diversity. People who behave in an acceptable way—our acceptable way—we tolerate. It is diversity when people do not behave in our acceptable way—and we agree to live with it. They are not we; we are not they. At its best, this kind of diversity opens a third way not otherwise accessible. At least it reminds us of the most profound truth—people are different. They are very, very different—on the surface perhaps, underneath for sure. And they still belong here.

Our principle follows "right of conscience" with "democratic process," which crucially reminds us there is a collective process, a way to form and act on conscience as a group, as an act of relationship that at least ameliorates the self-centered individual. It reminds us we are human, and not ever perfect. And it reminds us that, because we are human, push does come to shove. Agitation, demonstration—engage fairly as needed.

But proceed with hope. My body-art buddies did take down that nasty symbol of slavery and insurrection and 100 years of legal hatred. Did they realize it assaults many Americans directly, and all Americans indirectly—or was it just embarrassing?

So, I will keep my faith—with conscience both individual and also relational.

Amen. Blessed Be. Shalom. Salaam.

Denying the Dream

14 Jan 2018

In a few weeks it will be 50 years since Martin Luther King Jr. was murdered in Memphis, Tennessee. I remember how I got the news. After dinner I had gone into my parents' bedroom to talk to my girlfriend on the extension phone. Sometime during what was probably a two-hour conversation, her mother interrupted with news that had just been announced on television.

1968 was that kind of year. I opened the New York Times to the famous front-page photo of the street execution during the Tet Offensive. I saw Lyndon Johnson announce he would not run for re-election on a store window television late at night on the way home from a concert at Philadelphia's Academy of Music. My brother woke me on Senior Skip Day with the news Bobby Kennedy had been shot. I watched the brawling Chicago Democratic Convention on TV. I stayed up all night until Richard Nixon was eventually declared elected as the next President of the United States.

1968 was also the year I got my first car, fell in love, graduated from high school, went off to college and discovered Pabst Blue Ribbon was health food. Drinking beer at 18 was legal in Wisconsin then, and the frat house where I roomed had an open tap.

So, what kind of year was that—half a century ago? Was it traumatic and despairing—or was it exciting and filled with adventure? What do you remember?

We already know what kind of year this one is—angry and afraid, just like last year and the one before. The people who want it that way are not running the table but they are still in control of the game. The "signs of the times" are alarmingly clear. Too many others are willing to go along with it, heedless of the peril to civil society, to the body politic and even to physical safety when slander, insults and fear-mongering rule the rostrum. More than half of all Americans were born after the year 1968. They have no living memory of that episode of "the end of days."

Likewise, they have no memory of Martin Luther King as a living man. Yet the deepest and most turbid pool of ignorance and animosity is among those who do—or at least should. "Signs of the times" and "the end of days" is Biblical language. Dr. King spoke and understood it. He believed the world to be made by God, to be filled with both good and evil. He proclaimed men and women capable of doing the one and withstanding the other by strong character and right action. He understood the universe to have a trajectory in quite old-fashioned terms, an arc toward justice.

Now Dr. King's time comes again, as it has not in such urgency since his death. One of the distinguishing marks of the great figures of the American past is how they arise again and again to speak to a new age. Our history doesn't let us off the hook and Martin Luther King's greatest legacy is that he doesn't either. He still demands justice.

To begin at the roots of the evil, how do you think Martin Luther King would react to the ubiquitous use of the term "illegals" to describe 11 million people who live in this country? Do you think he would express outrage at the obvious parallel to long years of millions of Americans being routinely described as "colored"—and the smug certainty that term conveyed everything worth knowing about them? How timely that we now have "shithole" countries. It is deliberate—who belongs here and who does not—to some twisted minds. Demeaning and dehumanizing language has a purpose. It is debasement of others to get them away from the table, off your block, out of your way.

Some of us remember the horror of the Berlin Wall, and the agony of watching people being shot, blown up, savaged by dogs and cast into jail for trying to get across, around or under it. What do you suppose it means that the Orange Emperor demands just such a structure of terror, to be used in just such fashion? We will hear the tweets: We are now all safe; freedom has triumphed; America is great again; what's your beef?

Do you think Martin Luther King would be indignant that elected officials and their enablers can say with a straight face that an entire world religion is noxious and illegitimate? Some 1.6 billion believers are apparently less than acceptable in the eyes of God. Dr. King would make clear this is not his God. Millions of Americans are not unworthy because they practice their religion. Dr. King would call our attention to Amos and Isaiah, Reinhold Niebuhr and Gandhi, to the Founders and to Abraham Lincoln. Who, he would ask, invokes God's name on behalf of ignorance and exclusion?

Martin Luther King would certainly have proclaimed long and loudly that 50,000 refugees somehow threatening the "survival of our country" is at best a pernicious delusion and at worst a recipe for vigilantism, persecution, extortion and human tragedy on a colossal scale—that it is a betrayal of the American character and will cripple for decades any claim to a noble national destiny. He would name it the evil of denying the dream, not for falling short of our better nature but for turning our backs conspicuously on the very possibility of having a better nature. Those so quick to trumpet American exceptionalism are deaf and blind to that on which any legitimate claim must rest.

Martin Luther King gave his life for garbage collectors. Okay—they were "sanitation workers" even in 1968, but they were on strike against miserable working conditions. They were almost all black and they were fired for demanding better treatment and thus he was in Memphis, where James Earl Ray trapped him for the kill.

This is critical knowledge, but not because some of us remember those days. It is not because, thanks to Taylor Branch and many others, all of us have the opportunity to know that history. Now we are called again to live our understanding of it in full.

It is critical knowledge because destiny does not allow us a pass, and neither does Martin Luther King—or any other great man or woman. What happened then matters because it must influence how we act now. It always does. Who we choose to be, what we choose to become, must be shaped by how we understand what took place in the past. Our dreams inspire our accomplishments, and they are always rooted in what we think we have been— in who we think we can be—in how we choose to act.

Dr. King chose to act against an America complicit in the existence of a permanent underclass. He did not fight for voting rights, for employment rights, for an end to Jim Crow in the law and segregation in the culture as ends in themselves. They were a means to accomplish the ultimate goal. Dr. King saw an America free at last of people who could never expect their lives to be better, who could never live with the same opportunity and dignity all Americans are promised. He called us as one people to account for that promise, and for the essential nobility of the American dream, that all our people could one day live in this way, rich or poor, black or white, old or young.

What do you think Dr. King would call it when 11 million people in America cannot drive a car, hold a job, go to the hospital, call a police officer, attend school, get a bank account, live where they like, travel when they will, appear in a court of law, or congregate in public or private? I think he would call that a permanent underclass.

He'd tell us what we have decided we won't do is always impossible to accomplish. We won't integrate? Then we can't integrate. We won't assimilate? Then we can't assimilate. Now is our time to call each other to account for what we do want.

Dr. King is dead but not gone. Now again we do demand his dream as our own.

Amen. Blessed Be. Shalom. Salaam.

Gilded Splinters

21 Jan 2018

Harry Emerson Fosdick was a famous preacher who had a powerful friend, as ministers sometimes do. When his vestry kicked Fosdick out of the pulpit for being too liberal, his friend built Fosdick a new church for his very own. It is the Riverside Church on the Upper West Side of Manhattan. Ninety years later, it remains an edifice of liberal religion—sustained by a public parking garage the church operates under the building.

What Fosdick preached was called the Social Gospel. Christian faith was to be embodied not primarily in personal piety or the grace of salvation, but as an engine of social reform—of making better the world we live in. "God of Grace and God of Glory" is Fosdick's wonderfully resonant hymn. UUs don't sing it often but you recognize the tune and the refrain: "Grant us wisdom, grant us courage, for the facing of this hour," and in the second verse, "for the living of these days." Almighty God is to "shame our wanton, selfish gladness, rich in things and poor in soul."

Our Unitarian and Universalist forebears were among many Protestants who wanted to believe it would happen—that it was happening. We still do, and we should.

Unfortunately, as with all things within the human sphere, some assembly required. The Social Gospel—and the hymn—appeared just in time for the Roaring Twenties—the largest, loudest, most lavish and lascivious binge in American history. The rich got richer, the middle class got so much stuff they felt rich, and bootblacks and waitresses played tips on the Stock Market.

Did I mention the name of Harry Emerson Fosdick's generous friend? It was John D. Rockefeller of Standard Oil, a pious man who gave out shiny dimes to children. I will mention also a book called *The Fundamentals*, published originally just before World War I as a series of essays in fervent defense of Biblical orthodoxy against every aspect of liberal thought and religion. It's how we got Fundamentalists. It's how Fosdick got bounced, after preaching a sermon called, "Shall the Fundamentalists Win?"

This is an example of the tendency of new arguments suddenly appearing, to be actually recapitulations of old arguments. I'm not sure how much comfort there is in the moment, but the disagreement about "faith versus works" dates from the gospel of John.

In any event, we are pretty clearly less along the grace and glory spectrum—again—and more along the path of what I call "gilded splinters." The image is from a 1968 song by Dr. John the Night Tripper, who was from

New Orleans by way of barrelhouse piano and authentic gris-gris. It was called, "I Walk on Gilded Splinters," and I played it a lot on my all-night radio show. The good doctor—real name Mac Rebennack—has six Grammy awards and an honorary PhD from Tulane University.

Congress has thoughtfully provided the latest splinters. It is impossible to agree the Federal government is important enough we should pay for it. It is impossible to agree 700,000 Americans should not be deported out of the only home most have ever known. It is impossible to agree nine million children in the richest country on earth should not go without health care. It is impossible for either side to agree compromise always looks bad until there isn't any, and certainly it is impossible for anyone to suggest with a straight face that President Chaos will do anything else but hand out pitchforks.

The gilding is also painfully apparent. The Tax "Reform"—also known as "Down Is Up"—is larded like a cheap fruitcake with rewards targeted to the donation-enabled, by definition neither poor nor powerless. Health Care "Repeal and Replace" (remember, "Down Is Up"!) never had any legitimate "replace" element at all, and still failed. No problem—pull the protections, narrow the access, cut the funding—a guarantee that ordinary people will benefit muchly. Inequality? We've got that covered—wealth inequality, income inequality, voting inequality, racial inequality, religious inequality, gender inequality. You could float the Queen Mary in this newly overflowing ocean of inequality. We probably will—and whose name will be on it?

Speaking of dissociative disorder—I grew up when you could only buy cars from the Big Three in Detroit, watch television from the three national networks or pump gas from the "Seven Sisters" oil companies. Your telephone was firmly fastened to the wall, accessed by hooking and spinning a dial with your finger, and it was in thrall to everybody's mom, Ma Bell. Imagine my shock last week in Best Buy! There were hundreds of brightly flashing screens, some of them the size of my car. Stuff to feed the screens was heaped up for blocks, almost none of it comprehensible to me. There was a distinct roar of eager customers. I freaked. Maybe the customers weren't exactly roaring—more of a blare of beeping sounds—but Sally had to guide me out. We are not exactly clean of hands. The polling is in the bag—the once uber-idealistic Baby Boomers have clearly and decisively turned into, "I Me Mine." Did I mention Uber?

Meanwhile, nobody knows how many poor people there are in the United States. It's not a counting problem and certainly not a problem of finding them. It seems the experts can't agree on how to define poverty. The official definition from 1963 measures the average value of food needed for a week and multiplies that by three. Spend more than a third of your pre-tax cash income on food and you are officially poor. A newer Census Bureau method adds cash and non-cash income like the Earned Income Credit and food stamps as well, and then subtracts taxes, medical care and child support. Does this make your eyes roll back? Bottom line: If the government switches from the first method to the second, millions of children will lose benefits. They will no longer be poor. Wait—millions of the elderly will gain benefits. They will have become poor.

Aside from the obvious—it matters an awful lot to people in both those groups—does anyone care to make that decision? Are we feeding Junior or Granny? I won't even mention the people who think we should feed neither—or the methodology they espouse. Well, I will—even objective experts point out poor people today have a lot more stuff than they used to. If you have a cellphone and a color TV, are you poor? Are you worse off or better off if you can stroll into Best Buy for a lot of stuff you can't buy?

Whatever path we take, it is looking more and more like gilded splinters every step of the way. "All God's children got shoes on their feet," goes the old gospel song. Won't we be glad if we are among them?

And seriously, who are we in this new and uncertain world? I confess I do not know. I suspect we will have to do what people have always done, which is find new and more effective ways to take care of each other. I admit the possibility we will do so in some larger ways—science and government and yes, even businesses and religious institutions. These are ways of organizing human innovation, effort and energy proven to yield wide benefits. Many of those benefits have lasted, though not all—and not without some pain. To give up on our ingenuity is to give up on humankind.

As Annie Dillard reminds us, there is only us. Some of us see God troubling the water—I do, for instance. But still, we must walk out into it. Midrash says the Red Sea did not part for Moses until the People were in it up to their necks—or their noses. I imagine we will cross, but I am certain we will have to do some walking. Some we must prepare to carry. Some must carry us as we falter. Let us do so. Watch out for splinters.

Amen. Blessed Be. Shalom. Salaam.

Pass the Ballots

27 May 2018

When I was a kid my father would go bear hunting every November in the Pocono Mountains of northeastern Pennsylvania. He and his buddies would spend a long weekend at a lodge one of them owned on Lake Wallenpaupack. Most years Dad never fired his gun. What he liked was four or five days with the guys, playing poker and cribbage and not shaving. I was always disappointed when he came home—no bear.

Then one year he got a bear. They all got a bear—the same bear. My father brought home the trophy photograph, but he never went bear hunting again. "Not much bigger than a German shepherd dog," was how he described the bear. It panicked and ran into the middle of the group of hunters instead of away from them. "We basically shot it to pieces," my Dad said. Perhaps to avoid appearing overly sentimental, he'd later explain he'd survived the Germans at Anzio and the Colmar Pocket and add, "I'm damned if I'll be shot in the woods by my friends!"

So it's already election season all across America—another glorious display of flourishing democracy. Yes, that was a gag reflex. Any one of us could be standing in for the poor bear. Staying out of the woods no longer keeps you safe from being shot—those gut-punch incidents are now as common as bad car wrecks. Voters too have been blasting away, metaphorically of course, but with language almost as lethal. It is a kind of madness. Nobody is just wrong anymore. Everybody else is an enemy. Bad hunters. Bad voters. Memorial Day should perhaps be for all of us this year, for all the wounded.

Anger and anxiety are obvious results when common sense and what has historically been characterized as America's "civil religion" are blasted to smithereens by shameless manipulation, stupidity and belligerence—not to put too fine a point on it. Now it's a "circular firing squad" and the shots are being aimed. One way or another, we are all becoming targets—and many millions of Americans are blazing away.

For what cold comfort, this has happened before. Two centuries ago, American elections were literally riots—torches, eggs and assaults upon persons and property were routine. In 1884, one candidate's mobs chanted, "Blaine, Blaine, James G. Blaine, continental liar from the state of Maine." The other candidate's mobs responded with, "Ma, Ma, where's my Pa?" Illegitimate child or not, Grover Cleveland squeaked through the popular vote after one of Blaine's supporters got overheated at a giant rally and denounced the Democrats as the party of "Rum, Romanism and Rebellion." Irish Americans were not amused. After the election they marched through the streets, responding to the "Pa" question by chanting, "Gone to the White House, ha, ha, ha."

"Men, it has been well said, think in herds; it will be seen that they go mad in herds, while they only recover their senses slowly, and one by one." Please forgive the anachronistic language, but the book was published in 1841. Charles Mackay, a writer for the Glasgow Argus—Glasgow, Scotland—called his book, *Extraordinary Popular Delusions and the Madness of Crowds*. It is a history of remarkable events like the Tulip Craze and the South Sea Bubble, and a taxonomy of individual follies and delusions that feed these social contagions. Mackay's book has never been out of print. Of course, it helps immensely that we keep seeing both the mass outbreaks and the individual manifestations of what he was explaining. We had a Housing Bubble not ten years ago—check the box. Now we are having a resentment craze—check the box.

It's easy to point fingers. There are, by general agreement, voters—or at least potential voters—who didn't go to college, who don't think they have a political voice, who want to protect themselves from outsiders and tend to live in the parts of the country where Google searches for racial slurs and jokes are more common. Then there are the voters who, also by general agreement, are in debt from college, who don't think they have a political voice, who want to protect themselves from outsiders, and who live in the parts of the country where they have broadband access so they can go on-line and complain vociferously about anybody who doesn't quite agree.

The larger point is first, the two groups are intermingled. Second, everybody across the board is indulging in resentment and outrage. Few candidates have clean hands in stirring it up, and we as a people are letting it fly with absolute abandon. That is the really scary part. A whole lot of people are quite clearly venting a whole lot of anger rather than admit they are frustrated, disappointed and—most of all—afraid. In the "man bites dog" category, the very conservative ideologue Tony Perkins, he of the Family Research Council, was quoted during the late election as saying, "You can't be fearful and thoughtful at the same time." Thanks, Tony. It's a good point.

My favorite yardstick of the "madness of crowds," as Mackay said, is the curse of "low information voters." This slur goes back to the John Birch Society, when it meant anybody who did not know traitors like President Eisenhower were aiding and abetting the global Communist threat—even as we slept. Back in that day, in his classic, The Paranoid Style in American Politics, historian Richard Hofstadter called this mindset "suspicious discontent"—the vague but vociferously expressed conviction you are being screwed over, absolutely-and-insert-the-suspect-of-your-choice-HERE! Pervasive Dread? Suffocating Anxiety? Choose your pick and pile on for the smackdown.

Now we may think of these voters as "Faux information voters." "Fox and Friends"—yes or no? This is an easy answer for most of us, but this exercise does not uncover truth. If you are living and dying by Rachel Maddow or the Daily Kos, you too are living in a scripted reality. Most Americans say they'd pitch a fit if a child's holy matrimony included somebody from the "wrong" political party. This is not progress.

Free-range resentment is profoundly anti-democratic. The essential qualification for being a member of the polity is you live here. Of course, there are regulations, and the franchise was limited at first, but the Founders were clear about the framework of what constituted the community. They favored property holders but explicitly rejected other qualifications. Our whole history has been movement slowly and often painfully toward a vision of the ideal—all are created equal and have those inalienable rights.

And let me state my own view: Free-range resentment is profoundly anti-Unitarian Universalist. Our First Principle—the foundation of our history, practice and anything we might call faith, or even "beliefs widely shared among us"—is that every human being has an inherent worth, regardless of age, class or condition. Every human being has an inherent dignity, regardless of age, class or condition. Regardless as well, on both points, of anything that human being does. Aggravating as it surely is in practice, this is where deep theology intertwines with Enlightenment social order. We can be punished for what we do but we cannot lawfully or morally be deprived of our worth and dignity—or our opinions. We can't value humanity and not value humans.

I suggest, as Mackay said, our main obligation in this troubled and disturbing time, is to "recover our senses slowly, and one by one." Vote early, vote often, but don't forget about our values. You and I have rights and responsibilities. So does everyone else. Respect and persuasion is our value. Let us stand up for what we must believe. None of us wants to be the bear. Let's not gun each other down in the woods, either.

Amen. Blessed Be. Shalom. Salaam.

A Quantum of Forgiveness

23 Sep 2018

My high school soccer goalie was the toughest kid I knew. He had to be. Our defense in front of him was leaky. Jailbreak rushes were frequent. "Get out of the way!" he would yell behind us and then charge past to dive on the ball. He never flinched.

My high school soccer goalie builds display flower gardens for a living. What the heck? He's good at it—won the Philadelphia Flower Show the last two years. So I pointed Sally in his direction at our reunion. "Watch out," I added. "He's a Trump guy."

Quite innocuously, as Trump guys go, but the wise tread carefully everywhere.

And this then, is the question of our age: "How much forgiveness?" Should we forgive immigrants for ruining the country? Should we forgive racists for ruining the country? What about people screaming—for their own purposes and profit—how ruined the country is? Should we even consider forgiving them? I think not.

We are drowning. Up to our necks in crap, as we surely are, should we shovel or swim? All the resentments are seething, all the issues are boiling, all the identities are aggrieved, all the discourse poisoned—but all that looks like a "what to forgive" question. The dilemma is more essential: Whom do we forgive? When—and how?

Being only human creatures, it is not likely we can sustain either of the two extremes. Forgive everybody? Only Jesus and Buddha forgave everybody. We are not they. Truth is, they also left some significant fine print about the matter. I will discuss at another time. Forgive nobody? Only a psychopath forgives nobody, and by definition that is mental illness. So, we sort ourselves out somewhere on the spectrum in between. We likewise negotiate between forgiving everything and forgiving nothing. Again, no one can meet those extremes—in bestowing or receiving forgiveness. We are not gods.

Homesteaders who hoped to survive high plains blizzards would string wire between the house and the barn, so as not to get blinded and wander off to death. Some were known to string wire well out from each corner of the house, so as to find it more easily if caught out on the road when the storm hit. Of course, you have to mark which way is inbound, and so do we. Confronted with a blizzard, we need to mark the way.

This is a time of marking the way. Summer ended yesterday and autumn has officially begun. This year the timing of the weather is almost perfectly in tune with the celestial rotation and the human calendar. The temperature has dropped and there is real change in the light. It is a subtle but powerful signal the seasons are moving along. Like it or not, we are on the way to winter. As we move toward the tangibles of winter weather in New England—the dark, the cold, the snow and the ice—we also process inexorably toward the intangible winter that inevitably inhabits our lives. No one escapes seasons of despair. They are harbingers of the inescapable end of mortal life.

Yet we set markers of sustenance and renewal. Yom Kippur ended at sunset Wednesday. It is usually translated as the "Day of Atonement." The popular version is that Jews feel sorry for wrong things they have said and done the previous year. They begin the New Year fresh by admitting this. It is a time for repairing all relationships. But the acknowledgement of our wrongdoing must be more profound. Wrongdoing must be properly understood through prayer and solemn ritual as inextricable in human life, entangled in every moment from first to last. It is universal. Ashura concluded Friday at sunset. Sunni Muslims celebrate just these understandings, of humility and culpability. Mohammed drew on Jewish tradition. So may we. From our darkness comes the light. From our foreknowledge of death comes our deepest strength of heart. From our stained hands of wrongdoing comes the greatest power of our character, the power to forgive. It is our will that chooses it, and it is never too late for that choice.

In this time of troubles, I suggest it may be best to start small. Choose a smaller amount of forgiveness—a quantum, if you will. Forgive the whole creation or the whole human community or even the New York Yankees some other time when the job is not so overwhelming. That time will come. Remember small does not mean trivial. The difference is actually trivial between forgiveness of one human being and forgiveness of one billion human beings. What matters is the forgiveness of that one human being—instead of none. You know this threshold—it is the difference between being pregnant or not, the difference between being alive or not. The step from zero to one is what counts. It surely gets your name written in the Book of Life, at least for this year.

I suggest you find a quantum of forgiveness in an even more important way. The examen is obvious enough: What are you really sorry for? How have you fallen short—of what you intended or should have intended, of who you meant to be or should have meant to be, of what you should have said or kept silent about? What angry words have you spoken? What petty grudges have you carried? What part of your days was spent being selfish, small-minded or inconsiderate? How much were you—in every sense of the word—unloving, of family, friends and strangers alike? How many times have you assumed the worst of intentions, of those you know and those you do not?

Wait, whom are we talking about here? This is all about relationships, of course, and as you heard repeatedly, we are actually talking about you. There is one person we need to forgive first of all, most of all. You need to forgive you. I need to forgive me.

Putting ourselves at the center is not egotism. The great Process theologian Henry Nelson Wieman put it bluntly in a 1979 pamphlet he wrote for the UUA: The question is, in what way will you be different, not how other people will change. This is the central question of all varieties of religious life, answerable only by the belief we can be different and it matters that we make the effort.

I would add pragmatically that you couldn't possibly forgive anybody else until you have forgiven yourself. Neither can I. Nobody can. I suggest the possibility the person you have the hardest time forgiving—the one you don't let up on, the one who's never quite up to snuff at home or abroad—is sitting right in the pew with you, wearing your shoes. But wait, aren't we self-aware? Don't we see the excuses, the evasions and the rationalizations of all our everyday lives—the "self-privileging" with which we are beset? Of course we do. We are UUs after all.

And being UUs, we may need to be reminded that all these are the constructions of rational mind. They are not of the heart. They are not of the soul. They are not of eternity or the ineffable. They are a veneer. They allow our thin self-image as good or bad people. No true forgiveness can be rooted in seeing only appearances. Something so much deeper is needed to feed our hunger to be. I have already suggested that we must enter the deepest darkness to have any chance of a genuine light. We must accept our contamination with inevitable wrong before we have any true chance of doing right.

To forgive ourselves truly is to know ourselves truly, to lose our pretension that we are more or less good in favor of entirely belonging here. Once in a while it must come to that. Now is a good time to face ourselves and thus to know all others are of the same faulty stuff. Our crisis is an overwhelming need to forgive. Slowly, painfully, begrudgingly, the quantum of forgiveness we find can offer itself to them. Each of us has the power. Together we have the courage. The world still turns toward right.

Amen. Blessed Be. Shalom. Salaam.

Cloudy with a Chance of Meatballs

02 Dec 2018

At least the way Grandpa tells the story, the good people of the little town of Chewandswallow have a very good deal with the universe—or maybe it's just a special understanding with the cloud cover. In Chewandswallow, it rains food. Whatever the mealtime, appropriate comestibles come down from the sky—bacon and eggs at breakfast, PB&J sandwiches at lunch, spaghetti and meatballs at dinner, and more. They never have to cook, or food-shop, or store anything edible.

For some reason, Chewandswallow sounds like a Rhode Island kind of place—or maybe the Jersey Pine Barrens. It is certainly not Massachusetts—apparently nobody stands up at Town Meeting and complains about pancake syrup on the front lawn.

But as is sometimes the way with miraculous things, one day the rain of food turns into torrents of food—way too much for the people. The food turns to stuff nobody actually wants to eat. It comes down in huge sizes and bizarre combinations. Chaos ensues. I'll leave it there. *Cloudy with a Chance of Meatballs* is a great book for kids. Mine loved it. I loved reading it to them right up to when they could read it too.

The "chaos ensues" part we already know about. We are drenched in spaghetti sauce. Donuts the size of truck tires are bouncing down the street and squid is squishing on the sidewalk. The checklist of awful stuff is like the Mikado's little list, unrolling and unrolling. No end is in sight, and who wants to see how bad it might be? Let's not look.

On the other hand, we have to live with this, at least for some time. It may be a long time. In a possibly perverse way—but I prefer to think of it as hopeful—this may be good news. Taking the long view is almost always the most essential first step of surviving hard times. Bad events are no less bad, but they are events—things that happen. "This too shall pass," says the Bible, and any knowledge of history will sustain that wisdom. "No fair!" was my mother's complaint about the Great Recession. "I've already lived through this once." Of course she had. It was much worse and followed immediately by World War II. The first half of the twentieth century was the bloodiest epoch in human history—and in almost 75 years since, no global bloodshed at all.

We are keeping our fingers crossed so hard they hurt, but nonetheless… And let's note, in forty years abject global poverty has plummeted to the lowest levels in history.

Closer to home—let's consider the midterms. Be sure to count all the absentee and mail-in and provisional ballots before assuming you won. California Republicans are learning this the hard way and are, of course, whining big time. The Petulant Toddler may still think it was the greatest result in history, but pretty much everybody with a pulse knows otherwise.

This is, as we should perceive, the purpose of midterm elections. They are course corrections built into the system. They work reliably both ways. Remember that long- term view. We are fortunate indeed to live in a democracy that is incredibly deep. There are tens of thousands of local units of government in the United States. People vote all over the country for dogcatcher, for Pete's sake. We vote for legislators and executives and even the bureaucrats like clerk and treasurer and road wardens. You get to stand up and say your piece at your town meeting, your city hall, your school board and your tax assessor. It would be easier to put the Great Pyramid of Cheops in your trunk and drive away than it would be to truly run off with the government of this country.

This is important. No other country—even major democracies—is organized this way. It's crazy bad for efficiency and clarity, but it is whammo for making sure the king is always dead and there will be no other. That was the real priority—and they meant "King Mob" as well. All you and I have to do is raise our hands. Anywhere we do that, and demand for all the right to keep doing that, no matter how big or small the stakes, we are better off than any other people in history. It is a messy system and Your Mileage May Vary, always, but it is a dynamic and fluid system—New England weather in organized form. There may even be meatballs, but wait 15 minutes. You'll get bagels.

Look around also today, and realize you are sitting in a civic association— I mean, church. First Parish is one of tens of thousands of religious organizations, and there are literally hundreds of thousands of social, political, cultural and hobby groups all over—everything from Baha'i to bonsai. You name it; somebody's organized it, or will. Almost 200 years ago de Tocqueville remarked upon it as an exceptional quality in America, and to this day no other country comes close. You can literally sit here and see it: In 1839 the congregation of this church picked up the whole building and turned it from facing North St. to facing the small common out front. They raised the building and dug out what we call the Vestry. Why? Religion had changed, and they needed space to accommodate the social activities of emerging modern congregational life. Potlucks!

They also built a fashionable new Greek Revival façade onto the church— with all the architectural elements and, as necessary, all those steps. With the new orientation, you could then stand back and admire the building—very important for attracting newcomers and proclaiming your proper place in the social structure. They had to compete. Thank you to the Dedham Case of 1828, which disestablished churches in the Commonwealth. I always remind people when pledge time comes up: You own this edifice and this community lock-stock-and-barrel. You must obey the law, but nobody can otherwise tell you what to do here. The heart of civic association is—you are free.

Let me make this point about living in our own hard times. As you are free in your associational sphere, you are free as well in your hearts. This is your community, and it will feel the way you choose that it should, just as it operates the way that you choose it should. Our community is who we are to each other. We feel distress and despair. No human life—and certainly no human community—is free of these events. But we have control of who we are to each other. We choose how to greet each other. We choose whether to listen to each other and care about what we hear. We choose how to act in the world—face to face and far away as well. None of us is perfect, but each of us has the power of choice in these ways. No, it is not often easy—it never has been.

"Politics is downstream of culture," said the late Andrew Breitbart. The website he founded is still a font of rabid rage. His way of thinking leads to the alt-right and much else that is angry, belligerent and conspiratorial in our current world. It is a license to hate the Other. It is a template for vigilante conformity. We can see and feel it in the attacks on so many people and on so many values of a liberal democracy.

It is a moral black hole because it is backwards logic. Politics is a structure and process to create opportunities for diverse cultures and identities. In America, politics is not who you are, it is a way we negotiate the public space and our differences. It is how we map out the future. It is not and never can be a zero-sum game. It is not an end state—no matter how desirable or necessary any particular end state may seem. It is always wrong to confuse ends and means. Politics is a means. It cannot become an end. No political end can validate corrupt, cynical and selfish means. In our world it is harder and harder, but above all we must remember our first identity is human—all others flow from it. Bring your umbrella. There will be meatballs, but we will certainly persevere.

Amen. Blessed Be. Shalom. Salaam.

The Winter's Tale

06 Jan 2019

Part I: Hands and Hearts

January is the time to hear a special note. It is the best time—in the clear and the cold and the quiet outside—to hear what is inside. Now is the time to find your harmony with the stillness. Harmony-in-stillness is just as essential to the natural order as the movement of the other seasons. The special note is of birthing and renewing.

The old year is past and gone. Whatever we dreamed, whatever we hoped, whatever we worked for over the past twelve months—well, the Book of Life has been written to completion for the page of 2018. That finality can be hard to accept. It is harder particularly if our attention is glued to all those things we inevitably did not achieve to our satisfaction. It may be that the better list—the list of accomplishments and abundances—seems to shrink in our sight. It may vanish in a blizzard of regrets.

Yet the special note is quietly sounding. It is a season of gathering-in and of letting go. In the depths of our hearts a small fire glows. This can be a deep season of profound creation. It can be, as Emerson proclaimed in the Divinity School Address, "a refreshment of rest in the transparent darkness," rather than a visit to the gloom of night. He looked up and saw the stars pouring forth their splendor, and so should we.

Now is the time to gather in—to look into your heart and see what is good. What lives there in the quiet of this hour? What will grow and bear forth if nourished with the fuel of attention and practice in the coming weeks? Who might you be—who might you become—in this year that stretches out ahead? We are not in charge of everything, remember—but we do have charge of who we are. We cannot determine the events of our lives, but we shape every moment before us by how we choose to live it. We arise every morning with the power of gods—the power to make the day. Now we begin.

And what would you like to let go in the New Year? Will you not take a necessary moment to let go the disappointments you bear about yourself? Forgiveness must always begin at home. Will you not spend one precious moment to let go of grievances you bear toward others? Ill will ill becomes us. Will you not unveil your own powerful generosity of spirit? By your heart will you surely give and receive this ultimate gift.

Will you not allow yourself to lay down at least some small part of your burdens and enter into greater freedom? We are not in charge of everything, but we do have charge of who we are becoming. We cannot live without grief and cares. They come like the seasons, but we do not have to be driven by them. We can name our fears and cast them away. We can make them gone, away from the sustaining center of our lives.

Always, God breathes without and within. Here before you is a chalice of "Hands and Hearts," an artifact to remind us of profound truths. It represents our community—all those whose hands and hearts hold us, as we hold them. Whether we know them by name or not, they exist. I invite you to contemplate and record what you will gather in or let go in 2019—what should now pass through this spiritual portal into All-Being.

Reading: Philip Simmons: "Winter Mind"—UU World, Jan/Feb. 2001

I want to tell you about the sound of winter wind through a New Hampshire forest. … It's the sound a whole forest makes, unlocatable and everywhere, near and far, intimate and impossibly remote. I don't mean a storm wind, full of high drama, but the gentle, subtle voice of a forest as it speaks of winter peace and winter desolation.

The forest where we live is mixed hardwoods and conifers: maple, oak, beech, and birch; white pine, spruce, and hemlock. Two mountain ridges lie between me and the interstate highway 20 miles off, and with no sizeable town in earshot, I can hear the sound such a forest makes when gently dithered by winter air. Leaves are down of course, so it's the pines that matter most. They stand tallest and catch the wind. Theirs is a finely sifted sound, a soft hiss through unnumbered needles. Stand by one as it takes the air, and you'll know how God breathes. Hear the accumulated sounds of such trees coming at you over the miles, and you hear something like the breath of Being itself, the very sigh of our becoming and passing away. Unless the ground is covered in snow, the sound is accompanied by shrub turbulence and dead leaf scuttle. And there's more: hardwoods, their bare branches stiffened, provide an undertone, low and harder edged, the barely audible drag of sticks through cold air. And last, close by, the rattle of dead beech leaves still clinging to their boughs.

Part II: A Mind of Winter

"A mind of winter," is a phrase of the poet Wallace Stevens:

One must have a mind of winter
To regard the frost and the boughs
Of the pine trees crusted with snow;

And have been cold a long time
To behold the junipers shagged with ice,
The spruces rough in the distant glitter

Of the January sun; and not to think
Of any misery in the sound of the wind,
In the sound of a few leaves …

Philip Simmons hears the forest speaking of both "winter peace and winter desolation." How can these exist in one? To reconcile them is indeed to understand both mystery and miracle. Everything beyond human understanding is of course mysterious. Every encounter with the divine is of course miraculous. These must be true, by definition.

The mind of winter brings us encounter with the divine as wildness, even desolation. There must be moments when we feel isolated, separated, detached, incomplete, inadequate and unrequited. Some time or another we must each live through the inescapable bleakness of disconnection. How else can I understand myself, other people, and the very nature of creation? Without dark there can be no light.

Yet the wildness of the divine also offers us peace. The mind of winter invites the soul's contentment—to feel connected, bonded, involved, whole, sufficient and rewarded. At the very moment of emptiness, we can be filled. In the harshest climate, in the most painful circumstance, we still love and are loved and we understand these foundations. We grasp the shape and substance of the universe. We comprehend the architecture of the cosmos beyond time. We tell each other once more the Winter's Tale.

Wallace Stevens again:
In the sound of a few leaves,

Which is the sound of the land
Full of the same wind
That is blowing in the same bare place

For the listener, who listens in the snow,
And, nothing himself, beholds
Nothing that is not there and the nothing that is.

Stevens called this poem "The Snow Man." We have our chance to heap up the snow to be our own witness, and to be simply certain that "the nothing" is also enough.

Amen. Blessed Be. Shalom. Salaam. Happy New Year!

Anger Management

27 Jan 2019

If you ever saw the 1988 movie, "Mississippi Burning," you remember the double-edge razor blade. The camera tracks right in close on its gleaming menace. Behind it is a man bound and gagged in a chair. He has just been reminded by the man holding up the razor blade about what terror has already scarred human bodies in that time and place. "There was so much blood," that man says, with cold malice.

In the next scene, Gene Hackman takes a folder from the man who held the razor blade and passes it to William Dafoe. Hackman is the outside-the-lines FBI agent, and Dafoe is the by-the-book idealist. He fumes and sputters with outrage—evidence by such tainted means can't stand up in court. Hackman's response is ferocious: These people come from the gutter. "Maybe it's time we get down there and stop them."

These two scenes are entirely fictional. Squeezing informers—and paying—is what solved the 1964 murders of civil rights workers Andrew Goodman, James Cheney, and Michael Schwerner, as the FBI readily admits. It took three years—not movie time.

These are examples of a kind of "anger management." They are the deliberate deployment of base methods for worthy purposes, or what purports to be worthy purposes. They are defective management, but just before the razor blade appears there is a scene of much more unambiguous testament to the power of human feeling. It is a church packed with sweating people. It is a funeral—the coffin is in front of the pulpit. In that pulpit, surrounded by weeping and defiance, the preacher is heard to declare, "Now I feel anger. Angry is what we are today." This is historical, although not fact.

Angry is what we are today. Can anyone doubt it? We are daily reminded of our on-going contagion of outrage, hinged or not, connected to reality or utterly unmoored. Tenuously connected to reality might be the best summary of most of what most of us are feeling most of the time. Yes, there are quite plainly real causes. Yes, there are dangers and grievances and abuses both large and small—and slights never ending. There is ample fear to go around. There is broad anxiety and individual uncertainty and many reasons, if you are not worried all that much about yourself, to be worried a lot about all those other people. Those folks seem to have totally lost their minds, whoever they are and whatever they want. "The paranoids are out to get me," was the old joke.

Standing as we do in the long shadow of the life of Dr. Martin Luther King, Jr., we can have no illusions about the weight of his anger. It was deep and it was directed. Like many noble people he struggled to control his temper all his life, but he was capable of explosive words and short-fused actions. Some of his telephone conversations, even with national leaders, are legendary for their fulmination—sometimes apparently calculated and sometimes clearly not. Those close to him knew he could be volcanic.

He was, of course, not one bit paranoid. His phones were tapped. His most private moments were informed on. People were out to get him. Some were just powerful in their willingness to bomb or shoot or stab. Some were more dangerous—holders of institutional power determined to block or thwart him and the cause he embodied. The ones he most famously lost his temper with—or barely controlled it—were the ones who claimed they didn't want to thwart his cause, but couldn't understand why it all had to be so very urgent. Why these demands? Why these tactics? Why now?

Dr. King drew deeply on the Biblical prophets. This is a strength sadly lost to us skeptics, except by his example. We can be sure, because he often said so, he was not blind to the imperfections of those prophets and to their generally poor "life outcomes," as we might call them today. His belief was that most wonderful of faith constructs, profound but not deluded—unless hope for human betterment is itself deluded. He remembered the prophet Amos, who named the unjust and doomed Northern Kingdom. Amos was only a shepherd—although he wrote beautifully. He appears in the Hebrew Scriptures, and then disappears—back to his flocks, presumably. Amos was an inspired Everyman, and lucky. Jeremiah was neither—his persistent berating of the royal and priestly establishment gave rise to our expression, "a jeremiad," and got him thrown in a hole and stoned. The conquerors pulled him out before they carried off the People—mostly the very ones he had been hammering for their failure of moral leadership.

And there was Isaiah. In his lifetime he foretold disaster, but his prophecy called out to the People a century later during the Babylonian Exile. They heard in this Second Isaiah a covenant with God unbroken. They heard the promise of return to Jerusalem.

The central business of the prophet might be said to be good anger management. All these are examples of just that preoccupation. There has to be a driving sense of wrongdoing—either present or approaching unheeded. The words and the actions have to happen—private speech and personal resolutions have no weight in the public square. It helps a great deal to have a pipeline to higher authority, which has to be believable to the people you share it with. They won't much like the sharing, because it will be riddled with anger—anger at them, at their complacency and their faithlessness and their self-interest and shallow accommodation of what should be truth and clearly is not. The "clearly" is usually the difficult part. If they aren't angry before, they surely will be after you point it all out. Managing the anger is the key. To manage yours and to manage theirs—and there are only consequential outcomes no matter how a prophet rides the whirlwind. There is great danger always lurking, as Dr. King well knew.

How are we managing our anger? Let's agree on a euphemism—"Needs Improvement." It's okay to laugh. Once we've had a good chuckle, it might help to remember that anger has three vectors: They are Intensity, Duration and Proximity.

Good anger management requires proportionate Intensity, because generating meaningful ferocity takes a fearful toll on our emotions and our bodies—and, I would say, our souls. The God of Small Things reminds us that most everything is actually pretty small, even good things and certainly bad things. So don't have a cow, Homer.

Duration matters. Please, give yourself a break—and the people around you. Being one of the Perpetually Aggravated isn't going to yield much out of life except grief. It isn't very genial company, and whatever good might be done is often incidental to judgmental preoccupations that can amount to pissing in the communal soup. Take a breath, take a walk, take up the ukulele. Stay human. Of course, things move only when pushed, but nobody moves a piano except by moderate effort skillfully sustained.

The bottom line rests with Proximity. Yelling at the TV doesn't do any good. Neither does yelling at people on your smartphone. The president can't hear you. The people you are berating on Facebook are only going to berate you back—and who wins?

The rule is to push where the pushing's good. Petition, witness, demonstrate, vote—we leave in a world, thankfully, where those things matter. Get as close as you can to the people you want to hear you. Stay civil and look reasonable and of course that means use your inside voice. You don't like being yelled at—why would anyone else?

And finally, remember this: Most of the good you can actually do is actually in your immediate vicinity. Live right, right around you. You don't have to announce it; we'll pick it up. Slowly, it may be, but everybody near you will notice. I promise.

Amen. Blessed Be. Shalom. Salaam.

Future Discounted

24 Feb 2019

The water was vaguely slimy and iridescent—bright colors of green, red and yellow punctuated with rusty cans, broken bottles and discarded tractor parts. Even as a boy I was quite unwilling to touch it. We called it, "the swamp"—down the street and behind the houses—but it was only a small dump for the commercial greenhouse on the front of the property. God knows what was actually in that water.

We didn't, and didn't care much. We also ran blissfully through the DDT fog from the mosquito spray truck when it came around on summer evenings. We visited my father's stone yard and my brother helped pour out the used crankcase oil to "settle the dust." The 1950s and early '60s were far from perfect but they were optimistic, and incidental chemical consequences were either not apparent or not much discussed.

Now we know better. Shout out to Gaylord Nelson, senator from Wisconsin. The first Earth Day and the Cambodia/Kent State riots took place within a few weeks of each other in the spring of 1970. I was there. Talk about your alpha and omega of hope and something else entirely.

This year, this month, this day we seem to be engulfed in the "something else entirely"—a climate catastrophe unimaginable a few decades ago, even to scientists. "Duck-and-cover" is how elementary school kids once practiced for nuclear war. Now we duck-and-cover for wild fires, hurricanes, snowmageddons, poisonous food and water, and an apocalypse of mass extinction coupled with mass human migration. Somehow we must hope, to live our lives and have any chance of saving our civilization or the earth—or, we respectfully request, both of the above. Where will the hope come from?

Color me skeptical about the Green New Deal, whatever it actually turns out to be—but we certainly need policy hope. What might we actually do that might work to at least slow down the juggernaut? More critically, we need political hope—how might we actually persuade people to board available life boats and also hammer together the rafts needed to save us, instead of assuming this huge, fast, luxurious vessel can't sink?

I prefer good decisions made more likely by good decision process. It's never flawless, but we can steer in the direction of better than the alternatives—the perfect not allowed to eradicate the good-enough-for-government-work of dodging the Big Jam.

Let's start with the stunningly obvious: What is the future worth, anyway? Why exactly should we try to save the earth? What really makes human civilization so valuable? Well, it's the only earth we have—that is rather important. We live in civilization. The lack of it is not good for children and other living things. It is, in fact, quite catastrophic.

Still, "because" can't be the answer. It is intellectually lazy and tinged with, "I know better than you do." We're smart people. We ought to have answers. You will also notice in our day that people saying because are generally not being treated with the deference formerly given to experts, to institutions, to establishments and to norms of all kinds. Boss Plunkett of New York State is the one reputed to have said, "The people have spoke, the bastards." So they have, and they will. Enlightened communal self-interest is not winning this race. "I'm a climate scientist and I'm here to help you," is not getting to the hard-core resistance—as climate scientists now freely admit.

"Sooner or later," sang Bruce Springsteen, "it all comes down to money." Of course it does, and that reality can't be dodged. It shouldn't be, either. Even Democratic Socialism uses a monetary system to allocate costs and benefits. What should the future cost? Or, more pointedly, what should we here in the present be prepared to pay for it? Go big or go home may be inspiring the zeitgeist, but ordinary people are going to quite sensibly demand some actual figures. "What's in it for me?" is stubborn human nature. It is probably the biggest factor in why many people are foot-dragging. History reminds us people dragged their feet about the New Deal and World War II, and this challenge will clearly be orders of magnitude greater. Please let's not indulge for a moment the utter delusion that everybody is going to suddenly "get it." That didn't happen then and it won't now. Bernie can wave his arms as much as he wants, but at least 40% of the electorate will never vote for him, or anybody like him.

They have to come along, too. At least most of them do—probably with some degree of reluctance, but that is quite acceptable in our political tradition. After we get some handle on what the present and the future are worth relative to each other (What will we get then that we are able and willing to pay for now?), the next question is obvious: Is this huge series of changes going to take place through our system of representative democracy? One lesson of human history should be obvious—the most dangerous people are, time and again, the ones claiming the world must be saved and they know how. The fatal attraction of ends justifying the means rears its ugly head.

A big factor in hard resistance to climate action is clearly an instinctive aversion to government by experts. Expertise is a wonderful thing and should be indulged in frequently, but it has a very mixed track record when set loose without the constraints of common interest and consent. Let me mention the word "eugenics" and leave it there.

The civilization worth sacrificing a great deal to save is one that rests on the assumption that ordinary everyday folks can understand their best interest and will act on it. We must commit to citizenship up front and every damn day thereafter. If you don't buy that as a philosophy, please regard it as a strictly practical incentive. People sacrifice a lot more when they agree. Every mother knows the human race would literally not be here at all if this were not true. There are no shortcuts and we must resist the temptation to take them, even as the flames crawl into the backyard.

I read two articles this week that relieved some of the gloom. The first was an interview with a man named Hal Harvey. It was posted on Vox in January. Harvey's written a book called *Designing Climate Solutions*. His focus is how to get there from here—what are the low-carbon energy policies that grab the most benefit? He points out that only 20 nations produce 80% of global carbon emissions. He calculates that action in only five policy areas—like electricity—would give us a fighting chance at the two degrees benchmark. His Energy Policy Simulator demonstrates what happens in response to various initiatives. Harvey says this is all, "get-going-Monday-morning."

Concentration of effort on getting carbon out of the air seems like a bottom line, but the state of our hearts and our souls may be the biggest problem. In an interview published Friday in The Atlantic, David Wallace-Wells repeats the mantra from his newest book, *The Uninhabitable Earth*. Climate catastrophe is coming fast. It will affect everybody and be much worse than we have been willing to admit. But Wallace-Wells also talks about the shock of history—that the ingrained human optimism for the future may be giving way to a trajectory of despair that causes both pain and paralysis. He names demonization—of oil companies, specifically—as the worst manifestation, and do-it-yourself solutions as the most misguided. Wallace-Wells believes in narrative—especially the new one we must have. Story is the most powerful influence on human behavior and therefore on human potential. It must play a key role in how we get there.

Change the story; change the world. Start soon—time is pressing us.

Amen. Blessed Be. Shalom. Salaam.

Standing on the Rock

31 Mar 2019

It was a shock to realize that Dr. Martin Luther King, Jr. would have been 90 years old this past January 15. This week—April 4—will be the 51st anniversary of his murder. I remember the day. I remember how I heard the news.

Some of you do also, I am sure, but the vast majority of Americans have no memory at all of Dr. King as a living man. It was all very long ago.

This may not be a bad thing. To become a postage stamp, a holiday, a street name, a monument, an exemplar and an inspiration, is to leave behind the inevitable imperfections of being an actual person. This is bad for history but good for us. Icons are, by definition, flexible. They come from where they were to meet us where we are, where we have need for them in this moment. Joe DiMaggio came to meet both Mr. Coffee and Mrs. Robinson. Dr. King is closer to the stubbornly relevant Washington and Lincoln. Like them, he asks us, as Americans—as individuals and as a people—who are you? The question cannot be dodged. The answer can never be an easy assumption.

On the wall just to the left of the pulpit at the Unitarian Society of Germantown, PA, where I was student minister for two years, is a brass plaque commemorating Dr. King's sermon there in 1963, the year he wrote "Letter from Birmingham City Jail."

Dr. King is a hero obviously, but in what way? Not long ago *in what way*, but now?

"Injustice anywhere is a threat to justice everywhere." We enshrine this phrase in the second of our Seven Principles, and call upon it also in the Fifth and Sixth (see page iii). Our exact words are a congregational covenant to "affirm and promote … justice, equity and compassion in human relations." Most Unitarian Universalists would declare this to be a central belief. It is deeply and honorably idealistic and inspiring, and it is our living truth in this world. It lives, of course, only if we have the courage to insist on it.

In the Letter, Dr. King followed his assertion of the coordinates of justice with these words: "We are caught in an inescapable network of mutuality, tied in a single garment of destiny." This was not happenstance. You will recognize our Seventh Principle: "Respect for the interdependent web of all existence of which we are a part." I like Dr. King's more poetic language, but even our words are something greater than a noble ideal. They are a radical expansion. They are a statement of the authentic nature of the cosmic order. They express knowledge of the ultimate reality—of the way things really are. They are a statement not of belief, but of faith. "Justice" is a rock on which we stand. It is what we are challenged to do or to make. A "single garment of destiny" is a rock in which we take shelter. It is where we find refuge against the storms that blow against us, where we touch the transcendent—the place beyond any human artifice or action at all.

What did Dr. King find at that great portal? Here is his testimony:

> *I am convinced of the reality of a personal God. It is a living reality that has been vindicated in the experiences of everyday life. God is a living God, with feeling, will; responsive to the deepest yearnings of the human heart…able to make a way out of no way, and transform dark yesterdays into bright tomorrows. This is our hope for becoming better human beings. This is our mandate for seeking to make a better world.*

Those words appear in Dr. King's most widely read book, *Strength to Love*.

They present us with a conundrum. A man we revere as a saint in our time turns out to be, well—*saintly*. He experiences a deep and very personal connection with the Divine. His God doesn't just intervene in human affairs—but "breaks into" the human world. His God hears our needs, and carries us "across the Jordan"—away from suffering and into abundant life in a better world. Empowered by this certainty, Dr. King worked what any reasonable person would have to judge to be miracles.

Our days are troubled also, and likewise in need of miracles to sustain memory and hope. I suggest we be willing to accept that the mainspring of Dr. King's greatness was his deep Christian faith in God, without feeling at all that we must agree with him. Most of us probably do not agree with him, but it is not a debate. We do not need to give up any part of our conscience to Dr. King's personal God. We should still be filled with awe at what that God—by his own witness—enabled Dr. King to accomplish. That phrase, Strength to Love, summons us to the deepest well of courageous action.

How strong was Dr. King? How loving? Strong enough to lead a moral, political and social revolution against oppression so entrenched and powerful it seemed impervious. Strong enough to carry on despite being bombed out of his home not once but twice. He was strong enough to simply stop counting the death threats.

How loving? Loving enough to declare from the very start that the change to which he was utterly committed would happen not just in the lives of the oppressed, but also in the hearts of the oppressors. Loving enough to declare non-violence to be an absolute—and make it stick. Loving enough to endure all the suffering in the desert, from the vicious dogs to the FBI harassment to the backbiting from self-styled "militants." He was loving enough to declare— the very night before he was murdered—that he was and would be safe in the arms of his God.

Dr. King was strong and loving enough to declare a faith that is not intolerant or exclusionary, a faith that mobilizes without fanaticism for action in the world, a faith that connects all people of good will to the cosmic order without the strictures of sect or creed. Those words were visionary then. They are positively heroic now, when faith and faithfulness are being so twisted and abused in all those ways.

In the Birmingham letter Dr. King names with persistent practicality the "four steps" of a non-violent campaign—get the facts, negotiate, take action. But wait—the facts being explored, he says, are indicative of whether "injustice is alive." This is very significant. Even more so is the enumerated third step—before the "direct action" must come "self-purification." This is a thoroughly religious understanding.

Dr. King asked us first to see injustice as a living thing, not an abstract nor yet a thing from which we—as living things—can separate. He directs us to negotiation—to engage in community, most especially with the oppressors. And then he draws on the most ancient and pervasive ritual of the soul—the embrace of humility in body and mind, the purge of arrogance, condescension and pride. No ideals can be true without this step. No just demands can be made upon others without plumbing our own hearts.

Dr. King's heroism is a "soul-force"—what he emulated in Gandhi. He is heroic not because he believed in equal opportunity, but because he had an unshakeable faith in destiny. He was a martyr not because he was assassinated, but because he absolutely expected every day to be murdered. His covenant was an individual and social will-to-change that is moral in essence, compassionate in presence and righteous in activity.

We renew that covenant—justice and mercy intertwined in a way that compels action in the world. We renew it in our hearts and our souls, in our minds and our words, in our deeds and our examples. We too can be "co-workers with God," as he put it. However we may see God, we know that hope springs from our awareness of cosmic companionship. "The time is always right to do right," and to have the strength to love.

Amen. Blessed Be. Shalom. Salaam.

Why Does This Matter?

By Winter's Light

12 Feb 2017

"Tell all the truth but tell it slant" is a famous line from that famous American recluse, Emily Dickinson. Nobody is sure why she never married or even courted—as they would have called it then. Nobody knows why she stayed upstairs when guests came and, in her later years, seldom left her bedroom. A handful of poems, much altered, were published before she died at the age of 55 in 1886. No one knew there were 1800 more. Her "complete works" were published in 1955, but still more have been found.

"Slant," then—the truth Emily Dickinson discovered and wrote down in glittering fragments was very much on the slant. Eccentricity—even by the standards of spinster New England ladies—characterized her life. Her poetry was radical in form for its time and is still unconventional. She instructed her younger sister to burn the all the scraps of paper on which she jotted poems, so it is the slant of pure chance we enjoy her legacy.

Maybe there is a lesson for us, especially at this time and place.

The light of winter is still pale as the sun slowly rises from its lower course along the horizon. Many of us still leave home in the morning for work or school in the dark, and return in the same circumstance. The pitch of cold temperatures has just reached its steepest—the summer heat of earth and ocean is finally gone. It is cold and dark enough, and it is plenty stormy enough to drive us mostly indoors. It is dark there, too.

Like Ebenezer Scrooge we have been delivered by baleful mystery into a past of fragile jollity, a present of turbulent prosperity, a future of shocking dread—all, it seems to us as it did to him—unfolding in a single night. No wonder we scrabble after truth.

Scrooge famously awoke to a bright morning of second chances, of what we are all supposed to be saying and doing at the Christmas season—full focus goodwill and, in America at least, a tidal wave of shiny stuff. No such opportunity prevails this year. The long crash of winter following—of January and February and maybe even March—is not going to be relieved by pitchers and catchers heading to spring training, or even Daylight Savings Time and the crocus and snowdrops already coming. *It is dark there, too*—by which I mean the darkness is inside us, and it will not pass of its own accord.

It was Matthew Arnold, the Victorian poet, who famously cast the image of humanity faced with a "darkling plain, swept with confused alarms of struggle and flight, where ignorant armies clash by night." The poem is "Dover Beach." Norman Mailer used the image for "Armies of the Night," his

171

impressionistic account of the tumultuous march on the Pentagon in 1967. Oddly enough, Arnold's poem was written in two different parts, and the first one of them was—as often with Dickinson—written on the back of a sheet of paper containing notes about an entirely mundane matter.

Surely we must and will march and ready ourselves to march—hoping but no longer certain it can be done peacefully and effectively. It might help to reread "Dover Beach." That first part is a sparkling description of the natural wonders of the beach at night, and then an evocation in words of endless ebb and flow of the human condition in the passing ages of history. The long view, in other words. Arnold wrote it second, after he already had the closing section with the "darkling plain." His manuscript shows it is to connect to this emphatic declaration: "Ah, love, let us be true to one another!"

Arnold is believed to have written those lines on his honeymoon. His hope we might call the hope of winter's light. It is short and it is also slant. What we have to do is look more closely to see it, and the radically different way everything we see shows up when illuminated from something close to sidelight, instead of the glare of high noon and long hours of summer. We can escape compulsive anxiety in moments when we can take advantage—take refuge, which is certainly needed—in the slant of winter's light.

The trick is to look sideways into your heart. This may seem counter-intuitive. Scrooge certainly needed to get reconnected to humanity, but that was an extreme case exaggerated to make a cautionary lesson. Most of us are, most of the time, entangled in the opposite problem. We are too encumbered with the everyday, with matters demanding focus and purpose and even matters of relationship too roped up with expectations and who we think these people we may love are supposed to be—instead of who they are. Now we live in an age when what is not everyday comes at us continuously, irrationally and dangerously. We do need to stare it in the face and to act against it. Too much is at stake to do otherwise. But we must also take heart in the people around us. We must know and rely on, as always, their wisdom and courage.

Have you ever had a test for peripheral vision? You put your head inside a big white sphere and the doctor flashes lights all around it—a few in the center but most around the outer circle of your visual field. Then they tell you how many flashes you didn't pick up. The number goes up as you get older and your eyesight tunnels.

No physical barrier limits what we may see at the outer edge of our vision when looking into our hearts. What might we see, just out of the corner of the eye? What might we be feeling at the edge of the center spot? No—don't look right at it. Everyone knows that will often make it fuzz up or even vanish. Your best vision—your most accurate picture of the world actually comes on the outer edge, because that is the area least controlled by what your brain thinks it is supposed to be seeing. Take advantage of slant—reminded by the winter's light—and welcome what you know about how you are feeling and who you are, not when you are staring at yourself, but just when you are peeking around the edges. You may be quite surprised by the quantity of truth. Carl Jung constructed his whole idea of the Shadow around this proposal—that truth is often precisely as Dickinson stated, not something we can at first look straight at. Or, if you wish, catch up with one of Joseph Campbell's DVDs, popularizations of the same idea. Things are going on with humans—all humans—below our immediate consciousness. They matter hugely. They ground us. They comfort us and inspire us.

How much might you suddenly know about the people in your lives, from the most intimate relationships to the merest encounters, not by staring at them but by slowing down to let them show up in the periphery of your observation. Like physical eyesight, it works better because the brain is less dominant. What you are supposed to feel is less dictated and more truly observed. What hunch do you have, when you admit to having hunches about people? This is not some reality TV police drama. It is not designed to "out" people in any way, shape or form. It is designed to set you and them on a path a little more open to what is asking to happen—asking, not shouting. You remember the classic description of God as speaking in "a still, small voice." If God can be heard best that way, why not those you love? Who are they when you are not telling them—we all do it—who they are supposed to be? Who are we?

In the world itself, think winter's light. How many things rest just at the edge of our view, from a distant ship to a flitting bird to a stealthy fox to the reflected light on canyons and mountain and the distinctly different motion in the wind of every plant?

How lucky we are to be reminded for months on end—maybe now when we most need it—the bounty of existence is burgeoning all around us. How lucky we are to have the winter's light to remind us. All the truth remains there if we have faith to tell it slant.

Amen. Blessed Be. Shalom. Salaam.

Lighter Than Air

16 Apr 2017

"Invocation" is the name of May Sarton's poem, from which our Opening Words today were excerpted. Spring is entirely an "invocation," and Sarton's luscious language is especially wonderful for this time of year. "Dark earth," "pure air," "this light-possessed atmosphere." Whose soul would not respond to such an invitation?

Indeed, we all do. Except for the Winter Solstice—the shortest daylight of the year—at no other time in the annual cycle can we be as certain to feel so completely struck by the season, almost no matter what the current circumstances of our lives.

"For now the winter is past, the rain is over and gone/The flowers appear on the earth; the time of singing has come." These are the words of ageless amazement from the Bible's "Song of Solomon." If we are under heavy burdens, we feel lighter. If under ordinary burdens, we feel lifted. If free of life's constrictions, if young or simply young at heart, we are prone to almost dizzying flights—into passionate love, into gratitude, into a current of blessed satisfaction. We find ourselves, in exaltation or quiet content, being filled—for once, with having enough. We are here and so is the spring; it is good.

My younger brother was the famous flower-eater when we were small boys. My mother will still tell of coming out of the house to find him sitting delightedly among the iris and chrysanthemum along the fence, munching happily away. What I remember about her flowerbed is digging it up for small treasures of old glass or lost toy soldiers. I didn't eat the plants, but I'm not sure I did any less damage.

When we were just a bit older, the real seasonal priority was that atmosphere. "Light-possessed" it was, calling irresistibly—and we were dedicated kite-flyers.

In the late 1950s and early 1960s, that was a pretty simple endeavor. It meant spring had arrived when the kites appeared in the five-and-dime store, rolled up in a bin near the cash register, like kid-size furled umbrellas. They were two balsa-wood sticks, wrapped in the bright paper that would form the kite itself. We always tried to get a favorite color. String you had to buy separately, and we saved up to get as many rolls of the special lightweight stuff as possible.

Some assembly required of course, and there were a few painful lessons. Balsa-wood isn't very strong, and securely fastening the cross-piece without breaking something was not a given. Tearing the paper was even worse. Taping it back together was difficult and made the kite too heavy anyway. Begging for a replacement—or having the funds—was not always successful. After early lessons in aerodynamics, we focused on getting the right materials in the correct quantity to form a good tail—the secret to any successful kite.

We flew them from the street in front of my house. There were no trees, but there were some Charlie Brown moments. Without the proper launch, into the proper wind, with the proper tail—see above—the kite would beat itself to death on the pavement while you ran along trying to get lift-off. I remember kites fluttering down because the knot wasn't right, or flying away because somebody lost hold of the string or even—at least once or twice—let the end sail clear through the hand.

A washer tied on would help, but losing the end was commonly caused by hoped-for but not entirely accomplished success in a crucial maneuver. Coming to the end of your ball of string, you had to thread another ball onto the first. This was not easy, even with a brother or friend willing to help. Unfortunately, because of competition, fraternal grudge or petty politics, help was not always forthcoming when needed. In fact, it could be—and often was—strategically withheld. Hard cash, favorite possessions, or punches on the arm then became coin of the realm. IOUs were not generally accepted.

I also watched a few kites dishearteningly disintegrate in high winds, but what will powerfully resonate to the end of my days was the unalloyed excitement and wonder on the few occasions when a kite would simply soar higher and higher into the clear sky of early evening, the most favorable time. We would tie on two or three balls of string. We would exclaim at the vanishing speck of color. We would fantasize about tangling with one of the lumbering C-130s—prop-driven "Flying Boxcars"—that sometimes rumbled overhead in those days.

In the end we would almost always lose the kite, but the thrill has never gone. So maybe it is with life—in the spring and every season in its own way. Life's mechanism is simple but the procedures are complex. You break things. You tie a bad knot. You fumble the launch. You don't get enough help. The wind is contrary—or absent, or too strong. The string slips through your hands—as does, in the end, everything mortal.

And yet there come blessed moments lighter than air. May your spring be one.

Amen. Blessed Be. Shalom. Salaam.

God's Best Friends?

28 May 2017

An online article from The Atlantic invited me to revisit "The Trolley Problem," one of the most famous thought experiments in post-World War II philosophy.

Here is the problem in its classic form: A runaway streetcar careens toward five track workers who don't see or hear it. They will be struck and killed. On a branch line is a single-track worker who would be killed if the car goes that way. You are the trolley operator. What do you choose? Do you divert the runaway car to the branch, or not?

Most people throw the switch to cause one death rather than five. This may seem obviously "correct," but isn't it mysterious how the infinite value of one human life is less than the infinite value of five human lives? If you want to have real fun, imagine your spouse or child or best friend on that track alone. Now consider your answer again.

The Trolley Car Problem originally involved a runaway "tram." A philosopher named Philippa Foot invented it in 1967, in Oxford, England. Foot, who died on her 90th birthday in 2010, was teasing out the difference between causing harm and allowing it to happen. She was actually addressing the permissibility of abortion. A philosopher at MIT named Judith Thomson developed the trolley terminology and also the special challenge of losing somebody you love as collateral damage in the dilemma.

Foot, who was a granddaughter of President Grover Cleveland, became a very influential ethicist—a specialist in that branch of philosophy called ethics. Put simply, ethics is about what is "right." How do we know that? What does it mean?

Foot shaped modern ethics as a reasoning process. It is not necessarily rational. In fact, ethics often teases out why human beings from very different cultures seem instinctively to agree on the right action under defined circumstances. Our emotional response is universal when our loved one is on that trolley track. Ethics is linked to but not the same as morality. Morality is a culturally determined construct of good or bad action. Is it good or bad, for instance, to marry your sister? That's morality at work.

We have ethical aversion to the taking of human life—the Sixth Commandment is strikingly blunt. It is morality—our social or cultural norm— that defines when "killing" can be accepted. What are the moral exceptions to the rule? What are the degrees of culpability in taking a life? Is it self-defense, or manslaughter, or homicide?

Why Does This Matter?

Without the challenge of ethical problems, we have little chance at understanding the authentic complexity of right or wrong. We must also need morality, because every human society chooses what is good or bad about what we are considering doing—or have already done. With morality we enter the realm of how we feel about our choices—happy or sad? Have we broken the rules or not? We are judged—and shunned or sustained—accordingly. There are social consequences. Without ethics, morality can seduce us to ignorance of human beings and humanity, to a narrow and blinkered self-righteousness. Without morality, ethics is possible, but it fails vital human questions: What should I do? How should I feel? How does this work in my everyday life?

Philippa Foot, incidentally, is most famous for "virtue ethics," her consistent assertion that ethics must be useful in the real-world search for what is good and right.

And here I remind you Kermit the Frog was correct. It is not easy being green. As UUs, we are prone to saying—usually around pledge time—that "a free church is not free." But money isn't the half of it. Our "free and responsible search for truth and meaning" means we must consistently engage with ethical dilemmas. We can't solve them, but we absolutely can't ignore them. Our truth is plain: It is complicated.

And it matters where you stand, and when. UUs do not just accept the varieties of moral system—we embrace them. How other people see things is not fundamentally right or wrong, it is just how they see things. That applies to other cultures, other histories, and the person sitting next to you. Our morality must be diverse and dynamic. It can't come from tablets or scrolls or people in robes or tinfoil hats. It comes from us.

This is what I refer to as being "God's best friends." No particular belief in the divine is necessary to see this is a heavy responsibility we take on, to live both ethically and morally. It is to partner in the unfolding of all of it—whether to some divine plan or not. It is to seek to be good and do right without a map—or, to put it more properly, with many maps. Not, as has been said, many paths up one mountain, but many paths up many mountains. I am never more proud and glad to be a UU than when any of us, by design or happenstance, accepts both the opportunity and the responsibility we are offered every day in this special faith. It is a very important way to be in the world.

I do believe something else is needed also, something just as essential as ethics and morality. If we rely on them alone, something crucially helpful will still be missing, something filling a need embedded deep inside us and in all human communities.

Let me return to the Trolley Problem. Suppose you really are the operator of that runaway trolley, and your only choice is, how many people will it kill? A cynic might say this is paradigm for human existence. Down one path is bad. Down another path is worse—and there are only two paths. "Life is hard and then you die," the bumper sticker says. Cynical that might be, but it is also a truth unchangeable and inescapable.

On the other hand, what would it be worth to be at the controls of that trolley and absolutely sure you have done nothing wrong? You didn't, for instance, forget to check the brakes. You didn't even ask to be on board—and you are not one bit responsible for the universe and existence being what they are. You didn't put the track or the track workers there. You—you in your sole human capacity, with your mortal strength and heart and mind—are only asked to do the best you can under these circumstances.

You are on board the trolley car, in other words, but Original Sin is not. You are not guilty of the wickedness of the world, for the evil and despair you did not make.

Moreover, your best means something. If it is a choice between bad and worse, you can choose. We make such choices every day. We choose not to do harm, not to lie or cheat or steal. We choose not to speak falsely or harden our hearts against others, or live without gratitude for what we are given and what we have. We choose to love and we choose to prevail in the days we are given, by what means are accessible to us.

We do not have to be alone. We can choose to exercise the religious sensibility intrinsic to human beings. However we feel it, name it, or echo it, something at times speaks to us beyond our imagining. Our experience and our will have the capacity of limitless wonder, of connection to purposes and capacities far beyond our short time and limited horizon. How or why none of us truly comprehends, but something there is that cares about us—about you and me. When you are hurt and begin to mend, when you are ill and begin to recover, when you are despairing and begin to hope, when you are glad and caring and creating, something beyond the ethical frame of right and wrong, something beyond the moral instruction and judgment of good or bad—something feels what you feel. We need that, and all those around us need it as well.

What could be more important than to care enough to live this way, in our own lives and in the world? Caring is what joins us to the Divine—nothing else will do. Who are God's best friends? God's best friends are you and me.

Amen. Blessed Be. Shalom. Salaam.

Praying Toward Home

05 Nov 2017

The fall garden has come to pass. In November it is fully accomplished and reclining to rest. The peak garden of high summer has been and gone—some years rapidly and some years less so. It followed the spring garden, blossoming in release and potential. In a month or so will be the winter garden, spare in form but ticking over with resilient life. These are endless cycles we know—of the natural world and of our lives. But if a garden has in any way a beginning, it is there in the dead of winter. There—in our climate, at least—in the snow piled everywhere. There in the cold; there in the deepest dark. Call it rest and ski season alike—these are proper words inviting actions. They beckon fuller participation in the richness of existence.

Still, every gardener holds a prayer: Help me believe the garden will come.

Every garden itself expresses the process of prayer. A garden invites us to live now and in a better future. In the planning and planting we must plumb possibilities and steer a course. We get down on our knees, dig in the earth and enter that flow of the seasons—both partner and participant in the vast energy of all life. We must tend what comes, nourishing and protecting. A gardener is invited—indeed, required—to accept results may not be as wished for or even wanted. Good, bad or indifferent, no outcome is a given. No outcome rests on us alone—for which we should be properly grateful.

This is the larger context in which all prayer should reside. Answers do come: "The answer to a prayer," we may still find ourselves saying. We hit the black ice and don't skid off the road. Yes, that was a split-second prayer—no actual words necessary. The new baby is here—a prayer certainly answered, and celebrated in every culture.

What are your prayers these days? Are you praying to get something? You probably are, even if reluctant to admit it. Are you praying about something? You probably are, even if reluctant to admit it. Admitting that is easier: Praying about seems less like a Christmas list than does praying to get something. I encourage you to disregard this distinction—it is wholly artificial. Entering into prayer through the portal of gratitude is in no way a lesser path, with this sole condition—you at least ask to be grateful. You may not feel it, but that moment of humility is the transformation.

Here is the easiest way to see that: Pray for or about a person. It doesn't matter whom. It could be an individual or a group or the whole human race—past, present or future. It could be a face in the crowd, a face in your heart or in your dreams. It could be a face at home or work or at First Parish. It could be anyone you know well or no one you know at all, or anybody in between. It could be someone you like or someone you can't one bit get along with. The latter is the most challenging. It may also be the most useful of all the intentions and purposes of prayer. I respectfully invite you to consider: Every religion teaches this at its heart. The legitimate claim of any religious figure rests ultimately on the ability to enlist us to this truth. The merest instant of truly prayerful consideration of someone we find deeply difficult changes our whole relationship with that person. However minutely, it changes who he or she is for us, because it changes us. When we change, even in a small way, a distinct ripple spreads across the cosmos.

Does this sound like some kind of very un-Unitarian Universalist mumbo jumbo? If so, please chalk it up to my inadequate explanation. It is not a misfire of truth. We are the people who anchor the first of our Seven Principles in the worth and dignity of every person, and the last in the interdependent web of all existence of which we are a part (see page iii). These are points on a compass; they are connected to each other in an endless circle and cycle of going and coming, of setting out and returning, of honoring the tide at ebb and flow, the seasons, each life and all that lives. This is our understanding of wholeness, as best we can express it. They are the alpha and the omega in good old Biblical language. We should not hesitate to claim the concept as also our own.

We have many rational humanists in our denomination. You may recall my story of encountering congregational life and UU faith in a church founded by—literally—rocket scientists. They were from the General Electric Space Center in Valley Forge, PA. Our minister was an atheist—and didn't hesitate to say so. On the surface, a less prayerful place you could hardly imagine. Underneath, all those very smart people were still people—still flesh and blood creatures making an erratic and uncertain journey. As a denomination UUs for some decades indulged a smug superiority—only stupid people would practice religion. "Faith" was for fools. That isn't wrong, but it is a mistake.

My rationalist compatriots deserve credit. They were precisely smart enough to comprehend and admit how much human beings do not understand. They were willing—that atheist minister often played a shrewd role—to embrace in their own way the vast universe human beings will never understand. They got right that very important part.

"Now I lay me down to sleep; I pray the Lord my soul to keep. If I die before I wake; I pray the Lord my soul to take." These words may be familiar. The text is from the *New England Primer* of 300 years ago. The Lord's Prayer goes back 2000 years, though in the company of believers you will still be asked, "debts" or "trespasses"?

But the praying is from my childhood, when my brothers and I knelt down every night before bed. We alternated the two prayers day-by-day, like clockwork. My mother generally joined in with us. My father would sit by occasionally. He never prayed and seldom spoke. One time he berated me cruelly for whispering a joke to my mother in his presence and stubbornly insisting it was not for him to hear.

You can tell this memory is complicated. God the demanding, powerful and sometimes scary—that was my father. God the loving, attentive and comforting—that was my mother. Proud of remembering all the words, giddy with the adventure and solemn with the responsibility—that was who I thought I was in particular. All three boys were of course the company of sinners, though we seldom confessed to anything.

I bet your religious memories are complicated, too. If you say not, I will believe you, but ask you to keep the thought under consideration. Complicated memories are the ones that have the deepest hold on us, precisely because they have so much nuance, so much texture, so much amazingly vivid color and scent and sound. They are indelible but never entirely clear to us. Neuroscientists say they are the most emotionally fraught—my respect for my father all tangled up with my fear of him. That glare of intense feeling is why we see so clearly, like the pop of a flashbulb however long ago.

In a Unitarian Universalist context, I suggest the virtue of prayer is a particular kind of reconciliation. "Faith is for fools," I said, is not wrong. Rationalism cannot be wrong, if honestly believed—not in our faith. Whoops, a slight paradox there. It may seem our faith holds faith to be worthless. That would be what I declared a mistake. To believe what you believe is right; it is wrong to disbelieve what somebody else believes.

Your journey may be this one: Religion is complicated, compromised—even contaminated. You leave it, or it leaves you. It is like that for some time and then it is not. You do not know anymore, but you do ask. Whatever you call that, however you do it, whatever in the end you think it is really about—in the very big picture, like "cosmic" and "eternal"—it is praying toward home. You are heading that direction. We all are.

Amen. Blessed Be. Shalom. Salaam.

Faith and Its Discontents

03 Dec 2017

Our worship this morning has included singing, as it almost always does. You probably didn't notice anything unusual about hymn #6, "Just as Long as I Have Breath." There is really no reason you should, so I won't even ask a rhetorical question. It is a good song for congregational singing and we do sing it several times a year. It has a simple 4/4 rhythm—always a virtue in a UU church (and many others). It has a straightforward melody, although based on a German organ piece more than 300 years old. The words are—as UUs also notoriously prefer—both simple and straightforward enough to read ahead as we are singing to make sure we are okay with them.

Ah—the words: There is "breath," "vision," and "heart." In the end, there is moving affirmation: Despite "pain," "dark," and "disappointment," we are able to "say yes" to "life," to "truth," to "love." They are good words; they are good beliefs; they affirm what all of us probably agree would be a good life. What do those words mean?

A few years ago, the New York Times had a front-page story about the Holocaust. After several years of combing through archives, a study group counted all the ghettos the Nazis created, and all the "work camps"—the places where Jews and others were beaten, starved, mutilated and killed. The researchers counted over 42,500 such places in Germany and occupied Europe—some ten times the number previously accepted. No one could have gone far without literally running into a "Jew house" or slave labor gang.

Ah—those wonderful words. What do they mean? Evil is pervasive in human history. Evil happens every day right in front of us. Looking away or refusing to see cannot hide this. After two turbulent and troubled years, including self-proclaimed Nazis right in our faces, we may hope all this is really somebody else. It must be somebody we can't explain or understand and hope never to encounter. It must be a tribe afflicted with unreasoning grievance, stuck in some malevolent unreality.

I will tell you that a large wooden signboard hung in the attic of my Saco church. It had hung outside for many years to proclaim the church's identity to the world. It declared—as Unitarians so enthusiastically did—absolute belief in "the progress of mankind—onward and upward forever." The words were beautifully gilded nonsense. James Freeman Clarke invented them in the Victorian era, which you can tell.

But this is "faith"—a firm belief in something that does not exist. The words in "Just as Long as I Have Breath" are also a statement of faith. So is every one of our Seven Principles (see page iii). Start with the "inherent worth and dignity" of all human beings, to grasp the essential. Our long-ago signboard also proclaims—as many Unitarian churches did—our fidelity to the moral teachings of Jesus and the "brotherhood of man." We have mostly banished this sexist language. We mostly banished Jesus and God. In recent years a perhaps more sensible balance has returned us to what has been called for centuries "broad church." But don't underestimate the serious and aggressive intention with which this purge was carried out, and the continuing legacy of UU antagonism to what we have lately taken to calling, "the language of religion."

"Just as Long as I Have Breath" has no sexist language. It also has no words of any religious association (unless you count "breath," and maybe we should). It scarcely nods in the direction of any community larger than the individual striving for self-actualization, with a climactic vision of "they" saying we did well. Is it Final Judgment?

It's probably not. Let me be clear: There is nothing wrong with believing in life and truth and love. There cannot be any good case for belief in Jesus or God or Ganesh if you do not. To sing in community is to worship in community; to worship in community is to live in community. We really don't need to obsess about words or rituals. Our religion is strong and faithful to human experience and human aspiration. Our core conviction is that words and rituals have power but none has ultimate power, and none has legitimacy through coercion. To live in community is to be both enough and more than we can ever completely fulfill, which is how aspirations should be. Maybe someday UUs will have this affirmation: Our religion feeds hungers of the human heart that cannot now and never will be adequately fed with words. Won't that be an amazement? It will be a miracle when it comes—the best kind: spontaneous.

While awaiting the day, my point is this: We are people of faith. We cannot be otherwise. We do indeed believe in things that cannot possibly exist. No amount of cleansing of any word or any ritual—no housecleaning of orthodox or even mainstream Christian expression or even theology can break the commitment essential to our world. We too live in willing suspension of disbelief, in a sturdily constructed reality that is not. The argument for faith is not just that we indeed want and need it. There is also the pragmatic: It is the way the world works; the way humans are wired. It too is pervasive.

So, then we too must engage the discontents of faith. They are our discontents. Again, if you can't accept the argument from cosmic nature or the argument from human socialization, you may just as fruitfully grasp the argument from experience. To deny we struggle with a crisis of faith is to risk denying there is any struggle at all—paging Mary Poppins. It is to muddle along at least a few times a day wondering what the hell is this struggle we are almost certainly feeling at least some of the time. You know: What am I doing, why am I here, why is the car not starting, why do I not feel bathed in love every moment of every day? Could it be cancer?

I remind you of the wisdom of Rumi: "In times of sudden danger most people call out, 'Oh my God!' Why would they keep doing this if it didn't help?"

What about the Holocaust then? Was that us? More important, is that us? Is it what we too might aid and abet if the same malignant set of circumstances ensnared us?

Was that bad people? Was it evil—as in, the Devil? Or was it normal people—ordinary experience and expectation, hope and fear somehow plunging into an abyss of unspeakably bad behavior? Almost unspeakable, that is. Is it what we are or what we do? That is a question central to the nature of faith—the answer is always yes.

And nearer to our ordinary lives: I spent a summer as chaplain intern in a very large city hospital. I worked the trauma bays and the Neurological Intensive Care Unit. I watched people die. They died by accident; they died by sudden illness like stroke, but mostly by some long wasting into a shrouded goodbye. They died by knife and gunshot wounds. I held hands and prayed and kept silent and even talked—yes, words—with their families and friends, and sometimes with the dying themselves. I never saw any lack of faith. Disasters breed despair but they did not cause us to erupt in disbelief. Often faith was explicit. Other times it rested, present and ready, sturdy under strain.

I strongly suspect most of us would find the same. Life as utter futility, complete randomness, endless effects with no cause whatsoever?—not a place people will ever willingly go. Philosophers and scientists say we should, but no one volunteers and few of us agree to be recruited either. What I encounter every day in my life—you are likely no different—is the small stuff. Where is my faith today? What is my faith in this moment? What of my ordinary and hopelessly normal life—even in its most quixotic—is faithful living? That discontent is the one we must all overcome. It helps to admit it.

Amen. Blessed Be. Shalom. Salaam.

How Do You Love?

10 Dec 2017

Maybe you did "walk 47 miles of barbwire" to get here. You have my sympathy. If you "wear a cobra snake for a necktie" or "live in a house by the side of the road, made out of rattlesnake hide," please refrain from snacking on any of our members or friends.

Maybe you instead recognize these exotic images from the 1950s rock 'n' roll classic, "Who Do You Love?" You might be able to see the late Bo Diddley in cowboy finery, wearing thick black glasses and holding his famous rectangular guitar. I hope you hear the eponymous "Bo Diddley beat"—"bomp-diddy-bomp-bomp, bomp-bomp."

Scientists, with considerably less danceability, advise us we are really only a mobile set of genes looking to perpetuate themselves. "Who do you love" would seem to be the central question of human existence. While no individual outcome is certain, as a species we do find mates and create offspring—under whatever illusions about "why."

But wait, even the white coats now acknowledge a second question is at least as critical: "How do you love?" If we fail to nurture offspring, they are significantly less likely to survive. The genes lose and so do you. Bond with others, in a family, a tribe, a community, and offspring are much more likely to successfully nurture their own offspring—and we are all winners. The turning point in human history is simple: A predator grabs for a baby by the fire but everybody chases it off, not just the mother.

How do we love? After the romance or independent of romance entirely, we love, as we must, by sustaining relationships. It is easy to say and hard to do. Like a dog that finally catches a car, after the thrill of the chase we wonder what to do with the prize.

Valentine's Day is our pop cultural answer. There are lots of pop psychology answers, from "pick up your socks" to "never go to sleep angry." Herewith what might fill a deeper hunger, a more profound need, but one just as practical if viewed correctly. It is advice from four religious traditions—from Islam, from monastic and from poetic Christianity and from a saint of the Catholic Church. You might say this is, as in good Unitarian Universalist theology, only four of many answers to the important questions—"what is worship?" and "what is sacred?" They are a little more serious than Hallmark.

All four, by no coincidence, are rooted in mysticism—that is, direct encounter with the Divine. Each perceives the Holy as immediately present and accessible to us.

Other parts of all religions are about sin and salvation, the Creation and eternity, the place and purpose of humanity and indeed all existence. Mystics are about relationship.

Two voices you have already heard: Hafiz, the author of our Opening Words today, speaks from the Sufi tradition of Islam. Few terms could be more intimate in address than "Beloved" and "Presence"—each word capitalized. The Beloved is to be known; the Presence is to be felt. The Beloved Presence is to be beautiful and gladdening, to bring greatness to every heart and be "the breathing of the world."

The hymn we sang has verses from George Herbert, dating to England's Puritan era of the 1630s. Herbert was a courtier turned West Country parson and sacred poet. He was not "puritan" in the aggressive and even destructive stringency of religious and civil strictures on behavior and belief. His faith was Pietism—focused on the purity of his own relationship with Divinity. His sentences are famously stripped to their essence, every word economical as he advised believing and living to be. Every word is intricate with meaning, and with intimacy, immediacy and imagery. What is transcendent is just that, but also and essentially right here, right now, close as—that word—"breathing."

We will sing words of Hildegard of Bingen, abbess of a large monastery almost a thousand years ago. She famously held her own, wily and skillful in a violent and misogynist world—no sheltered saint at all. Still, her heritage is not of worldly success but of amazing visions, set down in what she heard and prayed. Her Divinity is directly connected to us, both parties glowing— "blazing sun" and "blessed verdancy," she said.

We will hear words of Kabir to close, an Indian Holy Man from almost as far back as Hildegard. His images are cosmic—literally. One after another, the elements of all creation are contained within—of all things—a simple domestic artifact, marking the first material evidence of human society. Listen to what else Kabir declares to be within.

All three of these voices are well within the mainstream tradition of Unitarian Universalism. Some teeth will rattle at the word "God," but still we know UUs are famously Pietist—even a little Puritan in our insistence on altering society. UUs are famously cosmological—those million self-declared UUs are mostly not in our churches because they actually worship the Grand Canyon and Waldo Emerson a bit more self-referentially than we do. We know UUs have long been attracted to the exotic, although we are more sensitive to what we now admit is often cultural appropriation. Didn't Rumi write romantic poems? No, he did not, except to God—whom he deeply loved.

Both hymns and both readings are in our hymnal, but you won't find anything by St. Ignatius of Loyola. Maybe we should broaden our thinking. Spiritual Exercises, which Ignatius wrote some 500 years ago, is a masterpiece of Christian mysticism. Ignatius become "warrior of the Pope," but his discipline of meditative prayer flows far beyond the boundaries of his ardent orthodoxy. Practice—how to actually do religion—is notoriously elusive in Unitarian Universalism. How to do relationship with what is transcendent and also those immediately around us, is the great hunger gnawing at contemporary life. Relationship—how do you love?—is a ritual, a planned behavior. It is not best defined, or even properly defined, as spontaneous human will or preference.

Ignatius advised more than prayer. In fact, what is called the "examen of consciousness" he considered sustaining beyond prayer, because it is focused on relationship, not petition or penitence. It is for a vital link with God, but also with one's self and with others. Here is an abbreviated version for your private, quiet moments:

Speak first of what gift you are receiving—everything is a gift. Say thank you.

Speak then of how you are being revealed to yourself as time passes. Ask for help with the obstacles. There are always obstacles, mostly of our own making. Admit it.

Speak of the Presence in today—what has happened, what has been felt, what call has been heard, what response has been given. It is not a contest. It is just your life.

Ask forgiveness. Know you are loved. Ask for healing: Of what event of this day would you especially like to be healed?

Trust and affirm. These are verbs. Trust there is powerful loving flowing through and around you. Affirm it also flows from you—claim the gift you wish for and believe it is available to you. You do not have to know how, only why, and the why is…because.

Who do you love, in this or any other way? It could be God called by any name. It could be an intimate partner. It could be a family member or friend or the entire human community. It can certainly be the Grand Canyon.

Whoever you are addressing, this is worship. This is sacred, because it boils down to phrases: "Thank you… Help me… I love you… I'm sorry… Be with me." This is what we say to any person we truly love, such that love may truly flourish the only way it can—in the nourishment of relationship. In only a few minutes—alone or together—we can throw down the barriers in the heart. We can feel them falling in the world.

Amen. Blessed Be. Shalom. Salaam.

Heaven or Whatever

04 Mar 2018

The best-selling author Bill Bryson, in *A Short History of Nearly Everything*, has a charming little digression about our immediate human relationship to atoms. Atoms are of course very small—half a million could "hide behind a human hair," Bryson notes. They make up everything that is. Atoms are virtually indestructible. Each one may exist 1035 years—an unimaginably long time.

Here is the fun part: Every atom present this morning as part of a human being has been someplace else before—lots of someplace else. Each one of us almost certainly has atoms from several stars and millions of organisms—along with a billion or so from every historic personage you could name. As Bryson notes, this does not include Elvis Presley—he's too recent—but you don't have to go back far before the recycling kicks in.

Atoms live forever, but none of them is exactly alive. We live for a century at most, but are utterly alive that entire span. Is this a good tradeoff—life for eternity? That quandary has challenged humans from before we even had a campfire to warm us.

When we die, our atoms go on to other careers. Where do "we" go?

I apologize for introducing two head-splitting questions on a day in early spring, but there is a fascinating recent wrinkle in what Americans say about that second one. Most Americans, as I'm sure you are aware, think we go someplace rather loosely defined as heaven. Some laxity in the definition of heaven aids and abets the very human willingness to anticipate heaven for oneself at a significantly higher rate than for others outside members of your immediate family. This connects to George Carlin's joke: People who drive faster than you are crazy and those who drive slower are clowns.

Not anymore. Heaven, I mean, not driving. The Pew Forum on Religion and Public Life looked into this not long ago and found 70% of Americans think other people's religions could indeed result in eternal life. There was a predictable squawk from the predictable squawkers—people, they claimed, must not have understood the question. So Pew asked again, and found 65% saying yes, they meant what they said.

Pew also asked, which religions? The answer was—in essence—all of them. More than half the respondents thought Catholics, Jews, Protestants, Muslims and Hindus will all go to heaven. More than half the respondents even agreed "people with no religious faith" would get eternal life. Almost half— very close to half—said atheists would go to heaven. I wonder, will the atheists turn this down? You may remember I said UUs couldn't go to heaven if we don't believe in it. Apparently, I was misinformed.

Among the major groups—white evangelicals, white "mainline" Protestants, black Protestants, and white Catholics—even the white evangelicals agreed Catholics and Jews would get there, and half of Catholics plan to share a cloud with the atheists.

It was Groucho Marx who famously quipped he wouldn't care to belong to any club that would have someone like him as a member. Maybe eternal life has become a lot more like "whatever" than heaven—at least for Americans. My theology professor used to say the overwhelming majority of churchgoers are Pelagian, although few have ever heard the term. They recite traditional creeds and affirm historic confessions, but what they actually believe is that we are saved by being good people and doing our best.

Apparently, the Pew survey found almost as many self-identified Christians who agreed with this plan as declared a belief in Jesus to be necessary. It comes as no surprise that when asked about the authority of the Bible, 39% of Christians called it the literal word of God. Yet some 18% declared it written by men and not God's word at all.

What could be troubling about this evolution? It affirms the long-term pluralistic arc of American life. It's ugly out there right now, but still we are more used to getting along with people who are not like us, even if we don't visit in their homes very often, even if we discover shocking segregation from real differences of opinion or circumstance. Despite the current tide of bluster from you-know-who, the long movement of our history continues—as it has since the Gilded Age in the 1890s—away from sectarianism and outright bigotry and toward tolerance and even institutionalized celebration of cultural diversity. Everybody is Irish on St. Patrick's Day. Cinco de Mayo, Kwanzaa, Rosh Hashanah and even Eid al Adha now appear on mass-market calendars.

These are good things without question, if we maintain a proper humility. But even without the stain of excessive self-congratulation, there is a troubling complacency not far below the surface. In long-standing middle-class tradition, we expect to be rewarded for our efforts to be good. But, as we are lately being reminded, ordinary goodness without moral rigor cannot withstand perceived threats to our physical safety.

It is also a long-standing American tradition to disassociate ourselves from the rest of humanity—all those not-so-special people in "foreign" countries. We have little real grasp of their dismal poverty. One billion Chinese peasants can now hope to buy a bicycle or a radio, but most Americans are sure they stole our jobs. Forty percent of the world's people have not a pot to piss in— as my father would say—let alone indoor plumbing, but we now careen into bitter invective about who gets to flush where.

In long-standing liberal tradition, we assume immediately the perfection of these poor circumstances is something human beings are going to provide.

The solution must be more education, or government agency, or the Bill and Melinda Gates Foundation. More people must become reasonable and responsible and enlightened—like us.

Unfortunately, these concepts are often diluted to the point where they are so vague, they have no real meaning at all. This is not a mote I detect in your eye without acknowledging the log in my own. I'm as sure as anybody I'll be rewarded for trying to be good, America is a special place and society can and even will do better for all people. Like you, I want these beneficent assumptions to be true, but they rely too much on us.

We should not be fooled. I am no advocate of eternal agony for human failings. The Universalists had it right, I believe. No human—by definition imperfect, often appallingly so—can be capable of evil so vast as to be scalded for all time. But 2009 was the 500th birthday of John Calvin, who made a compelling case that we are just so condemned. The Unitarians said no, but they argued with vigor, not casual dismissal.

And the Universalists did not believe there was no punishment—only that it did not go on forever. In fact, they came—under the stern rod of Father Hosea Ballou—to agree the punishment for our human failings is meted out in our human lifetime. Our agonies of loss, misfortune and fear are our inevitable blows from the lash of mortal fate.

For myself, I am no fan of floating around forever strumming a harp. That's not a heaven I can believe in. Look to the Universalists again: Eternal salvation is certain because it is the nature of God to forgive us. It isn't something we do—not even at our most determined, selfless and inspired. God—the energy of the divine at the heart of all—wants to be present to us in the here and now, and reconciled with us in the great beyond. That reconciliation is not just for humans. It is for all creatures and indeed the entire shebang. Everything will return to divinity, as to its whole and essential nature.

You don't have to agree with me. None of us has to agree with anybody else. But it is crucial in so many ways that we not allow the alternative answer to be "whatever."

Amen. Blessed Be. Shalom. Salaam.

So What?

01 Apr 2018

Most Easter egg hunts of my childhood were conducted indoors. We did not live in some gangland neighborhood, so I suppose this was mostly because the Easter Bunny wasn't keen on prowling about the yard with a flashlight at 1:00 in the morning. My memories are of locating bright eggs and chocolates stashed under the sofa and behind the drapes. Three boys pounding through the house certainly meant some wear and tear on the furniture and my parents' nerves. I know there were sometimes tears and sharp words, but the vivid recall is of happiness and specific moments of intense joy. It was a reliably glad day in a family not oversupplied with them.

How memory does serve us and save us. I want to remember the happiness of Easter, and so I do. As a parent, I tried to recreate it for our children, although Sally did most of the work. I was delegated to hide the eggs, which renewed the special part that was fun for me. I also got—and still do—my own Easter basket. The big kid still lives at our house, and I hope always will.

We did most of our Easters—more than a decade's worth—in Florida with my parents. There was always "inside Easter," but the new wrinkle was two editions of "outside Easter." The condo association where we stayed on the beach held their hunt on Saturday. The homeowner association where my Mom and Dad lived took the traditional Sunday slot and we'd drive over for it as the first part of the full day's visit.

Now let me advise you hunting for Easter eggs in Florida requires some special ground rules. First, stay away from the pond. When they say "water hazard" in those golf communities, they aren't kidding. There are alligators in those ponds—and you have to watch out even for drainage ditches. Most of the time, spotting the gator was part of the fun, but they do appear unexpectedly and they strike quicker than a snake.

Actually, the far deadlier hazard is the fire ants. If you've never encountered them, I hope you stay lucky. Fire ants love nesting under all those "brick" paths and driveways so helpfully and tastefully provided by developers. They nest everywhere else in the loose, sandy soil. Fire ants, as you may know, have an absolutely spooky ability to sense your presence. You don't have to touch the nest or even step very close to it. They will be up your leg or arm in seconds. Well, we were always lucky on both counts.

We were lucky also the kids were young enough to enjoy the egg hunting but mature enough to know it was not life or death. They were energetic but not pushy and they always ended up with a more than adequate reward. Kate in fact won the age group prize several times at one or the other event. That kid had some nose for Easter eggs.

Then we'd pile into the car and go with Grandmom back to the house, where Granddad would be getting ready to cook Easter dinner. My mother to this day believes I have a special fondness for leg of lamb. I do not—but I never say so. It's a ritual, you see. The lamb and the peas and the small broiled potatoes and the mint jelly and my father's favorite ice cream—it's something the family did for years and years. I would never be so dumb as to express anything but gratitude for her effort—and his—in preparing and serving Easter dinner. Their parents did it before them; but we will not.

"So what?" is the question of the season. There are big answers. For Christians the answer is cosmic in scope. Tony Campolo tells a story of preaching a vigorous Easter sermon to polite applause in a large black church. He was followed by an elder whose entire sermon was this: "Friday is here...BUT SUNDAY IS COMING!" The church erupted immediately in shouting, singing and dancing in the aisles. Sunday is for sure.

For Jews, the answer is cosmic but intimate as the family circle. "Why on this day?" is the youngest child's question at the ritual meal. The answer is about long ago—because God freed us from bondage in Egypt—and also about here and now—from all our oppressions, God's power frees us right now. Pagans too, understand both the long rhythm of the earth and its seasons, and the power that flows from another world into this one. All of us can see that power, and all of us can celebrate it, as we will.

I am a member of a very human family across several generations. You are as well. Some are here or nearby; some are far away or gone away lately or long ago. Some are yet to come. When I think about the question, "so what?" I think about my family and me. The control I have about what is past is in how I choose to remember it. I can continue, or change, or end what was. I create the present, as do you. But none of us in that creation is unaffected by the free energy of the past, the urge to becoming expressed in every instant. We can't actually tell our children what to remember about Easter. They will remember what they remember. So, to tell the truth, will we.

So what, then? Life is irresistibly new every moment. We have reason to be glad.

Amen. Blessed Be. Shalom. Salaam. Happy Easter!

Suffering Too Much

29 Apr 2018

My time as a Cub Scout leader was short but probably as satisfactory as it could be. Our Webelos den seemed to function well enough and everybody went on to become Boy Scouts, which was the goal.

But one Saturday morning the Executive Committee commented briefly on a boy in a nearby state who had been dismissed from a Scout troop for refusing to affirm a belief in God. A serious failure of leadership, we all agreed. "All they had to do was use 'Supreme Being,'" my co-leader declared. "Everybody believes in a Supreme Being."

"Not me," I piped up. "I'm an atheist." I must have been channeling Dennis the Menace. The results were anyway, as benignly humorous. I was politely ignored.

Today atheists are not ignored. They write best sellers, hit the talk shows and blog at a furious pace. Perhaps you have read or heard Sam Harris, Richard Dawkins or the late Christopher Hitchins. Maybe you are an atheist. That's perfectly okay with me.

It is a compelling conclusion in answer to one of the knottiest questions of human existence—why do the innocent suffer? The atheist response is obvious: Undeserved suffering exists because God doesn't exist. It's open and shut. A genuine divinity—a Supreme Being—wouldn't allow the misery and pain we see all around us. Q.E.D.

This question is one of "theodicy." Thus, the Bible's Book of Job. My father used to say "poor as Job's turkey" to particularly emphasize the degree of someone's material deprivation. In the story, Job is a righteous man victimized by what appears to us to be an almost frivolous wager between God and Satan. God will allow Satan to strip Job of his prosperity—of his sheep and cattle and servants. God will allow the death of Job's ten children. God will allow Satan to strike Job head to heel with all manner of bodily afflictions. God bets Job will remain a faithful believer despite all trials short of death.

The name "Job" is translated from Biblical Hebrew as a question: "Where is the divine Father?" It is just as well translated as: "[the] hated/cursed/reviled one." Bible scholars say this ambiguity may be deliberate. The tension is the heart of the story.

Job struggles mightily with theodicy, aided by three friends who (not) helpfully suggest he must have done something wrong, or maybe God has some divine purpose to allow such atrocities, or maybe these awful things just happen and we don't have a clue.

We could agree with any one of these propositions in answer to the challenge of theodicy, but what Job does not do is become an atheist. He does something radically different—he challenges God to account for his persecutions. You may be surprised to hear this happens often in the Hebrew Scriptures. Yahweh gets a good what-for.

God's answer is framed as a legal one, but it emerges from a whirlwind in verses of beautiful, poetic imagery. The short version is this: I am God and you are not.

I am God and you are not. Job has to hear it twice—he is a stubbornly righteous man—before giving way. "I have changed my mind," he says, "about dust and ashes."

Why might we consider the same answer to be best for us? Let's evaluate the alternatives. If you get sick or injured, if someone you love dies, do you really want to believe you did something wrong—even if you don't know what that could possibly be? Or even if—more likely—you know vividly every single thing you have ever done wrong, but why are you of all people being punished so terribly? I don't think we want to or should say we just deserve to suffer for the faults of being human, or for no fault at all.

How about the second possibility? Does God have purposes we can believe, even if they inflict terrible loss on us? Does He (God is always He when this language is used) really "need beautiful angels in Heaven," so that's why children get fatal cancers? In the maelstrom of grief, any of us might say or do something deeply awkward, but when we are reasoning, will anybody solemnly propose such a response makes any sense at all?

Finally, there is the third proposition. Call it the atheist's proclamation. God does not exist. Undeserved suffering clearly does. The latter is absolute evidence of the former. One question: If God is cleared away so completely, where does that leave us?

Is it truly just a matter of "not nice to mess with Mother Nature"? Does she get even with earthquakes that bury hundreds, tsunamis that sweep the shoreline bare for miles and hurricanes that cause billions in damage? We do name hurricanes, and check how often we slip into addressing them as malevolent actors, which is of course absurd.

Or are we indeed living in a universe of random disaster, of cataclysms that fall upon us without rhyme or reason? Who would affirm such an utterly purposeless existence? It may be true and correct, but does anybody want to be reminded of this?

If we don't check these clichés of calamity, we can take on too much suffering. We add to disaster the poison of shame, fear and anxiety. We rub salt in our own wounds. We carelessly replicate an "explanation" that does us nothing but harm.

Almost twenty years ago I careened straight through a red light into the busiest intersection in Chester County, during morning rush hour no less. It is a miracle no one was killed. No one was even injured. When the police officer asked me what happened, I told him the truth: "I drove through a red light. I have no idea why."

Neither does Job. What does either one of us deserve? I got two seconds of terror and a $150 fine—did I suffer too little? Job has lost everything. Did he suffer too much? How would we know? How could we possibly judge? Did God deal fairly with me and harshly with Job? What human mechanism could weigh this conundrum?

Job is a character in a 2500-year-old story, not a person, but the riddle of theodicy is just as much beyond our comprehension as it is beyond his. We are not God. We are too often not particularly good human beings. What we should know is when we do wrong and cause suffering, we must own that entirely. When we do less than what is right, we must own that as our own shortcoming. These are well within our human capacity. But we are not responsible beyond our capacity—beyond "dust and ashes."

I am God and you are not. Job finally "speaks in agreement." Some experts detect irony—a hint of continued defiance about the shortcomings of divine justice. God grants Job's plea for his three insulting friends—the rabbinical tradition says Job's forgiveness is what recovers his prosperity. God admits responsibility for Job's travails, and restores his wealth twice over. He fathers ten more children and lives 140 years.

Possibly Job spends his days considering the wisdom and justice of the divine, pondering an energy that belongs only to the divine. It is shared with us, but we do not make it, grant it, or withhold it. We have no compelling case to even understand that energy. There is absolutely no possibility of bargaining for it. No matter how good we may be, we cannot obtain for certain a single preferment. No matter how bad, we do not any of us "deserve" our suffering. When we are afflicted, we are simply afflicted. There is no need to add to the burden by overloading ourselves with shame, guilt, or fear.

Jesus asked, "Can you by worrying add a single hour to your life?" Buddha's enlightenment rests on the understanding all existence is by definition impermanent. If we insist on suffering because of this, we have only ourselves to blame. And God does not answer to our judgment, only in mystery, like the deepest ocean or the farthest star. The universe is not about us in the end—or anywhere in the middle for that matter.

Amen. Blessed Be. Shalom. Salaam.

Neither Here nor There

14 Oct 2018

The thunderstorm on the Indiana Toll Road was sudden and fierce. I hit a patch of wind and water, and the old Plymouth Barracuda did a quick-as-a-blink 180 spin—counter clockwise, if I remember. For a moment I was looking straight through the windshield at the semi-trailer bearing down on me. I am about to die is what I thought. But the car kept right on spinning, all the way around 360 degrees, pointed back in the correct direction, in the correct lane even. The semi went barreling by, horn blasting.

Skating across the trapdoor to eternity like that is one thing. Standing on it, with the clock ticking, is an entirely different circumstance. None of us really wants to be there, but almost all of us will. Many of us will in a lifetime stand there more than once. This is actually good news by most measures. Death by catastrophe is rare in the United States and rapidly getting more and more rare. This is cold comfort if it does come to someone you love, as we obviously do not overlook for even a moment. Loss is loss—and a shocking loss still is and will be one of the worst events of all our days.

Nonetheless, what medical ethicists began a generation ago to characterize as "dying slow" is what will be the final episode for roughly 97% of us. When I was a chaplain intern in 2003, Arthur Caplan, one of the earliest and still most prominent of those "bioethicists," warned our team bluntly of the impending disaster. "Society," he told us, "is totally unprepared for death that takes months or even years, instead of minutes. And so are we," he added.

We know the plight of the oldest old. They are too often kept alive seemingly by hook or crook even when accelerating physical or mental debility—or both—is snarling them and those around them in tangles of frustration, confusion and despair. The "we" I am instead thinking of is someone I know who was diagnosed this year with a rare blood cancer. "This will kill you," the doctors said, "but we really don't know when. It could be two years or twenty years." I don't think they actually added, "We'll just have to wait and see," but that macabre humor was clearly the apparent in the situation.

Men with prostate cancer have been getting this cheery news for years of course, but now it is much more common. There is more early diagnosis. That means more people get to know they are really sick even if they have few or mild symptoms. There are more treatments. Some of these do avoid the scorched-earth campaigns of older days. There are also, thankfully, more "wait and watch" opportunities, and more willingness to use them at least as long as possible. So, as it does, life goes on—sort of.

196

But how does that happen? How do we ride a train we now know has a station stop too soon for our plans or preferences? If we hear the wire snap—the one that holds that piano high over our heads—do we stop for the impending impact, or keep walking?

The first step into what we might call "adjusted expectations" is likely to be this: You will ask if you are dying and the doctor will not actually answer the question. They almost never do. For one thing, they often really don't know—not with much clarity anyway. Medical circumstances are complicated. That's just on the course your condition may take and the options available to respond. And who knows how you will respond? Each of us is a unique organism. The answer you will get is usually something like "x percent of patients were alive x number of years after diagnosis." This sentence is predictive of absolutely nothing, but most of us will ignore this inconvenience. There is no reason to feel guilty—ignore is what human beings do. It is undoubtedly necessary.

But the next day, or the next week or the next month…there you are, blowing in the wind, neither here nor there. Your old life has ended, at least metaphorically. Your "here" is not what it was. You aren't exactly "there" either. Wherever you think there is, it hasn't happened yet. The trapdoor has not sprung and you are not gone.

"Why?" is probably the overwhelming question—"Why me?" The historic answer, from every arena of human thought, from theology to statistics, is the same: "Why not? Why not you?" Why not me? Why not any of us? The contingency of mortal existence is inescapable—although, again, we ignore this inconvenience. This is undoubtedly necessary. None of us would get much sleep if we looked for comfort to a metaphoric image of life as a flying arrow falling inevitably to the ground.

One recommendation is this: Start your spiritual practice now. Every spiritual practice is about this trajectory—how to engage it, how to understand it, how to lighten the burden, how to live in its shadow without losing the light of life itself. A second recommendation is this: Start your spiritual community now. A spiritual community is any group of people, any number or relationship of people—including those otherwise strangers to you—who are willing to live in the acknowledged awareness of this reality.

Your family might get it—or at least some of them. It is shocking however, how many families do not, so don't take it for granted. Don't take it for granted either that you are clear to them on this crucial matter. Your friends might get it, but consider carefully whether you could stand up during the seventh inning stretch and blurt out, I think about dying and I'm afraid. If one of your friends did that, how would you respond?

I hope you know your church does get it, or at least we understand we are supposed to and are willing to try. It is why we have a minister. It is why we have a Pastoral Care Team. It is why we remind ourselves that subjects of such weight are acceptable here. In church the dark substance of our lives is not an interruption to cocktail chatter or sports talk. It is why we are here, more than any other reason. That matters. I hope you feel it is true. If not, I assure you we will absolutely keep trying.

I also urge you to feel no guilt or shame or embarrassment about the why and why me questions. Don't waste a moment feeling bad that you are feeling bad. I remind you of the central principle of sitting meditation: The thoughts come; don't fight them; let them open up and then dissipate like the passing clouds they are. Repeat as needed. For a more concrete example, this advice: If a tornado approaches, open the windows and doors so the sudden change in pressure is less likely to blow the house apart.

Storms come and go. So do you and I. If the going part seems to be coming, I suggest skipping the "bucket list" reflex. Of course you should do things you need and want to do—send us a postcard from Paris. But try not to indulge mere busyness. Try not to run away. "Try" is the operative word here, but do remember that when you are indeed gone, you will be gone from the lives of real people. Who are they? Who have you been to them, and how? What hole will you be leaving in their lives?

Most important, what can you put in that place now, while you are still here? When they go on in this world, what part of you will they carry along? We are seldom given any other meaningful heritage. All our works turn to dust. The dedication of our lives is what matters in the end, not what we may have accomplished—large or small. No material accomplishment can really cause people to miss you in their hearts.

The love and care we give to others has meaning long after our hour has passed. No saintliness is needed, and for that we must be glad. If we locate ourselves in a web of relationships, we can never finally be lost. No minute is ever too late, even the last one.

Amen. Blessed Be. Shalom. Salaam.

The Live-Lamb Nativity

23 Dec 2018

For a parish minister, there are certain especially enjoyable gifts of the moment. I look forward to a lively congregation on Sunday morning, and it happens a lot. I look forward to beautiful music then too—and we are generously rewarded. I look forward to laughing children and we have them in abundance. Did I mention Coffee Hour?

And I do have fantasies of a full house—which is pretty reliable on Christmas Eve. On several other occasions there is what might be called a "fullish" house, and that's probably as often as you or I could actually stand it, if truth be told. The Christmas Eve service does hold one impossible dream for me. I want—just once—a live animal nativity. I don't mean a dog wearing antlers but the real thing—sheep! Oxen are a little too large. Camels have notoriously bad tempers and they spit. Cattle are much bigger and clumsier than you realize until you get next to them. They can be spared. Horses I have never trusted since the days when they tried to take me under the fence. Doves do what birds do, and we have carpet problems enough.

A lamb is what I'd like—a baby sheep. Just one will do. They are small, soft, gentle and plaintive when they cry. I'm not sure they are hypoallergenic but we could probably manage, and how much mess can a lamb make?

Well, some other year maybe. I'm not really disappointed. Metaphorically of course, there is always a lamb in the nativity—the image of Jesus as the Lamb of God is one of the earliest attached to him. This is partially because the lamb was embedded in the religion, culture and economy for a millennium before his birth. It is more deeply revealing to recall the lamb was a preferred sacrificial animal for many of the practical reasons I already mentioned—much easier to manage than a brace of oxen for instance, which was at the top of the list if you had done something really bad.

The point of the lamb is not its harmlessness, of course, but its almost total vulnerability. It is at least one way of reminding us of the essential vulnerability of all life. The Nativity Story is a sacred origin story, if more widely known not necessarily more compelling than many other sacred origin stories humans tell each other. The litany of perils is long and we all share them in one way or another. What many are lifting up in our day—properly so—are the acts of tyrants. It is the tyrant Caesar Augustus who levies the tax and compels the difficult mid-winter journey of a heavily pregnant woman on the back of a donkey to a distant city of her husband's lineage. And we think the Department of Motor Vehicles is onerous! It is the tyrant Herod whom the Magi must dodge to save their lives, returning home "by another road." And the same Herod orders the slaughter of every baby boy in fear of this one baby boy. We see again that at the core of every tyrant is someone willing to inflict horror for the sake of power.

And the family, momentarily safe around the manger, must then flee into a far country to save their child. They are refugees from violence. Apparently, the authorities of that place of relative safety believe them. That refuge is Egypt—the land that held the Israelites enslaved and then tried to annihilate them. The long-ago hearers of that story would not have missed this epic irony. And in our day, some churches and many others are not missing the painful reality that refugees in our day do not receive such respite.

UUs can't put out a crèche with barbed wire over it because we have vacated our claim on that symbol. There are good reasons, but a price is paid when symbols are lost.

Thankfully the symbol of the lamb in safety remains richly with us. Of course, it—and all the other animals—are in the barn. It is winter in the story and it is deadly cold in that time of year in those lands. The shepherds are not out in the fields keeping watch over their flocks—they are in their homes, which they share with the animals on which their lives depend. They keep close what is dear to them and so should we.

I'd have the lamb to remind us of this important lesson within the larger story. Of course, it is meant to apply to people. All animal stories are actually about people.

Another lesson might be the most crucial of the cycle of stores woven into this larger narrative. You already know the details are different in different places in the Bible. But let me point out the entire fabulous account is of a universe in good order, from the cosmic to the quotidian. The lamb safe is only a fragment.

A star in this orderly universe moves to light the way. Not where we live, right?

The timelessly awkward circumstances of an unmarried woman who is pregnant and can't or won't name the father, is solved without bloodshed or even scandal—perhaps an even greater miracle than the star. And look! In the order of this universe he is "of the House and lineage of David." Daddy Warbucks is not nearly so well qualified. That matter-of-fact assertion of Joseph's clan ties is certainly not mentioned at random. Nor is the attention of the Magi, the most learned and respected people of their day. Hey, Brady, Gronk, and even the grumpy hoodie guy are coming to your house—bringing gifts, no less! In our universe it would be almost as unlikely that all the animals are gathered and nobody is trying to eat anybody, or kick anybody, or spit at anybody. It doesn't mention the snake, but I fearlessly assume this goes for him as well. And if we are keeping an eye out for wolves, they are at least not huffing and puffing at the door. Please note also that alongside the regal Magi are the shepherds, almost the poorest and lowest people of their day, and they certainly had not bathed recently, if ever.

The journey has been made without illness, or accident, or robbery and despoliation—in our era of run-flat tires it is easy to lose track of this miracle. The longer trip to Egypt is noted without any incident at all. That innkeeper doesn't have a room but they are not driven away—another hard-to-grasp miracle. They are safe, if in the humblest of circumstances. Homeless shelter, anyone? Let's not forget a virgin has given birth. I'm not alluding to the Immaculate Conception—that's the easy part. I'm talking here about the grueling, painful and very dangerous birthing itself. She hasn't done this before, although maybe she has helped someone. Maybe Joseph has also, but there is no other help of any kind apparent—not even running water or clean sheets.

I haven't even mentioned the angels, but I'm sure you already have the point. The universe of this story is not the one in which the people of those times actually lived. It is not the one in which we actually live. It is orderly in the most comprehensive meaning of the word—every important element is aligned on the miraculous, on the good, on the safe, on the prophetic, on the bond between the creatures of all kinds, on kindness and gentleness and generosity and the words Mary keeps deep in her heart. And also, the wonder—the surpassing wonder: Look what has happened! Look what we see and hear! Look what a vision we have been given! Look what a great promise for all and for all time to come!

Some assembly required. Evil has not been banished. It is only held off for a time. Privation has not disappeared. Violence has not abated, let alone ended. The stars return to their courses and so do the people, as people will do. They are good and bad, busy and idle, cunning and caring, going on about their days and their fates. Yet, somehow, they remember this concatenation of miracles. They remember for all the years that this special universe did exist. They hope it will exist again. So should we.

Amen. Blessed Be. Shalom. Salaam. Merry Christmas!

Being Wrong Religiously

28 Apr 2019

We had a frank exchange of views over brunch with the in-laws on Easter Sunday. Actually, the whole family was frank in their dismissal of my views, so here is a joke: What's the difference between a pessimist and a cynic? A cynic is more likely to be right.

I agree that is not exactly a knee-slapper, but what we are living with is hardly humorous. Scientists are debating whether the Anthropocene officially commenced in 1950, but the truer epoch of this day is the Age of Idiocy. Somebody will need to help me with the Latin for that, but can there be any doubt? What isn't screwed up?

Not long ago, a New York Times front-page story was the introduction of the Green New Deal. I went to the comments section to check out public reaction. No scientific sampling, but I jotted down the comments "most recommended" by readers. The first was somebody who said since we put a man on the moon, we could certainly afford this new expense. The second declared the country to be in the hands of fossilized white dinosaurs. Third in line was "absolute poppycock—defeat Trump first!" Fourth was a reminder we "can't leave nuclear out of the equation." The fifth most popular response— fifth—was the first one both relevant and rational: We need a lot more information to understand the whole thing. Thank you, gentle reader. You gave me some small hope.

If a pandemic of being wrong might be considered our social body's response to the current state of despair, confusion and a drastic shortage of available runway, what matters about being wrong religiously? Why should anyone care? If the 21st century will indeed be the last century of civilization, why would religion matter?

Let me briefly introduce you to James Luther Adams, the great Unitarian theologian, teacher, writer and parish minister. He published in 1976 a book called *Being Human Religiously*. It was his life's work to believe such a thing was possible. That might be around the last time anybody in the intelligentsia made such a claim. Now we know the "human" of Modernism was already done. Classic deep-thinking Liberals such as Adams—and Reinhold Niebuhr and Paul Tillich, among others—had brought knives to a gunfight. They indeed epitomized the "fossilized white dinosaurs."

Consider this about the fire in Notre-Dame. The edifice is not gone, but it is certainly lost. It survived the Age of Reason and the Age of Revolution alike. The Age of Idiocy—the characteristic conceits for experts, technology

202

and cost analysis—did it in. We are left poorer for sure. Will we also be wiser? What is there available to rebuild?

James Luther Adams can still help. In this post-Modern time, when there are no undisputed facts, no objective truth or universal morality and no neutral parties, Adams still matters. He lived nine decades suffused in religion, not as a scholar only, but as a traveler through rich and rewarding experience. His father was a preacher of the hardscrabble Plymouth Brethren. Vigorous dinner discussion was of Jesus, the Bible, the End Times—no current events mattered. All his life Adams rejected that rigid doctrine but remembered the warmth of the prayer and the consoling small groups. All his life Adams remembered the parables. His remarkable impact as a teacher rested on his own mastery of myth and memory. Adams thought and taught in stories.

And the crucible of his adult faith was Nazi Germany. He was there before the Nazis took power and famously found himself dragged into an alley while watching a swastika parade. His rescuer told the flustered Adams the goons were on their way and would likely have beaten him to death for asking questions that provoked a noisy argument. In 1936, Adams went back to Germany and sought out every liberal Christian he could find, risking his life to associate with the Confessing Church—already banned and being rounded up into concentration camps to smother their faith resistance. Bad as things may be now, the 20th century was no walk in the park. We should remember.

Adams can remind us of the possible merits of being wrong religiously, as opposed to not. His indictment of liberal Christianity came directly from what he had seen. It lacked any "costing commitment." It failed to inspire concrete resistance from the heart, the place where the sacrifice must originate. It was disengaged from the messy disputes and disappointments of common life. It deferred to authority rather than generate a new and more robust order. It talked about justice instead of doing it. It chattered about faith—often dismissively—instead of tapping its strength and solace.

Our main heritage from Adams is the "voluntary association." He proposed that faithful people living in relationship with each other had the power to behave in the values they held, not just mouth them as words. "By their groups you shall know them," was his famous gloss on the saying of Jesus. Holding relationships together in the congregation gave meaning and matter to larger circles of relationship, out into the community, out into the world, with other people and other perspectives and ideas.

You will note that every element of Unitarian Universalism as a denomination is based on this insight. Every item of belief is voluntary, every participation is a chosen one, every human conscience is cheerfully—or sometimes not—assumed to be in high-minded formation to take responsibility as final sovereign of not only our own lives but also the earth and all that dwells upon it. Our Seven Principles (see page iii) provide ethical understanding and also a conveniently organized roadmap of how to relate, from the unique individual to the entire universe. You recall: inherent worth and dignity right on out to the interdependent web. Like Willie Mays, we catch everything that's hit out there, no matter how far we have to run.

But there is no outrunning the Age of Idiocy. There is no stepping into the safety of our herd immunity against the contagion of wrong. We too are spattered with performative this and that—identities frayed under siege. At best we are in the Red Sea up to our noses, hoping desperately it will part as promised. At worst—we are subject to the worst—we look around and wonder if we somehow got conscripted into what sure looks like pharaoh's army. It's hot and dusty and noisy and this may not end very well.

Fortunately, every Haggadah reminds us God loved the Egyptians, too. He took no pleasure in tormenting them. Adams came to the same essential conclusion and it might be the thing we should remember at the deepest level. We are not the Divine and the Divine is not us. The burdens of the Divine are not our burdens. The nature of the Divine is not human nature. Adams saw relationship there, too. So did William Ellery Channing, who stealthily sold that concept to all mainline American Protestants. Well, they sold themselves after he showed the way. The Divine is a not-us, which we can yet perceive. Adams was perfectly happy to welcome atheists—the "not-God" folks—on board the boat. They too hunger for and can put their hands upon what is not human, what can be felt in the heart as needed and necessary, no old-guy-in-a-bathrobe at all.

We are fated to be wrong a lot, in any age. The human capacity to screw up is richly documented. It may well be at floodtide right now, but it is always a turbulent current of our free will and our insecurity and our incredible hunger for possibility. To be wrong religiously—any kind of religiously—is to understand through relationship. There is more than us out there, and inside us as well. Other folks love their children just as much as we do. The world is a puzzle that isn't supposed to be solved. It's okay.

Amen. Blessed Be. Shalom. Salaam.

About the Author

David W. Chandler received his Master of Divinity degree from Lancaster Theological Seminary, Lancaster, PA in 2004. He served the Unitarian Church of Harrisburg, PA as Intern Minister and was ordained by them in 2005. In 2006 he served the Thomas Paine UU Fellowship, Collegeville, PA, and was called to the UU Church of Saco and Biddeford, Saco, ME. After serving them 2006—2013, he served as Interim Minister 2014—2016 at the UU Fellowship of the Eastern Slopes, Tamworth, NH, and at First Parish UU Medfield, MA 2016—2019.

David and his wife Sally live in Saco, ME. Their son Ben lives in Los Altos, CA with his wife Josephine and daughter Brielle. David and Sally's daughter Kate lives with them in Saco. The Chandlers joined the Main Line Unitarian Church, Devon, PA in 1991. David was president of MLUC in 1999 and 2000.

Made in the USA
Middletown, DE
26 July 2019